Advance Praise for *All the Presidents' Money*

"Presidents' personal finances open a window to their souls. In Gorman's perceptive telling, presidents pair up in unexpected ways: Truman and Coolidge were both worrywarts. Eisenhower and Truman both wanted to reduce taxes on their book profits. FDR lost $24,000 in the lobster business. This book is the right gift for anyone in finance or accounting."

—**Amity Shlaes**, *New York Times* bestselling author of *Coolidge*

"In this powerful book, Gorman examines the financial lives of American presidents and uses that as a platform to lay out clearly something that we all need to understand: the opportunity set for most Americans was greater in the past. But the insights she provides do not simply serve as a warning, they give us the understanding needed for a better future."

—**Richard Vague**, author of the *Wall Street Journal* bestseller *The Paradox of Debt: A New Path to Prosperity Without Crisis*

"Few topics are more humanizing and relatable than an honest review of our relationships with money. In a fresh take on presidential history, Gorman lucidly examines the personal finances of those who have sat at the apex of national power and influence, resulting in stories of humility, grief, prudence, splendor, and extravagance. The power of *All the Presidents' Money* is that within a few pages it becomes clear that every president demonstrates a thoroughly modern and relatable range of experiences with money and money management despite being the most powerful people of their respective times. The takeaways become more poignant when considering their mindsets toward debt, future discounting, and entrepreneurship, and how those are balanced on a wide-ranging continuum of financial fragility, outlook, and opportunity. This hard-to-put-down account should be required reading for anyone taking a personal finance or US history course."

—**Dr. Billy Hensley**, CEO, National Endowment for Financial Education

"*All the Presidents' Money* delves into the financial lives of America's presidents, revealing the behaviors and decisions that shaped their fortunes. As someone who studies behavioral finance, I found her insights both fascinating and instructive. This book is a compelling read for anyone interested in the intersection of history, psychology, and finance."

—**Dr. Daniel Crosby**, author of *The Soul of Wealth* and *The Behavioral Investor*

"Wow! Presidents are just like us. They worry about money, too! Or they don't worry...and go broke on bad gambles and good wine, as the case may be. This is a fascinating book, a fun read, a financial history lesson, and I'm sure one that will have tongues wagging in Washington."

—**Bruce Littlefield**, *New York Times* bestselling author

All the Presidents' Money

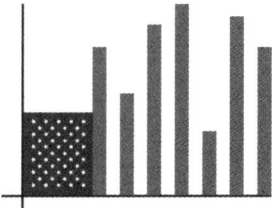

How the Men Who Governed America Governed Their Money

Megan Gorman

A REGALO PRESS BOOK
ISBN: 979-8-89565-276-3
ISBN (eBook): 979-8-88845-081-9

All the Presidents' Money:
How the Men Who Governed America Governed Their Money
© 2024 by Megan Gorman
All Rights Reserved

First Edition Regalo Press Hardcover: September 2024

Cover Design by Christopher Parker
Interior Design and Composition by Alana Mills

Publishing Team:
Founder and Publisher – Gretchen Young
Editorial Assistant – Caitlyn Limbaugh
Managing Editor – Madeline Sturgeon
Production Manager – Alana Mills
Production Editor – Rachel Hoge
Associate Production Manager – Kate Harris

As part of the mission of Regalo Press, a donation is being made to the White House Historical Association, as chosen by the author. Find out more about this organization at: www.whitehousehistory.org.

No part of this book may be reproduced, stored in a retrieval system, or transmitted by any means without the written permission of the author and publisher.

Regalo Press
New York • Nashville
regalopress.com

Published in the United States of America
1 2 3 4 5 6 7 8 9 10

*To my husband Roger for all the love and support.
You are my life. We are ours.*

*And to my nephew Elliot. May the hurdles in life be
enough to make you ambitious but not too high as to
keep you from the American Dream.*

Table of Contents

Presidents of the United States — ix
Introduction — xi

PART I: THE BASIC BUILDING BLOCKS

1. Thomas Jefferson Cordially Invites You to Dinner
   (or How Your Future Self Impacts Your Wealth) — 3
2. Abraham Lincoln Would Like a Library Card Please
   (or Education & Pedigree) — 25
3. Herbert Hoover Saves the Stanford Football Team
   (or The Art of Number Crunching) — 53
4. Don't Mess with Ike When It Comes to Poker
   (or Appetite for Risk) — 75

PART II: MONEY AND MEANING

5. Gerald Ford: Hate the Game, Not the Player
   (or Financial Confidence and Anxiety) — 101
6. Calvin Coolidge Is Rather Thrifty
   (or The Values of Money) — 129
7. FDR and Elvis Get the World All Shook Up
   (or Charitable Intent) — 153

PART III: THE WEALTH BUILDERS

8. Lady Bird Buys a Radio Station — 185
9. Meet George Washington—The Ultimate American Hustler
   (or Grit) — 215
10. Ulysses S. Grant and the Never-Ending Get-Rich Schemes
    (or Luck) — 237

Afterword — 259
Bibliography — 263
Index — 287
Acknowledgments — 289
About the Author — 291

Presidents of the United States

1. George Washington (1732–1799)
2. John Adams (1735–1826)
3. Thomas Jefferson (1743–1826)
4. James Madison (1751–1836)
5. James Monroe (1758–1831)
6. John Quincey Adams (1767–1848)
7. Andrew Jackson (1767–1845)
8. Martin Van Buren (1782–1862)
9. William Henry Harrison (1773–1841)
10. John Tyler (1790–1862)
11. James Polk (1795–1849)
12. Zachary Taylor (1784–1850)
13. Milliard Fillmore (1800–1874)
14. Franklin Pierce (1804–1869)
15. James Buchanan (1791–1868)
16. Abraham Lincoln (1809–1865)
17. Andrew Johnson (1808–1875)
18. Ulysses S. Grant (1822–1885)
19. Rutherford B. Hayes (1822–1893)
20. James Garfield (1831–1881)
21. Chester Arthur (1829–1886)
22. Grover Cleveland (1837–1908)
23. Benjamin Harrison (1833–1901)
24. Grover Cleveland (1837–1908)
25. William McKinley (1843–1901)
26. Theodore Roosevelt (1858–1919)
27. William Howard Taft (1857–1930)
28. Woodrow Wilson (1856–1924)
29. Warren G. Harding (1865–1923)
30. Calvin Coolidge (1872–1933)
31. Herbert Hoover (1874–1964)
32. Franklin D. Roosevelt (1882–1945)
33. Harry S. Truman (1884–1972)
34. Dwight D. Eisenhower (1890–1969)
35. John F. Kennedy (1917–1963)
36. Lyndon B. Johnson (1908–1973)
37. Richard Nixon (1913–1994)
38. Gerald Ford (1913–2006)
39. James Carter (Born 1924)
40. Ronald Reagan (1911–2004)
41. George H.W. Bush (1924–2018)
42. William J. Clinton (Born 1946)
43. George W. Bush (Born 1946)
44. Barack Obama (Born 1961)
45. Donald J. Trump (Born 1946)
46. Joseph Biden (Born 1942)

Introduction

Lobsters.

Louie Howe was focused on the lobsters.

As he sat down at his desk in the spring of 1924, he prepared to write another response to the attorney in Maine, Ensign Otis. He knew that despite everything going on, this business endeavor was important to the Boss. And right now, the Boss—otherwise known as Franklin Delano Roosevelt—was struggling to recover from polio.

There were fourteen main providers of lobsters in the United States, but the group that had stood out to FDR was Witham Brothers Inc., who had a plant in Rockland, Maine. The Witham Brothers had been in the business since 1912 and had not only consistently turned a profit, but their profits rose year after year. They were looking to expand and needed cash, and it seemed like a good deal at the outset. Not only did they have a strong balance sheet, but their lobsters had the reputation of being high quality. Furthermore, the Witham Brothers had patented their containers that allowed them to ship lobsters as far as San Francisco.

The deal FDR had put together in early 1921 was simple: he would invest in the lobster company and acquire shares for approximately $10,000. This capital infusion would allow them to provide fresh lobsters all around the United States. But by having control of one the biggest lobster farms in the country, they were also hoping that they could make a profit when the price of lobsters went up.

And FDR enjoyed investing in start-up ideas. True, his record on investing wasn't that strong. He had lost money on something called General Air that sought to establish a dirigible airship service between New York and Chicago. But this one, he had told Howe, was a good one. Unfortunately, six months after making the investment, FDR was stricken with polio.

Howe studied the letter from the company. At this point, three years in, it was not looking good. The Witham Brothers had misread the situation. They ran their business as a consolidator of smaller lobstermen. These smaller lobstermen were used to being paid cash right away. They didn't have the patience or cash flow to wait for the price of lobsters to rise.[1]

This misjudgment of the workers, along with haphazard accounting, had made this investment a mess for Howe to clean up. And now the attorney shared the bad news: "It is my opinion, after working up every outlook for assistance, that nothing can be worked out here that will come anywhere near getting Mr. Roosevelt's money back for him, and that he would receive no cooperation or consideration from the other creditors if he attempted to go ahead and work out their problems along with his own," wrote Otis.[2]

A few weeks later, after Howe updated the Boss on the situation, FDR himself wrote back. "I do not want, and cannot afford, to put another red cent into the company in the way of cash…I am a creditor to the tune of nearly $16,000, not counting my original investment in the stock of the company."[3]

By the time FDR got out of the lobster business, he had lost $26,000. That doesn't sound like much, but it's close to $450,000 in 2024 dollars. Clearly the transaction frustrated him, but it wasn't enough to really damage his personal finances. After all, he had significant trust funds to fall back on.

WHY THE PRESIDENTS?

When you go through the correspondence and paperwork of FDR's direct investing, it's hard to believe that the transaction happened just over a century ago. But the truth is, that is one of the most interesting aspects of the personal finances of the presidents: most of their money problems are just like ours.

---

1   Letter Ensign Otis to Louis Howe, dated April 10, 1924. This letter lays out the crux of the business issues they were facing.
2   Ibid.
3   Letter Franklin D. Roosevelt to Ensign Otis, dated May 1, 1924. Emphasis in original letter.

Introduction

Sixty-one years before FDR got caught up in lobsters, another man was assessing his finances before a big move. Abraham Lincoln was leaving Springfield, Illinois, for his inauguration in Washington, DC, on February 11, 1861. He was going to be leasing out his twelve-room, Greek Revival–style home on the corner of Eighth and Jackson. It was one of the nicest homes in Springfield, and Lincoln was designating his local insurance representative Robert Irwin to handle his bills. He listed his net worth at $10,000—or $292,000 in 2024 dollars.

It was a far cry from the young lawyer who came to town with two saddlebags of possessions in 1837. Even when he married Mary Todd, they could only afford to lease a room at the Globe Tavern on Adams Street for four dollars a week. But over the years, he scrimped and saved. He even purchased the home on Jackson Street when it was a one-story cottage, and slowly renovated it to the stately house it is today. And it helped that Mary's family was wealthy and was willing to assist them.

Finally, fast forward to the 1930s, where college student John F. Kennedy was very focused on where every penny went. Kennedy had grown up with money. His father, Joseph Kennedy, had set up trust funds for all of his nine children with a philosophy that they would be able to remain independent.[4] Yet despite the wealth to fall back on, Kennedy was never a spender. Even his closest friend, Lem Billings, noted that he was "very close with a buck."[5]

Billings recalled that during their summers in college, the Stork Club was the scene in New York. The club would attract the most attractive people. And they held fun events like Balloon Night where balloons were dropped from the ceiling containing $100 bills and tickets for free meals or a free bottle of champagne.

As exciting as being at the club was, for Billings, it was a financial stretch for his budget. Yet this never deterred Kennedy. Billings recalled that they would "order one drink at the table and then Jack and I would excuse ourselves and hurry over to Third Avenue. There was a bar where we would have a few beers and come right back. I only bring this up because Jack Kennedy tried to live within the budgets of his friends."[6]

---

4 (Billings 1964) Tape #2.
5 Ibid. Tape #10.
6 Ibid. Tape #3.

All the Presidents' Money

FDR, Lincoln, and Kennedy are all revered for their leadership. In fact, two of them, FDR and Lincoln (along with George Washington) usually rank in the top three presidents. But despite their abilities as presidents, all came from such different backgrounds.

FDR was born into great wealth, and lived off a trust fund managed by his mother. Lincoln started out as one of our poorest presidents. Yet he worked hard to learn how to manage money, diligently saving US Treasury bonds during the Civil War. Even though Kennedy also came from great wealth, he was known for being frugal when it came to money especially since "everybody thought he had it made." He would even "give orders to the butlers at the White House not to open bottles of champagne until the last one was finished" as a cost-saving measure.[7]

When it comes down to who of the three was most successful with their personal finances, the truth is it was probably Lincoln.

The stories of how the presidents handled their own personal finances are fascinating. Every presidential cycle, the potential contenders release their finances and submit paperwork explaining their financial lives. It's gotten to the point where there are law firms that specialize in helping with these disclosures. The subject is interesting partly because we want to know whether the individuals who run our country are fiscally sound, and partly because these financial disclosures often reveal more intimate (and at times, embarrassing) details of their lives.

We have a long history of our presidents being on our money—going all the way back to 1813 when James Madison appeared on $5,000 Treasurer bearer notes (and George Washington resigning his commission on the back).[8] In 1869, the US Treasury decided to put George Washington and Thomas Jefferson on the one and two-dollar bills respectively.[9] Since then, we have become accustomed to the presidents being the "face" of our currency, but ironically, we have little insight into how the presidents learned

---

7   (Salinger 1965) page 66.
8   (U.S. Currency Education Program n.d.).
9   (The Bureau of Engraving and Printing n.d.) The original picture on the first $1 notes when issued in 1862 was a portrait of Secretary of the Treasury Salmon P. Chase. For a fun history of the challenges of the $2 bill, check out St. Louis Bank Historian Mary Piles' article at https://www.cnbstl.com/about-us/news/the-history-of-the-two-dollar-bill. Wouldn't it have been fun if "Toms" had become more mainstream in their usage?

Introduction

the skills to handle their personal financial matters. In fact, we don't know their individual money stories at all.

Many of our presidents have been self-made and came from humble beginnings. Like Lincoln, they were able to climb to the top of the economic and social ladder in this country through a combination of ambition and skill—the classic American success story. But others struggled with a lot of the same issues we do with money today. Would you believe that Dwight D. Eisenhower supplemented his army salary for years with a one-hundred-dollar monthly stipend from his father-in-law? (And by the way, Ike would not want you to know that.) Conversely, William McKinley, upon winning his first law case, tried to give back the twenty-five dollars his senior law partner had paid him, as he felt it was too much.[10] (McKinley wasn't focused on money as much as the social mobility his career provided.) Or that Lyndon B. Johnson would write to a friend in the early 1940s that "I waked up worrying about money" yet still bought $195 custom-made suits on a regular basis ($4,000 in 2024 dollars).[11]

FINANCIAL FRAGILITY AND FINANCIAL RESILIENCE

In the academics of personal finance, two concepts that are regularly studied are that of financial fragility and financial resilience. In fact, when you read articles about personal finance, thematically, most focus on how we can evolve from a position of fragility into one of resiliency. It is a journey that most Americans struggle with—and it isn't getting better.

In modern times, we define financial fragility as "being unable to cope with [an] emergency expense in a short period of time."[12] A 2013 Federal Reserve study showed that only half of all Americans can handle an unexpected $400 expense.[13] Think about that—it could be something like a car repair or a sick child that could tilt many Americans into fragility. In fact, the number improved dramatically to 68 percent in 2021 and the Federal Reserve attributed it to the increase in the Child Tax Credit.

---

10 (Morgan 1998) page 38.
11 Letter Lyndon B. Johnson to O.J. Weber, dated February 16, 1942. Courtesy of Lyndon B. Johnson Presidential Library. Also in (Caro 1990) pages 81–82.
12 Definition from The National Endowment for Financial Education (NEFE).
13 (Federal Reserve May 2022) This is an update on the original study from 2013.

Financial fragility has been a constant for a majority of the US population since before the founding of the country. The United States started as an agrarian nation subject to the whims of nature. Most of the population teetered on fragility, and this fragility has not lessened with time.

Researchers noted certain patterns when tracking fragility. Fragility occurs typically in situations where there is lower income, lower education levels, and lower financial literacy. While it impacts all genders and races, it is no surprise to learn that women and minorities have a greater struggle. In fact, women have a 42 percent chance of being financially fragile versus men at 30 percent.[14]

Financial resiliency is the bookend of financial fragility. It is the "ability to withstand life events that impact one's income and/or assets."[15] Researchers typically point to a variety of factors that create such resiliency, including being positive, flexible, focused, organized, and proactive. Resiliency allows one to navigate the ups and downs of personal finance without forcing an individual into fragility. It is a learned skill, but as you can imagine, those with access to higher incomes have an easier, more direct path to achieving resiliency.[16]

In working with successful high-net-worth individuals, I focused on their financial decision-making, their ability to be resilient, and the key attributes that got them there. I also saw individuals who, despite the high level of income they generated, struggled to make that resiliency connection. They were wealthy but competed against the pull of fragility. It was often my role to coach them around these damaging behaviors.

The question became how to best share the insights I have gained about financial decision-making. I had no interest in writing a typical personal finance book because it's not a genre I typically read. The nuts and bolts of "how to" doesn't hold my interest. Further, storytelling about individuals who are not known to the public is harder to connect to. But it is only through storytelling that we can truly relate our financial situation

---

14 Raveesha Gupta, Andrea Hasler, Annamaria Lusardi, Noemi Oggero, "Financial Fragility in the US: Evidence and Implications," GFLEC, https://www.nefe.org/_images/research/Financial-Fragility/Financial-Fragility-Final-Report.pdf.
15 (O'Neill PhD & CFP 2011).
16 In assessing fragility, the most common question is, how confident are you that you could come up with $2,000 if an unexpected need arose within the next month? See (Hasler, Lusardi and Oggero 2017).

Introduction

to others. The book I wanted to write was more of an intersection where personal finance met history.

So, I returned to what has interested me since I was six years old: the American presidents.

THE PRESIDENTIAL FINANCIAL JOURNEY

The American presidents are a complex group to tackle. While they live in a mud-slinging reality on the way to and through their presidency, the moment their term ends, they become historical figures carved in stone.

But they started out as ordinary men, and their early money stories put them on a financial path that allowed them to climb the American political system. Many of them made the journey from fragility to resilience. Financially, they failed at times—and at other times thrived. For most, the journey was not linear, and the real lessons were in the peaks and troughs.

In deciding to focus on the presidents, to put their financial journeys in context, it was important to ask questions regarding the eras during which they lived. I had to define their specific money stories and more importantly, ponder the question of whether, if they were born today, they would find their financial journey the same, easier, or harder.

In many of the presidents' stories, financial fragility is a common theme. However, what is different today is that, for previous generations, there were ways to overcome fragility, especially through access to education, by either college or apprenticeship, in fields such as law. This access required financial decision-making, but it did not come with the same steep financial consequences that we see today, as evidenced by the student loan crisis.

For presidents like Ronald Reagan, Herbert Hoover, and Bill Clinton, access to education became their springboard to achieve a higher financial level in society and break the bonds of financial fragility. What kept them there was the ability to utilize skills they had developed early due to their money stories. You will see this theme appear again and again throughout this book.

Keep in mind that not all presidents started financially fragile. For example, Thomas Jefferson came from a wealthy and educated background, yet financial stability remained elusive—even on his deathbed. Thus, another theme that appears in these stories is that sometimes education and wealth cannot override outside and family influences. In such cases, financial fragility ends up as a destination instead of a starting point.

As we learn the stories of these presidents, we will find that the ability to be resilient was developed by some and not by others. Further, resiliency is a skill that is sometimes learned by watching what not to do.

Ultimately, financial strength is a function of experience coupled with personality and determination. From these money stories, we learn not just the financial beginnings of our presidents, but we gain an appreciation of the context for our own financial journeys.

METHODOLOGY

All of the presidents have been extensively studied, but examining their personal finances is a little more complicated, and biographies tend to gloss over that aspect of their lives.

In writing this book, my job was to search different presidents' stories for the occasional mention of a number or dollar sign. Once I could narrow down on a story, then it became a bit of a scavenger hunt through primary source documents to find more of the details.

Once you get to the original sources, you realize that the presidents are just like us. They talk about money all the time. And they worried about it. From Grover Cleveland's handwritten will to James Monroe's carefully cultivated shopping lists, they are all caught up in their own personal financial dramas. Further, through many of the oral histories available at the presidential libraries, their friends and families recount the money stresses they experienced. Money isn't easy for them, just like it isn't easy for us.

But while connecting with their stories is important, it was also shocking to discover how many of our presidents had made money from slavery. Twelve of our forty-five presidents were slave owners—more than a quarter of them.[17] Slavery is a horrific institution and one we should not want to glorify. As a result, while there are presidents who had very strong financial skills, we need to keep in perspective how their wealth was created.

---

17   While Joe Biden is forty-sixth, we have to remember Grover Cleveland had two non-consecutive terms, making him both the twenty-second and twenty-fourth president.

Introduction

Finally, in working through the presidents' personal finances, we need to keep in mind how much inflation can have an impact on numbers. Whenever possible, I tried to convert numbers to 2024 values in order to give context and scale to the story. For instance, when Richard Nixon started at Whittier College in the fall of 1930, tuition was $250. For our modern eyes, this is incredibly low. That $250 in 1930 has the buying power of $4,600 in 2024 dollars. But Whittier College's 2023–2024 tuition is now $66,500. So, in this case, not only has the buying power changed, but there is a relative change in the cost of tuition almost a century later.

THE IMPACT OF STORIES

But even with my passion for history and the presidents, in order to write this book, I also had to have an interest in money. Over the past twenty-plus years, I have had the good fortune to work with wealthy individuals and their families in managing their financial lives while working at Goldman Sachs, BNY Mellon, and finally my own boutique practice. While my background in law and finance enables me to provide expertise to these individuals in navigating their personal finances, I have been given a front-row seat in how Americans create wealth today. What I have found is that wealth is more than simply a reflection of someone's financial success. It is a fascinating story of talent and hard work, layered with the element of luck. I can't tell you how many times I have worked with someone with an eight- or nine-figure net worth who started out with very little. Peeling away the layers of these stories, I have realized that there is no single core belief or experience that enables an individual to succeed financially. Rather, there are both positive and negative experiences, usually beginning in childhood, that impact how individuals make financial decisions.

Here is a list of what I have found to be the main factors that contribute to the way an individual makes such decisions:

> Education
> Grit
> Risk-taking
> Future self
> Confidence

All the Presidents' Money

Values
Charity
Marriage

But then something funny happened when I was writing this book; I noticed a group pattern in the occurrence of these traits. Some grouped together differently than others. Further, when considering a certain trait, such as grit, it was important to tell stories of those with and without that trait and how it impacted their financial journey.

The first group are what I would call *The Basic Building Blocks*: Connecting with your future self, education, budgeting, and risk-taking. These foundational traits are accessible to most of us.

But skills aren't enough. We have to examine what I call *Meaning and Money*. Life is long, and there are a lot of experiences that impact how we react to money. As we accumulate assets, we attach values, confidence, and charitable impact to wealth. Navigation of these areas can make a difference in how your financial planning plays out.

Finally, there is the last category: *The Wealth Builders*. Early on in my career, I heard a radio interview with a well-known CEO. His advice was succinct: All your happiness in life comes down to two decisions: what you do and who you marry. Seems obvious, but it stuck with me. And I looked at my clients. I saw the ones who really were different financially had three characteristics: they had married the right partner, they had grit, and they were able to navigate luck.

So, as you read these sections, you want to be focused on mastering *The Basic Building Blocks*. If you are lucky enough to have one of these skills, embrace it. *Meaning and Money* are reminders that your financial philosophy has an impact on your satisfaction. And as for *The Wealth Builders*, if you have any of them—or all of them—you are well on your way to financial stability.

PART I

The Basic Building Blocks

Chapter One

THOMAS JEFFERSON CORDIALLY INVITES YOU TO DINNER
(OR HOW YOUR FUTURE SELF IMPACTS YOUR WEALTH)

William Plumer was impressed.

It was by far the most sumptuous dinner party the Federalist senator had been invited to during his time in the capital. Sweetmeats, European cheeses, exotic fruits, and other delicacies were served during the many courses, and naturally, because Thomas Jefferson was the host, the wine was superb. In fact, it was not unusual for there to be eight wines served at such a dinner party.[18] As Plumer later wrote to his wife, it was "the best I ever drank, particularly the champagne, which was indeed delicious."[19]

While Jefferson's guests indulged themselves that evening on the meal cooked by Honoré Julien, his steward, Etienne Lemaire, pored over the household ledger.[20] He wrote out in French, *roquefish* (rockfish), *esturgeon* (sturgeon), and *gallon d'huîtres* (a gallon of oysters), along with their respective pricing.[21] His ledgers also took note as to the wines being cellared and

---

18 (Scofield 2022).
19 (Plummer Jr. and Peabody 1856) page 246.
20 (Scofield 2022) Interestingly, while the ledger showed the food served, Jefferson did not keep track of the menus. However, he did keep a detailed list of guests and their dates of attendance. Lemaire himself had an interesting role with Jefferson. Not only did he keep the ledgers and do the bookkeeping, but he was also a sommelier and a part-time chef.
21 (DeWitt 2010) pages 152–153.

stored including Chateau Margaux and Hermitage.[22] He was confined to a monthly budget of $500, but given the president's predilection for French food, it was not uncommon for a single meal to cost $50—an unheard-of amount at the time. Extravagance and foreign-food influences abounded. Lemaire had to make the numbers work even though he shared with his household contemporary Edmund Bacon in 1809 that "Mr. Jefferson's salary did not support him while he was President."[23]

Such a bacchanal came with a hefty bill, and in an agrarian economy, the upkeep of this extravagant lifestyle would prove to be a challenge. But costs were a minor irritation for the president who had long believed that informal dinner parties often brought the best political results.[24] When Lemaire presented the monthly ledgers for sign-off, the president would barely glance at it.

As a financial manager and tax attorney, I sympathize with Lemaire. When you work with someone who can't stop spending regardless of what you do, it's like watching an accident in slow motion. You try to trim around the edges to prevent them from really hurting themselves financially.

Over time, Lemaire tried to influence the president to make changes, as did the president's daughters. Jefferson was convinced to cut his wine bill over the last years of his presidency from $2,600 in 1804 ($68,000 in 2024 dollars) to $75.58 in 1808 ($1,850 in 2024 dollars).[25] But his love of entertaining in high style—serving his guests the best in Havana chocolates, Parmesan cheese, and Maille mustard—could not be stopped.[26]

The year 1826 was the fiftieth anniversary of the Declaration of Independence, and that year an announcement of a lottery appeared on page 2 of the April 29 edition of the *Saturday Evening Post*.[27] It read:

> Messrs. Yates and McIntyre [of New York City] have
> the management of Mr. Jefferson's lottery. There are

---

22   (Hailman 2006) page 289.
23   Ibid., page 288.
24   (DeWitt 2010) page 152. Of course, Jefferson's predilection for a political dinner party would be immortalized in the Tony Award–winning musical *Hamilton*.
25   Ibid., page 155. This is also mentioned in (Hailman 2006) pages 262–265, which gives an inventory of wine and price paid by the Jefferson White House.
26   Ibid., page 153.
27   Lotteries were extremely common in Jefferson's day. Every weekly *Saturday Evening Post* had numerous listings for lotteries. In Jefferson's case, his lottery managers generously waived their fee.

Thomas Jefferson Cordially Invites You to Dinner

11480 chances at $10 each. The books for subscription were opened at Washington on Saturday, and it is said the tickets will be ready for delivery in a very short time.[28]

The lottery prize included mills, acres of land, and Monticello itself. A lifetime of poor money management had finally caught up with Jefferson. He was in debt for over $100,000 (or $2 million in 2024 dollars).[29]

It seems absurd that such a revered president could end up in dire enough financial straits that he would be forced to auction off his possessions. Yet, a lifetime of poor money management had taken its toll, and Jefferson's predicament was a good example of what I call the failure to connect with your future self. Many people are simply not able to look ahead and see the person they will be in the future, and as a result they make financial decisions based on a very near-term perspective, a.k.a. *present bias*.[30]

In financial planning meetings, we often ask questions like: Where do you see yourself in ten, twenty, or thirty years? What does an optimal retirement look like? What are your greatest financial concerns? In studying those who make sound financial decisions, researchers find that those who can answer these questions with relatability, vividness, and optimism have a strong connection to their future selves.[31]

JEFFERSON AND HIS WINE OBSESSION

If Jefferson had had access to financial planning help in his time, the concept of connecting with his future self might have sunk in. One problem was that in Jefferson's time, the average life span was around forty years.[32] From his father to his wife to his children, death was commonplace for him. His future self—decades into the future—probably seemed like a stranger to him. If you asked him where he saw himself in thirty years, he would probably have said quite simply, "Dead."

---

28   (Nilsson 2015).
29   Monticello's website has a number of references to Jefferson's financial dramas. They can be found at https://www.monticello.org/slaveauction/.
30   (Xiao and Porto 2019).
31   (Lurtz 2019) and (Hershfeld 2011) both discuss this in-depth.
32   (Wasserman 2013).

All the Presidents' Money

Jefferson had no way of knowing that he would make it to what was then considered the very ripe old age of eighty-three. In his mind, the future wasn't that far ahead of him, so he was good at negotiating with himself about finding a way to pay for things tomorrow. Eventually, however, the reality of his situation did sink in, and in a letter to his granddaughter that he wrote in 1811 entitled "a dozen Canons of conduct in life," he listed, "Never spend your money before you have it."[33]

As news of the auction became public, Jefferson's family members sought to help. A few years prior, in 1822, Jefferson had gifted his grandson, Francis Wayles Eppes, his Poplar Forest plantation.[34] But once the news was public, Eppes was shocked to learn that his grandfather was in such bad financial shape.

Immediately Eppes wrote to Jefferson. "It was with infinite pain my D[ear] Grandfather, that I saw your application to the legislature; the first information which reached me, of the immediate pressure of your difficulties: and I write as well to express, my unfeigned grief, as to assure you, that I return to your funds with the utmost good will, the portion of property which you designed for me:—and which I should always have considered as yours, even had it been, legally secured to me…when I learn that after the payment of your debts, but little of your property will be left.…I now with the greatest allacrity [sic] relinquish."[35]

He then added in a postscript: "P.S. May I ask, what your scheme is, for the lottery?"[36]

At eighty-two, Jefferson could finally assess his financial dilemma quite clearly. He responded directly to his grandson. He wrote, "[A] Virginia estate requires skill and attention—skill I had not, and attention I could not have. That was engrossed by more imperious calls, which after acceptance had a right of preference to all others. The wonder rather is that I

---

33   (Thomas Jefferson's Monticello n.d.).
34   Two years after Jefferson's death, Eppes would sell the property to his neighbor. More history of this property can be found at Thomas Jefferson's Poplar Forrest at www.poplarforrest.org.
35   Letter from Francis Wayles Eppes to Thomas Jefferson, February 23, 1826. https://founders.archives.gov/documents/Jefferson/98-01-02-5929.
36   Ibid.

should have been so long as 60 years in arriving at the ultimate & unavoidable result."[37]

And there, quite succinctly, in three simple sentences, he explains away his poor money management. Jefferson stopped keeping a ledger as early as 1770, when he was twenty-seven years old, and to be fair, he did have a lot going on in his life. While his peers were fighting the British in the colonies, Jefferson was sent to France to manage diplomatic relations with the French, who were just years away from revolution. Jefferson would spend his evenings at extravagant dinners where the courses were the height of fine dining. Women's hairstyles were large and decorated with flowers, jewels, and even live birds in birdcages. Perhaps what was most intoxicating for Jefferson was learning about wine. And not just French wine, but wines from all over Europe. (It has been argued that Jefferson was the first American oenophile.) For a young man from Virginia, it made a strong impression on him, and he was determined to bring the French way of life to the new United States when he returned.

As the eighty-two-year-old Jefferson stood on the precipice of total financial ruin, he decided he finally needed to get his financial house in order. His correspondence for the last year of his life was littered with references to this goal. He was aware that he had heirs who were depending on him.[38] Rather than feel shame or embarrassment about the auction of his possessions, Jefferson was relieved. But when they heard about the impending auction, Jefferson's contemporaries were horrified and immediately a plan was hatched: the auction must be canceled. Instead, they would simply find a way to help the aged and revered Jefferson avoid financial ruin.

And that's how Thomas Jefferson became the subject of what was essentially the first GoFundMe campaign in the United States.

But as with many campaigns, fundraising didn't go as planned. Only $16,500 had been raised—a decent sum, but not enough to help Jefferson avoid ruin. Meanwhile, the Virginia legislature felt that allowing the auction of Monticello was not a wise idea. They did not want to have such a vulgar event associated with Jefferson and felt there would be other ways to manage his financial issues.

---

37   Letter from Thomas Jefferson to Francis Eppes, March 9, 1826. https://founders.archives.gov/documents/Jefferson/98-01-02-5954.
38   Ibid.

Although the elderly Jefferson became focused on ways of paying off his debt, the behavior that led to his predicament continued unabated. His table at Monticello remained full of visitors, some he knew and some who just stopped by to see the legend. He continued his lifestyle of throwing lavish dinner parties where he served amazing wine.

In one of his last letters, Jefferson complained that his inventory of European wines was dwindling, and he "needed" to obtain some new vintages. The auction of Monticello faded quite quickly into the background, and his financial challenges were simply ignored.

Jefferson was engaging in what financial planners call *future discounting*, which is "the human tendency to place less importance on future rewards when compared to current rewards."[39] Even the last letter he would write was about buying wine on credit. Three weeks later, on July 4, 1826, Jefferson died, still in debt and with no financial plan in place.

Just a few months after his death, on a cold January day in 1827, an auction occurred at Monticello. Along with land and household items, the auction contained a tragic spectacle. With the exception of seven slaves freed under his will, the remaining slaves of Monticello were sold at auction in order to pay off the debt. A chilling legacy for all who witnessed it.[40]

Jefferson had an enviable existence as a key figure of his time, living a luxurious life few could afford. The truth is that he really couldn't afford it either.

WARREN HARDING ORGANIZES HIS FORTUNE

If Jefferson ranks as one of our most financially challenged presidents, we may be surprised by a president who ranks higher in money management. Especially if that president had one of the worst presidencies in our history. This is where Warren Harding comes in.

Warren Harding is rarely held up as a model president. In fact, in C-SPAN's annual rankings,[41] Harding typically ranks in the bottom quar-

---

39   (Lurtz 2019).
40   (Thomas Jefferson's Monticello n.d.).
41   Per C-SPAN's site: "In 2000, C-SPAN's original team of academic advisers devised a survey in which participants used a 1 (not effective) to 10 (very effective) scale to rate each president on 10 qualities of presidential leadership: Public Persuasion, Crisis Leadership, Economic Management, Moral Authority, International Relations, Administrative Skills, Relations with Congress,

Thomas Jefferson Cordially Invites You to Dinner

tile of presidents in comparison to Jefferson's consistent top ten appearances. Most Americans today only know Harding from the Teapot Dome Scandal in the early 1920s, when a member of his cabinet was charged with taking $400,000 in bribes. Harding was never personally implicated in the crime, but the scandal took a lasting toll on his reputation, especially since he died suddenly three years into his term. To some degree, his poor reputation comes from a bit of a "shooting the dead man" approach, as he was president for less than one term and was much maligned after his death. His legacy is not one that current presidents aspire to recreate.[42]

From a financial perspective, Harding was savvy and successful. The antithesis of Jefferson, Harding had a good gauge of his future self from an early age. He could see where things would progress financially and made the appropriate sacrifices that would likely benefit him down the line. If he were alive today, we would probably see him in Silicon Valley as a start-up entrepreneur.

But, like a lot of young visionaries, Harding was a restless young man. At nineteen, Harding was struggling to determine his career path. He knew he did not want to go into medicine like his parents. He tried teaching and selling insurance, but neither ignited his passion. Living in his parents' home, he bounced around town looking for his moment.

In the 1880s, technology was transforming industries, including newspaper publishing, to which Harding found himself drawn. The advent of the linotype machine meant newspapers could contain more news and be published faster, and the public ate it up. Also, newspapers had catered to the educated. But suddenly the focus shifted to the common man. And the common man craved sensational stories—from true crime to political intrigue.[43]

Despite his politics, he became a reporter for the local Democratic paper, the *Marion Daily Mirror*, making seven dollars a week. Harding took

---

Vision/Setting an Agenda, Pursued Equal Justice for All and Performance Within the Context of the Times. In 2009, 2017, and 2021, following a change in administrations, subsequent surveys have been conducted using these same 10 characteristics."

42 That being said, John Oliver on *Last Week Tonight* had a segment on Harding in which he had actors Anna Kendrick, Laura Linney, and Campbell Scott, among others, spoofing the life of the twenty-ninth president. You can check it out here: https://youtu.be/5cBV8KFFasY.

43 (McNamara 2020).

on any story—from wedding announcements to local news to advertisements. He fell in love with newspapering—but soon just being a reporter wasn't enough for him.

Harding studied the newspapers in his hometown of Marion, Ohio, looking for one that could be molded to his liking. Finally, he stumbled upon a sheriff's sale for a small newspaper that lacked the prominence of other papers.[44] It was quiet, sleepy, and ready to be disrupted. Harding was intrigued. The *Marion Daily Star*, or as it was known *The Star*, could be the vehicle he was looking for. The price was $300, which was the equivalent of about $9,000 today.

However, just because Harding had a vision didn't mean he had the liquidity to buy the paper. But he was an affable young man who had a lot of friends—including some Republicans. As he considered the project, he took two of his friends to lunch. Over oysters, Harding proposed purchasing *The Star* to Jack Warwick and John Sickel.[45] But Harding was no fool in making this overture. His reasoning for picking Warwick and Sickel was strategic: Warwick was an apprentice printer, and Sickel had recently inherited a large sum of money and was uninterested in being involved day to day.[46] The three young men agreed to the partnership.

Yet a month later, Sickel bailed out. It was going to be a 50/50 split with Warwick. Now, Harding had to come up with cash to buy his half. And what did he do? In modern parlance, we would call this a "Friends and Family" fundraising round. Harding went to his father asking for help. Now his father, George Harding, was a doctor who owned property around the town. Seeing his son's passion for the project, he sold a vacant lot to the bank and handed over $150.[47] Harding's days in the fourth estate had begun.

At first, his purchase of the paper was seen as a bit of a joke in town.[48] But it was soon apparent that Harding had a knack as a newspaperman.

---

44 This appealed to both Harding and his father, who were Republicans. We will encounter a similar story with LBJ and Lady Bird and their radio station.
45 (Warwick 1938).
46 (Hall 2014) page 20.
47 Ibid.
48 Interview with Sherry Hall, May 25, 2021.

Thomas Jefferson Cordially Invites You to Dinner

As the business grew, he bought out Warwick in 1885 after a rumored disagreement about adding an important piece of technology to the company: a telephone. In addition to that, being an entrepreneur was tough, and they often went without wages. Harding was conveniently living rent-free with his parents. Warwick needed a steady paycheck, so he stayed on as an employee.[49]

Harding studied all the area newspapers and came up with an idea: Ads were the lifeblood of newspapers, yet the local businesses advertised their wares the same way regardless of season. For example, snow shovels were promoted in the summer because the ads remained the same all year.

That is where Harding's vision was key. He made the daily rounds of the local businesses to earn their trust. He was an advocate for "buying local." As time passed, he began to discuss a novel concept: ad campaigns that changed frequently based on the season.

As his vision took off, the paper flourished and, as a result, so did Harding. His marriage to Florence Kling brought into the mix her brilliant business mind and allowed the paper to grow to national prominence.[50] Florence Harding was a unique woman from her day. Her father was incredibly wealthy and educated his daughter—particularly in the area of finance. Florence took steps with *The Star* that helped with revenue, including hiring paperboys directly as a way to cut costs and increase profits. Yet, as in the system of the day, despite running the books, her signature never appeared on the bank slips.

The Star was no longer a small, quiet paper; it was a powerhouse. The Hardings reveled in the financial success. But they saw the community and their success as a joint venture. It wasn't uncommon for Harding to invest in other small businesses in town.[51] He had a very generous spirit in trying to help spread the wealth.

But Harding knew he needed to take steps to keep his paper running smoothly. He focused on how to create longevity for the business. He believed employees would work harder if they were owners. He wasn't the

---

49 Warwick's departure in search of steady income illustrates something we still see today: entrepreneurship is really the world of the upper middle class and above who can afford to support an entrepreneur.
50 Interview with Sherry Hall of the Harding Library, May 25, 2021.
51 Ibid.

first business owner to do this. Companies like Sears Roebuck, JC Penney, and Procter and Gamble had programs where they would set aside stock to provide the employees income when they retired. This would evolve in the 1950s into a concept called an employee stock ownership program, or ESOP.[52]

Harding took the radical step of turning over minority ownership to a group of employees. In the early 1900s, 25 percent of the paper became employee-owned. Harding cultivated these young men and in return received incredible loyalty. It was "their" paper, not "his." To his team, he was affectionately referred to as "W.G."

Now, by this point, you may be saying, "Look, I get it. Harding was a great entrepreneur, but what does this have to do with financial planning?" And that is the odd thing about personal finance. When it is done well, it looks simple. Harding's story seems straightforward. Yet, he made choices and took calculated risks that tied in well with his future goals. If he lacked a financial skill, he wasn't afraid to get advice and follow it. Just imagine if Jefferson had done even 25 percent of what Harding did financially—he likely wouldn't have ended up at auction.

But connecting with your future self also requires you to change. As you grow over time and your values change, so should your connection to your future self. The Harding who bought the paper was not the same man in the presidency. His goals had changed. By the 1920s, he was looking ahead. He needed to think about what his next act would be post-presidency. He was focused on answering the question we ask in financial planning meetings: What does your retirement look like?

The second year of Harding's presidency, 1921, was a pivotal one. After nearly forty years of ownership, it was time to sell his beloved *Star*. And this is where the story gets interesting from a financial planning perspective. Harding displayed empathy—not just to his family but to his employees as well.

Now, you might be thinking: *Who cares about empathy? Isn't it really about the money?* But the crazy thing is empathy has a place in financial planning because it allows us to connect with our future selves and do the

---

52 (Menke 2011) Interestingly, the first modern-day ESOP was in 1956 with the Peninsula Newspaper Inc in San Francisco.

right things for our future goals. It also allows us to help others around us who we feel are in similar financial positions. Harding felt a sense of responsibility because he knew that his selling of the paper would have significant financial implications for all involved.

Humidity was high on June 20, 1923, when President Harding, his wife Florence, and their dog Laddie left Washington, DC, for a presidential tour. They were calling it the "Voyage of Understanding," and the first stop was St. Louis, Missouri.

The previous months had been difficult for Harding. Challenges within his administration were growing. Personally, he was struggling with his health. A bad cold in January had left him sluggish. He had long struggled with problems related to an enlarged heart. In fact, in reviewing his medical records, many modern historians and physicians believe he had an undetected heart attack in early 1923.

But despite his bad health, Harding was in mid-negotiation to sell *The Star*. He had concluded that at this point, the paper needed to grow and needed an owner who could really focus on it. The industry was going through consolidation, and Harding knew that he needed to take advantage of the environment to secure his future. His focus was on the presidency, and so he knew it was time to sell it, but he wanted to sell it for a significant sum. While he wanted to get top dollar for his paper, he had two other priorities: taking care of his employees and making sure he had a role post-presidency.

Initial offers started coming in at $350,000.[53] But Harding held strong to his conviction on value. He knew that having a president involved would be beneficial to any buyer. In September 1922, he invited a potential buyer to Washington, DC, and noted that the paper was "very successful." More importantly, he noted that while he owned 75 percent, the other owners were less interested in selling.

His negotiations worked. *The Star* went under contract to Brush-Moore Newspapers for $550,000 (or $9.4 million in today's dollars) in June 1923.[54] The press release reflected his sadness. Harding "let it be known he deeply regrets the release of the majority ownership…but he is certain of its

---

53   (Hall 2014).
54   Ibid.

true establishment and sure it will carry on under the new control, working with his associates of many years who have so successfully and progressively carried on the work since his public duties have taken him from Marion."[55]

It was a transaction of both cash and stock. While some would call this amount exorbitant, the valuation was roughly ten times the annual profit. In the year prior to the sale, that was $60,000. Also, he had known Louis Brush and Roy Moore for years, and they had values similar to his own.

Brush and Moore agreed to keep on his employees, who would be compensated and well-treated. More importantly for Harding personally, once he finished his presidency, he could still keep a hand in the newspaper business by serving as an associate editor who would regularly publish pieces for the paper. His future seemed to be set.

But while the letter of intent was signed, the deal had not closed when Harding left the White House on that balmy June day. He was feeling worse and worse. With all the changes he had made to his financial life, he knew he had to address his estate plan. He needed to update it to reflect the new facts of his financial life. Harding also knew it was integral for his finances to run smoothly after his death and to protect those he loved; he needed to plan proactively.

As the presidential entourage made their way to St. Louis, Harding sketched out his Last Will and Testament. Over the course of three typewritten pages, Harding drafted fifteen separate articles to support his wife, father, and other family members. There was even a small bequest for three employees of the *Marion Star*. His wife would receive the bulk of the estate, including real estate and investment income, but as they had no children, he protected himself by only giving her a life estate.[56]

This was pretty crafty of Harding. A life estate meant his wife could use the assets for her lifetime, but at her death, it passed according to Harding's wishes, not his wife's. That meant if she remarried, a future spouse could not inherit Harding's assets.[57]

We use this technique all the time in estate planning. It is often called a qualified terminable interest property (QTIP) trust. It allows the first

---

55   (The Daily Advertiser 1923).
56   Last Will and Testament of Warren G. Harding, dated June 20, 1923. Copy available on Warren G. Harding Presidential Sites.
57   It should be noted that this is a common technique used in estate planning, especially now in the day and age of multiple marriages and longevity.

spouse who passes away to give the survivor access to the assets yet still control where they go ultimately. Or as we like to say, it provides "dead-hand control."

At Florence Harding's death, the estate would revert back to his siblings. He also took care of his father, allowing him the use of one of Harding's homes and some investment income. He made two small charitable bequests to his hometown. In regard to his funeral plans, he was quite clear "that no part of my estate shall be expended for a monument other than a simple marker at my grave."[58]

Harding could not have written his will at a more appropriate moment. Less than six weeks later, while at the Palace Hotel in San Francisco, he suffered a fatal heart attack and died on August 2, 1923. The deal for *The Star* had yet to close, but it did after his death.

Just three months after his passing, Brush and Moore honored the "earn out" they had in their contract with Harding. They entered into a ten-year agreement with Florence Harding as a Special Correspondent for $13,300 a year for the *Marion Star*. In the event she passed prior to the end of the contract, the remaining funds would pass to the Warren G. Harding estate.[59]

The Harding estate was a lucrative one. In the final probate filings, his total estate was valued at $893,012.48. This would be approximately $16 million in 2024 dollars.[60]

Unfortunately, his wife passed less than a year after him. Lucky for his siblings and their children, Harding's forethought on making sure Florence only had a life estate was a wise one.

While Harding's process seems like a logical one, the piece that makes his story different from Jefferson's is that throughout his financial life, he was always looking ahead. He could see who he was going to be in the future and made specific plans for that. Even while president, he knew there could be a day when he needed to work; in Harding's time, ex-presidents didn't get multi-million-dollar book deals. While Harding is often seen as one of our worst presidents, in terms of connecting with his

---

58 (Hall 2014) page 200.
59 Harding Publishing Company Agreement, dated November 23, 1923.
60 Final Account from The Probate Court of Marion County, Ohio.

future self, he is arguably one of our best. In today's dollars, he turned a $300 investment into a $9.4 million sale of a newspaper.

JOE BIDEN BUYS (QUITE A FEW) HOUSES

If Thomas Jefferson and Warren Harding are at the opposite ends of the spectrum when it comes to connecting with their future selves, what happens when a president's experience is a little more typical? Although people can often see who they want their future self to be, sometimes other personality traits get in the way.

That's what we find in Joe Biden's money story. Biden has long been seen as "Middle Class Joe." In fact, he's spent a political career embracing this image. At times, he has prided himself on being the poorest senator in Congress and once said in a 2020 political debate in New Hampshire, "I've never focused on money for me."[61]

Despite this middle-class image, that didn't mean he was not connected to his future self. Biden was well aware of where he wanted to go. In addition to a connection to his future self, he also had empathy. But Biden's story is unique because trauma can disrupt the connection. It can undermine the decision-making process. And the Biden story is actually a common one for a lot of Americans.

The best way to understand Biden's financial story is to look at his real estate portfolio. Luckily, it is a pretty well-documented obsession that began when he was a child in Scranton, Pennsylvania. Biden's parents were decidedly blue-collar and lived paycheck to paycheck. The childhood home he grew up in reflected that. His parents didn't even own the house at 2446 N. Washington Avenue in the neighborhood of Green Ridge—his maternal grandparents did—but it was a place of great happiness with multiple generations living together.

Yet Biden's father had trouble finding work in town. He cleaned boilers for a living and the search for a paycheck was such that it took him 135 miles south to Delaware and was only home in Scranton on the weekends.[62] Eventually, when Biden was ten, the family made the move to the Brookview Apartments in the working-class town of Claymont, Delaware.

---

61 (Biden, et al. 2020).
62 (Owens 2022) page 27.

Thomas Jefferson Cordially Invites You to Dinner

Now, Claymont might sound like a nondescript place, but just eight miles south of Claymont lay Wilmington. The first things you note when you arrive in Wilmington are the stately manor homes and the lush greenery. If you live in Wilmington, it means that you've made it and that you are part of the town's long history of wealth. And in the town of Wilmington, the Du Pont family and its wealth cast a long shadow.

The Du Pont family came to Delaware from France in the early 1800s and started a gunpowder business. The success of this business turned the family into one of the wealthiest in the country. They had a tremendous impact on how the town grew over the years, and, at one point, employed 10 percent of Delaware's population. The Du Ponts often married their cousins, and so as Wilmington developed, it had the air of old money. Even today, due to the favorable banking and corporate laws of the state, it has an aristocratic atmosphere. The leafy green area, flush with country clubs and large estates, was a very different environment from the Scranton that Biden had left behind.

We can only imagine how Joe Biden first saw Wilmington when he arrived as a ten-year-old boy, but it must have made an impression. It was clear that there was a world out there beyond what he had seen in Scranton. In some homes, you didn't live paycheck to paycheck, and you didn't have to worry about whether your father would find work.

After college and law school, Biden returned to Wilmington and very quickly, he knew where he was going. He passed the bar, engaged in private practice, and then ran for and was elected as a local official. Biden was going places, and he was clear about his goals. He wanted the life of living in Wilmington, and he wanted it quickly. He dreamed of living in one of these luxurious homes.

Once married, Biden would drive around Wilmington with his wife, Neilia, and look at his hopes for the future. In those pre-Zillow days, those hopes often came in the shape of driving by a home and imagining the life behind its doors. Buying a home is usually an emotionally driven purchase, and a new house quickly becomes the symbol of an ideal life. In this way, some people tend to connect with their future self through real estate. Biden confessed in his memoirs about his house obsession. "My idea of Saturday fun was to jump in the Corvette with Neilia and drive around the Wilmington area scouting open houses, houses for sale, land where we could build."[63] By the time he was twenty-eight, his obsession caused him to buy and sell four different homes. These homes were financed by mortgages and loans from his father-in-law.[64] Biden struggled with being cash poor, but it didn't deter him. Illiquidity was not an issue as long as he was in the real estate market, but he was building a financial house of cards.

Then tragedy struck. His wife and baby daughter were killed in an auto accident right after his election to the Senate in December 1972.[65] A tractor trailer struck their car in an intersection while his family was out Christmas shopping. His sons, ages two and three, survived.

The accident set off a chain of financial events. While he had always been very focused on real estate, the trauma of his loss intensified his obsession. Researchers have studied brains that have gone through trauma, and they find that it directly impacts the decision-making process.[66] In fact, one study found "as various forms of trauma go unrepaired, the road network of the physical brain begins to develop places of semantic rigidity and semantic chaos."[67] As a result, those individuals who have suffered trauma were more predisposed to act with urgency.

Chaos and urgency. Those are two words I would use to describe what happened to Joe Biden over the years following his wife's death. I have worked with clients over the years who have had traumatic situations happen—death, abuse, addiction. One widow I worked with was shocked to find out after her husband's sudden death that she was worth $20 million. That's a lot to absorb—and upon finding out, she became extremely focused on endowing a $2 million scholarship in his name. It became imperative in working with her that while the endowment was a positive thing, we needed to slow down and talk through all the various outcomes—including whether or not she would have enough money to make it through her retirement. Now, it might seem like anyone with that kind of money shouldn't have money worries. But it all comes down to living expenses. If she was living on $600,000 or more a year, it would be tight. Luckily in this case, her expenses were more in the $300,000 range and thus she could afford to donate $2 million.

---

63 (J. Biden 2008).
64 (Bykowicz 2020).
65 (UPI 1972).
66 (Ross III and Coambs 2018).
67 Ibid.

Thomas Jefferson Cordially Invites You to Dinner

That clearly didn't happen with Biden. Part of his problem was that everyone around him was on his Senate staff. It's harder to tell someone that it might not be the best idea when they are your boss.

Grief-stricken, Biden spent his evenings driving around looking at real estate. While he loved North Star, the house he lived in with his late wife, he was also overwhelmed with the memories and what he considered "all our lost dreams."[68] In driving around, Biden was drawn to the most prestigious streets. Then one night on the way to a black-tie event in Philadelphia, he stumbled upon an abandoned manor home on four-and-a-half acres on Montchanin Road. Owned previously by the Du Ponts, the house came with a special panache despite having fallen into disrepair. A developer was going to tear down the house and sell the lots, but Biden had other plans for it.

Biden couldn't believe his luck. It had everything—a fountain, a pool, and even a ballroom. It was all of his dreams tied up in a ten-thousand-square-foot house. Paying no attention to his annual Senate salary of $42,500, he immediately started negotiating. He wanted the house. After haggling with the developer, a price was agreed upon: a mind-boggling $200,000—the equivalent of a $1 million home today. He sold his previous home, worth $46,000, and moved in with his two sons and his sister and her new husband.[69]

Although it appeared to be his dream home, upon closer inspection it was like a scene out of *The Money Pit*. Squirrels roamed the third floor, and asbestos was hidden behind the walls. Biden could barely afford the maintenance and started selling plots of land to cover costs.[70] His political filings reveal that while he had whole life insurance, he was constantly borrowing against it. Next to his political opponents, Biden's greatest enemy was illiquidity. Is it a surprise that he often appeared on lists as one of the least wealthy senators?

I can only imagine watching this play out. A person in Biden's position is so focused on the goal, they can't see the forest for the trees, and they become resistant to advice. They can't admit mistakes, and they double down on their behavior. Biden was frenetic about constantly renovating

---

68 (J. Biden 2008) pages 98–99.
69 (Cramer 1993) pages 285–286.
70 Ibid., page 287.

his home. He continually trimmed plots of the property to maintain some liquidity. But even in those decisions, he wasn't the most rational. One of his most off-the-wall decisions was that if he sold a plot of the property, he would consider "moving" structures from that part of the property onto land he still owned. Rumor had it that he had even considered this with the swimming pool. Many thought that Biden was a little crazed about his home. The house was nicknamed "The Station" due to all the comings and goings, and it became the center of the Biden political world.[71]

As a side note, when we see how frenetic Biden is about The Station, it brings to mind another president. Grover Cleveland bought a property outside of Washington, DC, when he was elected in 1886 and recently married. It was an 1868 farmhouse on twenty-six-and-a-quarter acres that he purchased for $21,500 ($690,000 in 2024 dollars). He called it Oak View. But unlike Biden, Cleveland was more frugal in nature (he had been a bachelor for many years) and had sufficient savings that allowed him to improve the property. Over the time he was president, he repaired structures as well as added to and updated the main house. By the time he was done, he had spent $13,000—a significant sum but not one out of his budget.[72]

While Cleveland loved the property, when he lost the election, he had to take a job in New York City. As he left DC, he initially decided to keep it, hoping to generate enough rental income to cover the costs. Yet immediately he realized he couldn't bear to have a tenant use his home and he put it on the market. He sold it for $140,000 in 1890 (akin to $4 million in buying power in 2024).[73]

A SECOND HOME BECKONS

This financial instability became his sense of normal, but after more than twenty years in the home, Biden, his second wife Jill, and their daughter were ready for a move. They sold "The Station" for $1.2 million. While this seemed like a great price for the property, keep in mind it was probably just a return of all the capital Biden had put into the home.[74]

---

71 (Owens 2022) page 142.
72 (Jeffers 2000) pages 225–226.
73 (The Washington Post 1890).
74 The sale of "The Station" is controversial on two fronts. First, he sold the home to the CEO of MBNA, a company Biden regulated in his time in the Senate. Further,

Thomas Jefferson Cordially Invites You to Dinner

Despite the sale, Biden still pursued his dream of being among the landed class of Delaware. He purchased land on Barley Mill Road and built a house. By the time he finished his two terms as vice president, he really only had his Senate pension to sustain him. Yet, Biden had one other real estate dream that he shared with his second wife, Jill: a beach house. Growing up in Hammonton, New Jersey, among the highlights of Jill's summer vacations were day trips to the Jersey Shore with her grandparents. To Jill, that time at the beach was about family. "I have a lot of wonderful memories about being with my grandparents; they'd take me to Steel Pier and to ride the rolling carts on the Boardwalk [in Atlantic City]."[75] And while Joe grew up in Pennsylvania, which was too far from the coast for beach trips, his memories of Scranton were filled with family happiness, and a big house near the ocean would be the perfect place to spend quality time with his children and grandchildren.

Most wealthy enclaves on the East Coast have their summer beach getaways, and for Wilmington, Delaware, the hot spot is Rehoboth Beach. It was here that the Bidens aspired to own a second house. But when Biden was a senator and then vice president, this seemed unlikely. Managing one primary residence was difficult enough financially for the Bidens. However, after leaving office in 2016, both Joe and Jill were able to monetize their White House experiences by writing memoirs, and Joe went on lucrative speaking tours and became a professor at the University of Pennsylvania. All of a sudden, the guy who could barely make ends meet due to his illiquidity had a net worth of $7 to $8 million.

(While this is a substantial number, due to inflation, Biden's net worth is really just starting to crack the threshold of high net worth. A net worth of $8 million in the 2020s is like having $2 million in the 1980s.)

In 2017, Biden and his wife purchased a home on the beach overlooking Cape Henlopen State Park in Rehoboth Beach for $2.74 million. It was a 4,786-square-foot home with six bedrooms and five-and-a-half baths, a gourmet kitchen, and an in-ground pool. Very impressive, but the real value the Bidens saw in the house was that it had the space and amenities

---

in the 2020 election, on October 17, 2020, Eric Trump tweeted out a picture of the house with the comment, "The salary of a U.S. Senator is $174,000 per year. This is Joe Biden's house… seems legit." Little did he know how financially crazy owning that house was for Biden.

75   Ibid.

to accommodate a large extended family, which was far more important to them than any prestige that came with ownership of such a property.

Today, when people see Biden, they see a man with substantial real estate. As he and Jill bike around Rehoboth (followed by the press crew), it looks like the path to this financial success was easy. But Biden is like most Americans in how he connected to his future self. He knew what he wanted, though at times his decision-making was flawed. Some of his decisions could have been better, and some were beyond his control. Yet, Biden ultimately positioned himself to monetize his considerable political experience and create more stable wealth. For many years his was a cautionary tale, but finally, after much triumph and tragedy in his professional and personal lives, he was able to manifest a happy ending to his financial story.

PLANNING FOR FUTURE SUCCESS

The desire for financial security has remained the same over centuries. We all seek financial resilience. It's easy to look at Jefferson and Biden and judge them. Jefferson's approach was to stick his head in the sand. Biden knew what he wanted, but his decision-making process was chaos-ridden. Their actions are emblematic of the struggle in all of us to connect with our future self and make the right financial choices. Without that connection, we become financially fragile.

Resiliency takes work. But the takeaway we saw with Harding is while forethought is important, empathy is also a key component for success. One thing that has struck me over the years with the wealthy families I work with is that while the media and politicians often describe them as "not paying their fair share," many of them are taking actions with money through empathy.

On this interesting topic, one story resonates with me. I work with a very wealthy CEO. He wanted to buy a home for his son in San Diego, California, during the recent housing boom. When it came time to bid, he gave me explicit instructions. The realtor had advised to put out a crazy, over-asking offer just to secure the property. He said, "Regardless of what the realtor says, I refuse to over-bid hundreds of thousands over the asking price just to win the home. If I do that, then I've changed the rules and

Thomas Jefferson Cordially Invites You to Dinner

am blocking others from ever accessing the housing market. It just doesn't seem right."

Mentally playing out how our financial actions will leave an impact is key. So, next time you are making a financial decision, don't just think about your financial goals, but ask: Am I acting with empathy toward the me that is ten, twenty, or even thirty years into the future? You might find it's a good guidepost on decision-making.

Chapter Two

ABRAHAM LINCOLN WOULD LIKE A LIBRARY CARD PLEASE
(OR EDUCATION & PEDIGREE)

John Adams was anxious. He hadn't anticipated that he would make the fifteen-mile journey from his home in Braintree to Cambridge, Massachusetts, on his own that day in 1754. His tutor was originally supposed to come with him but at the last moment took ill. Now, here he was on the journey, in bad weather, alone at age fifteen, to take the Harvard entrance exam.[76] "Terrified at the Thought of introducing myself to such great Men as the President and fellows of a College," he later confided in his diary, "I at first resolved to return home."[77]

For Adams, there was a lot on the line. His father, also named John, was a farmer and deacon. His father did not have the opportunity to go to college, and he wanted that for his son. Joseph, his father's brother, had attended Harvard. At the time, Harvard was a place where men studied for the ministry. Adams's father wanted him to be a minister and was determined that his son get a good education. Harvard would provide both—if he could get in.

Once the younger John was considered "fitted for college," he had to take the entrance exam that would determine his future.[78] Luckily for

---

76 (New England Historical Society 2022).
77 (J. Adams 1966) The early entries of his diary are often weather reports—hence us knowing he left for the exams in inclement weather.
78 (McCullough 2001).

Adams, he not only did well on the exam, but he scored so well that he was awarded a partial scholarship to pay for his studies.

Scholarships have long been part of education—since the time of the ancient Greeks. But they didn't reach the colonies until 1643 when Ann Radcliffe Mowlson, the widow of a wealthy merchant, left £100 to Harvard in her will for "the maintenance of some poor schollar [sic] which shall be admitted into…Harvards Colledge [sic]."[79] By the time Adams got there, a number of scholarships helped him cover costs, but not entirely. Where would he get the rest?

The Adams family had a financial philosophy: land was the best investment one could make, provided they never sold it. Since Adams needed the money for tuition and his father wanted him to attend Harvard, he made an exception and sold ten acres of land to cover the remaining costs.[80]

If I hadn't mentioned John Adams, you might have thought this was a modern-day story. While this financial transaction took place almost 275 years ago, it's indicative of how college is financed today: a student secures partial scholarships (or loans) to attend college, and their family finds ways to pay what isn't covered. Many of my clients have funded education accounts or 529 plans to help with their children's education. That land sale was the eighteenth-century version.

History proved that John Adams's father made the right bet. The ability to access Harvard changed the course of his son's life. A speaking engagement at Harvard convinced Adams to pursue the law instead of the ministry. And the benefits of his education allowed him to build his finances from a thriving law practice and in marrying a woman from a wealthier family.

THE EDUCATION EQUATION

So what does education have to do with wealth and money? The answer is quite simple: *Everything*.

In today's world, we may take for granted that everyone goes to college. And we all can easily recite the benefits of a college degree: higher income, greater wealth, better health and longevity, better mental states, greater

---

79 (Harvard University 2023), also in (Pallardy 2020).
80 (McCullough 2001) pages 34–35.

Abraham Lincoln Would Like a Library Card Please

chance of being married or partnered, and greater likelihood of owning a home.[81] Although not a perfect formula, this basic equation illustrates how many of us—presidents included—approach getting an education:

$$\text{Strategy} + \text{Sacrifice} + \text{Education} = \text{Greater Opportunity Set.}$$

In financial planning, we talk about opportunity sets all the time. An opportunity set is a group of potential options. And when it comes to gaining an education, we need to imagine someone at eighteen years old with their whole life in front of them and all the potential to build financial stability. At that point, everything is a possibility. As decisions are made, the doors close on some options, although the goal is to keep as many opportunities as possible.

This reminds me of a client couple of mine. They had been funding their daughter's 529 plan since she was born.[82] I remember crunching numbers with them to make sure they could fully fund it every year with the annual gift exclusion.[83] When their daughter was accepted to Duke, they had me sit down with her to explain how the 529 would finance the tuition. The plan had just over $280,000.

After we reviewed the analysis of how the plan would work and how she would graduate debt-free, the daughter looked up at her parents and said, "I cannot believe you did this for me. It's unbelievable." She was crying; they were crying—it was an amazing moment. She was filled with gratitude that her college education would be fully funded.

But she was also grateful for something else. Something more important than the 529 plan. It was gratitude for the opportunity set that they were giving her. Her decisions would not be dependent on whether she had loans to service. She could explore her career more and take risks. She could

---

81 (William R. Emmons 2019) page 297.
82 A 529 plan is an education account set up for the benefit of a beneficiary. The money is gifted to the account and grows tax-deferred. Provided the beneficiary takes it out for *qualified education expenses* the money comes out tax-free. These accounts were established during the George W. Bush administration and continue to be seen as the best vehicle to save for education.
83 The annual gift exclusion is how much a person can transfer to another without paying gift tax. This amount is adjusted for inflation by the IRS on a regular basis. In 2024, it was $18,000. This means a married couple can give their child $36,000 a year without incurring gift tax.

change her mind about what she wanted to do or even take a lower-paying job for a unique experience. Upon college graduation, she would still have all the doors open for her and all that possibility. She could start building her net worth right out of school. And that is a priceless opportunity set.

As our presidents navigated the opportunity set equation, some had an easier time than others. Traditionally, the track to college was for the wealthy (and arguably still is). Presidents like Thomas Jefferson and Theodore Roosevelt went to college because their families could pay the tuition. They went to school with other men from their socioeconomic class. It was a way to be educated and create connections.

If I asked you to tell me the perfect path to take through education, I'm sure your answer would be along the lines of: Attend a highly rated prep school for pre-college education followed by Harvard, Yale, Stanford, or another Ivy League school for college. This would be followed by a graduate degree, preferably from Harvard Business School (commonly referred to by those in the know as "HBS"), Harvard Law, or Stanford Law. And then of course, head to Goldman Sachs or McKinsey in the bid for an illustrious Wall Street or corporate career.

This isn't just the path to build wealth, but also the path to sustaining it. It's generational wealth building.[84] Beyond obtaining prestigious educational degrees, one would make connections with people that could lead to opportunities at successful companies—and all of that together helps one develop "pedigree." Without it, wealth building—and certainly generational wealth building—can be more difficult.

Nine presidents didn't attend college: George Washington, Andrew Jackson, Martin Van Buren, Zachary Taylor, Abraham Lincoln, Andrew Johnson, Millard Fillmore, Grover Cleveland, and Harry Truman. It's an illustrious list. All were born into poverty, yet all found ways to get educated without college. And interestingly enough, with the exception of John-

---

84 Generational wealth building is simply the passing of assets from one generation to another. But it sounds a lot simpler than it is. In many languages, there is a version of "shirtsleeves to shirtsleeves in three generations." The wealthy focus a great deal on it. Generational wealth building also factors into the racial divide in the United States. White Americans have greater opportunities than Black Americans to build wealth and pass it to the next generation. A 2021 McKinsey report found a "$220 billion annual disparity between Black wages today and what they would be in a scenario of full parity." See (Shelley Stewart III 2021).

son, all died wealthy men. And yes, Truman had money—don't believe the myth that he was poor (as we'll discuss in a later chapter), but Truman was the last of this group, and he was born in 1884.

LINCOLN TAKES A UNIQUE PATH

In 1858, it was decided that there should be a directory of all members who had served in Congress. To those who were living, a query was sent out requesting a biography. A response backdated June 15, 1858, stated:

> "Born, February 12, 1809, in Hardin County, Kentucky.
> Education defective.
> Profession, a lawyer.
> Have been a captain of volunteers in Black Hawk war.
> Postmaster at a very small office.
> Four times a member of the Illinois legislature, and was a member of the lower house of Congress.
> Yours, A. Lincoln."[85]

Lincoln himself drafted the words upon the request for a short biography to give his fellow representatives over a decade after leaving the Illinois legislature.

"Education defective" is not a term we associate with the author of the Gettysburg Address and our most popular president ever, though the humility is in keeping with his reputation. Lincoln's lack of a formal education weighed heavily on him, so he took it upon himself to remedy the defect by reading voraciously at every opportunity. He borrowed books from neighbors. When he moved to Springfield, he made extensive use of the state library. And when he finally went to Congress in the 1840s, he boarded across the street from the Library of Congress. Historian Hubert Skinner once opined that when Lincoln was serving in the House of Representatives, he was "a puzzle, and a subject of amusement to his fellows. He did not drink, or use tobacco, or bet, or swear. It would seem that he must be a very rigid churchman. But no, he did not belong to any church; and soon

---

85   (Lanman 1859) This is the bio that appears in the directory. However, it is also reprinted in the *Collected Works of Abraham Lincoln* as well as in a letter from Lincoln to William H. Henderson, dated February 21, 1855.

he became reckoned an 'unbeliever.' How did he occupy his spare time? He was mousing around the books of the old Congressional Library…'Bah!' said his fellow Congressmen, 'He is a bookworm!'"[86]

Reading and learning was Lincoln's ticket out of a life on the farm. For someone eager to learn who had been born in a one-room log cabin in Kentucky, the idea of a vast library in which he could wander and read books on a whim was a simply untold luxury. Lincoln had attended three or four rudimentary "ABC schools" that were on the western frontier, set up to provide a level of education to remote rural children.[87] But often those schools had teachers who were barely educated themselves, and he estimated later in his life that he probably had less than one year of formal schooling when it was all pieced together.

Fifty years later, he would write to a journalist, "Of course when I came of age I did not know much. Still somehow, I could read, write, and cipher to the Rule of Three; but that was all. I have not been to school since. The little advance I know have upon this store of education, I have picked up from time to time under the pressure of necessity."[88] He read, in other words, in order to achieve professional and financial security.

In his early years, when public libraries were few and far between, Lincoln borrowed books, and his father's second wife's dowry even came with a few books. He devoured the Bible, *Aesop's Fables*, and *Robinson Crusoe*. He even got his hands on a book that he read time and again: *The Life and Memorable Actions of George Washington* by Mason Locke Weems. Washington became not just a hero but a role model. College education wasn't the only way to rise in society for someone who was born in 1809. Two other future presidents born about the same time as Lincoln—Millard Fillmore (born 1800) and Andrew Johnson (born 1808)—who also could not go to school instead took apprenticeships with a clothmaker and a tailor, respectively. Only Franklin Pierce (born 1804) had what we would consider today to be a traditional education path; he attended both Philips Exeter Academy and Bowdoin College.

---

86 (D. L. Wilson 1991) page 52. See also (Miller 2002).
87 These schools were sometimes called "blab" schools as the students often simply repeated back the teacher's lesson due to the fact that many could not read or write.
88 Letter Abraham Lincoln to Jesse W. Fell, dated December 20, 1859.

Abraham Lincoln Would Like a Library Card Please

With his native intelligence, Lincoln would probably have had no trouble getting into any number of good colleges, including Harvard, which at the time required only a basic knowledge of English and arithmetic and a year of the classics in order to qualify for the school's admission examination. But even if he had passed the test, Lincoln simply couldn't afford the annual tuition of $55 plus living expenses of around $350. When Lincoln was college-aged, his opportunity set was very different. He was helping on the family farm with hard labor. Even after he left his father's home, he went from splitting rails to piloting a flatboat loaded with produce. Neither job left much time for learning.

Then, a unique opportunity unfolded by chance. While piloting the flatboat to New Orleans, it got stranded on a milldam. Lincoln took the lead in directing the crew and managed to free the boat. As a result of his calm, direct actions, the owner of the flatboat, Denton Offutt, took notice of the lanky twenty-two-year-old.

Years later, Lincoln would tell of this moment in the third person. "During this boat-enterprise acquaintance with Offut, who was previously an entire stranger, he conceived a liking for Abraham, and believing he could turn him to account, he contracted with him to act as clerk for him, on his return from New Orleans, in charge of a store and mill in New Salem."[89]

The opportunity to manage the store was like a golden ticket. The store would be in a little cabin overlooking the Sangamon River. Lincoln would be paid fifteen dollars a month plus the luxury of sleeping in the store, if he wanted. Now that he had reached adulthood, he was also not obligated to give his salary to his father.

But the job came with another key benefit. Managing the store would take only part of his time, and Lincoln would spend his off-hours walking to neighbors' homes to borrow books. While in New Salem, he tackled the plays of Shakespeare, William Grimshaw's *History of the United States*, a biography of Benjamin Franklin, and numerous other works.[90]

Although the New Salem store lasted less than a year, the habit of filling his leisure time with self-education through books became a permanent fixture in his life. He continued borrowing titles from neighbors and friends,

---

89 (Pratt 1943) page 9.
90 (Miller 2002) page 51.

branching out into practical subjects like surveying and, most significantly, the law. Diligent self-education became a way of life, and any time he had a question, he looked to books for the answer. His thirst for and acquisition of knowledge propelled him ever upward, becoming a lawyer, a state legislator, a US congressman, leader of the newly formed Republican Party, and finally, our sixteenth president. Between his successful law practice and the political offices he held, as well as his abstemious lifestyle, Lincoln was able to save money and grow his wealth, and when he was assassinated at the age of fifty-six, his estate was valued at $85,000, or the equivalent of $2 million in 2024 dollars.

While Adams went the way of Harvard and Lincoln was self-educated, in the early part of the United States there was a third path to education: the military. With the opening of West Point in 1802 and the US Naval Academy in 1845, another opportunity set was opening up for men to obtain their education. Ulysses S. Grant, Dwight D. Eisenhower, and later Jimmy Carter all took advantage of this system.

But the military academies have never been easy to get access to. First, you must have the grades. Second, the applicant needs to be able to meet the physical requirements of the school that includes testing to ensure the candidate has "strength, agility, speed and endurance."[91] Finally, you have to hope you are the best of the best as the acceptance rate is challenging. Grant's 1843 West Point class started with sixty cadets. Yet by graduation day four years later, the class was only thirty-nine cadets.[92] Today, both West Point and the Naval Academy each accept approximately 1,200 students.

Thus, a military education was, and still is, possible, but a very tough needle to thread for anyone looking to take this path. But that's probably what makes Ike's story so impressive.

IKE GOES TO (MILITARY) COLLEGE

Dwight D. "Ike" Eisenhower wanted to go to college in 1908, but it just wasn't in his family's budget. With a family of eight to house and feed,

---

91   (United States Military Academy West Point n.d.) The West Point test requires candidates to be able to do six physical requirements: (1) basketball throw, (2) cadence pull-ups or flexed-arm hang, (3) forty-yard shuttle run, (4) modified sit-up, (5) push-ups, and (6) one-mile run. The Naval Academy has similar requirements.
92   (National Park Service 2021) Almost eighty-five cadets arrived at West Point, but 30 percent immediately were cut due to not being able to meet physical requirements.

Abraham Lincoln Would Like a Library Card Please

asking for college tuition was like Ike asking to go to the moon. Ike's father, David, worked at the Belle Springs Creamery as a mechanic and foreman, a job that provided a decent income of $380 a year for the family, but they lived paycheck to paycheck.[93] David and Ida Eisenhower fostered self-dependence in the boys.[94] His mother would often say to them, "Sink or swim."[95]

When Ike and his brothers were school age, their father made them an interesting offer: They could each get a patch of the family's garden to grow whatever they wanted, then sell their yield in town. The money they made would be theirs.

Ike was an observant and clever kid. As they walked their horse and cart around, he took note that the two products that sold the most were sweet corn and cucumbers, so he devoted his patch to growing these products. And when he discovered that buyers were willing to spend two cents for the early-season corn and only one cent later in the season, he maximized his early-season crops to take advantage of the seasonal difference.[96]

The ability to work to attain what he wanted made an impression on Ike. As he and his brothers got older, they would also work at the creamery alongside their father. Years later, Ike would reflect that "one circumstance that helped our character development: we were needed. I often think today of what an impact could be made if children believed they were *contributing* to a family's essential survival and happiness."[97]

While Ike certainly wanted to go to college, the annual tuition of $150 was far beyond his means, and he expected to go right from high school into the working world. But then something happened that resonated with Ike. As he sat with the Abilene High School class's graduation ceremony in the spring of 1909, the commencement speaker took the stage. Henry J. Allen was a newspaper editor at the time and would eventually become a senator and governor. Allen looked out at the graduating class and said,

---

93   (Morin 1969) pages 10–11. It is important to note that Ike's father had failed at a business in Texas. This failure haunted his father and made an impact on Ike to be self-reliant when things were bad.
94   (D. D. Eisenhower 1967) page 33. Ike discusses this trait that was taught to him.
95   Ibid., page 38.
96   (Ambrose 1973) pages 14–15.
97   (D. D. Eisenhower 1967) page 33. Emphasis in original. This quote makes me laugh—could you imagine what Ike would say today about how children are?

"I would sooner begin life over again with one arm cut off than attempt to struggle without a college education."[98] That comment galvanized Ike into action.

Ike and his older brother Edgar came up with an ingenious solution.[99] They both wanted to head out to college, so they made a deal: one of them would stay in Abilene and work at the dairy, while the other went to school. After two years, they would switch places. Since Edgar was older, he would go to college first.

Years later, Ike would explain, "Ed and I had it all doped out…[we] just had one idea that summer: to get our hands on every cent we could possibly earn."[100]

And this is one of the points I love most about Ike's story. Ike was all about strategy. He understood patience and playing the long game. Sure, he would take longer to get through college, but it would also mean he and his brother would have degrees. And Edgar wanted to be an attorney. The strategy they set was a sound plan.

THE ICEMAN COMETH

Off to the University of Michigan Edgar went, while Ike worked at the creamery. He started as an iceman hauling three-hundred-pound ice cakes and loading wagons for deliveries. Through hard work and reliability, he was promoted to fireman. And when I say hard work, I mean it. Ike was working eighty-four hours a week from 6 a.m. to 6 p.m. in the furnace room pushing burning coal.[101] When he took this role, he was lucky to get four days off the entire year. Within the year, he was a second engineer at the creamery making ninety dollars a month.[102] He saved $200 for Edgar's tuition and living expenses.[103]

To increase his income, Ike also started to work as a night watchman at the creamery. To help while away the late hours, his friend Swede Hazlett

---

98   (D. D. Eisenhower 1967) page 102.
99   One funny piece of trivia is that growing up, Edgar was "Big Ike" and Dwight was "Little Ike."
100 (D. D. Eisenhower 1967) pages 102–103.
101 (D. D. Eisenhower 1967) page 104.
102 (Kansas Newspapers In Education 2017).
103 (Ambrose 1973) pages 24–25.

would come over. We all know how late-night talks as early twentysomethings can result in big ideas. And Swede planted a big idea with his buddy Ike. Swede's dream was to attend the US Naval Academy in Annapolis, Maryland. He didn't make it the previous year, but he was trying again. "Look at it this way, Ike," Swede told him. "Here's a chance for an education and you don't have to pay for it."[104]

The idea that college could be free appealed to Ike. (Remember I told you Ike was frugal.) At the same point, another passion stirred in Ike. The Naval Academy was a huge sports school with a big emphasis on football. Ike was a big sportsman. His two favorite sports had long been football and baseball. The Naval Academy could be a golden ticket for him, especially since his physique had gotten bigger and stronger due to his work at the creamery.

Ike had a bigger hurdle to cross than he did in making money at the creamery. An appointment to the US Naval Academy required a senator's support, and he was a nobody. How was he going to get the senator to pick him as a candidate for the academy? A methodical approach was necessary.

The Eisenhowers were a well-liked family in town, and Ike made the rounds to ask for letters of recommendation to both of his US senators. And every letter noted that Ike's father always insisted on paying in cash. In Ike's day, that was a sign of "unimpeachable honesty," and the implication was that the apple probably didn't fall far from the tree.[105]

The letters were sent off to the senators' offices, with the hope that someone would take notice. And Ike was in luck—Senator J. L. Bristow was interested in considering him for the appointment. As Bristow had gotten several candidates for the US Naval Academy as well as West Point,[106] he decided to have all the applicants take a test. Ike shrewdly didn't provide a preference for either, although he hadn't even thought about West Point.

While Ike had been a good student in school and liked reading history, as he later said, "No school subjects set me afire." In order to pass the test, he had to master more complex topics.[107] He went back to school to take additional classes in science and math. But he still had his commitment to

---

104 (Morin 1969) page 19.
105 (D. D. Eisenhower 1967) page 105.
106 West Point was founded in 1802 by Thomas Jefferson when he was president. The US Naval Academy was not founded until 1845.
107 (D. D. Eisenhower 1967) page 97.

his brother Edgar. Ike not only kept working crazy hours to make money, but he spent the next couple of months studying. He was in it to win it.

And win it he did. Bristow shared that Ike had gotten the top score for the Naval Academy out of the four applicants. But just as Ike was breathing a sigh of relief, bad news came. He was disqualified from the Naval Academy. He would be turning twenty-one at the time of matriculation and thus had aged out; you had to be no older than twenty to go to the academy.

Before the news could sink in, Ike found out that he scored second among the eight West Point candidates. However, the applicant that had scored the highest would not be taking the appointment. In his place, Bristow would be making his recommendation to appoint Ike to West Point. After passing an entrance exam, Ike was accepted, and as a result, he would obtain a top-level education completely covered by the US government. The pressure to pay tuition was alleviated. In his memoirs, he recalled that by the time he got to West Point, between spending money on his brother, his transportation, and his basic cadet uniform, he had five dollars left.[108]

And just to give context of how Ike beat the odds: he was one of only 164 cadets at West Point (and the Naval Academy only had 219 spots).

THE MODERN ERA OF EDUCATION

I don't want to diminish the value of Lincoln's and Ike's tenacity—you get the feeling that they both would have done well in any era—but Lincoln and Ike came of age at a time in the United States when degrees were not a prerequisite to higher-paying jobs. I'm not saying they weren't preferred; they just weren't required. But they stand at the demarcation line in our country's history. The rules changed by the early twentieth century, and by the late twentieth century and into the twenty-first, an even bigger challenge had arisen: the price of a college education was going up. In 1960, Harvard University cost $1,520 for tuition. That amount would have the same buying power in 2024 of $15,766. Yet for the 2023–2024 school year, tuition is $54,269. And when you roll in room, board, and other expenses, the total is $79,450.[109]

---

108 (D. D. Eisenhower 1967) page 108.
109 "Tuition and Fees," Harvard Faculty of Arts and Sciences, Registrar's Office, 2024, https://registrar.fas.harvard.edu/tuition-and-fees.

Abraham Lincoln Would Like a Library Card Please

Education and pedigree are foundational elements for wealth building and financial stability in the twenty-first century.

Before I get to more of the presidents' stories and the paths they each took, though, we need to understand the history of education in the US since the beginning of the twentieth century. Then, with that context, we'll look at two financial concepts that emphasize the connection between education and wealth building.

The World Wars and the GI Bill had initially shifted the dynamics of who could attend college and how it could be paid for. And it changed how some of our presidents were able to access education. Up until the beginning of the twentieth century, the path to education was either college (usually reserved for those with money), apprenticeships (and, since many presidents are lawyers, they usually clerk under an attorney), or self-education. But the United States was changing and the education path was as well.

At the end of World War I, soldiers came home and were given a train ticket and sixty dollars for their service. Over four million men flooded the labor market that was already being impacted by the post-war inflation and an economic retraction. Unemployment ran rampant. Americans across the country struggled to survive. Some of the most aggressive protests in US history (which continued well into the 1930s) occurred, as angry veterans marched on Washington, DC.

By the time World War II was nearing a close, both Congress and the White House wanted to be better prepared for the sixteen million men and women who would be heading home; they knew there might not be enough jobs to support them. As a result, just a few weeks after D-Day, the Servicemen's Readjustment Act of 1944, otherwise known as the GI Bill of Rights, was signed into law by FDR. Along with unemployment benefits and help with home loan guarantees, it offered higher education. Specifically, if a veteran had ninety days of service, they could get $500 to use toward education or a training program along with a living expense stipend.[110]

---

110 "G.I. Bill of Rights," National Archives Foundation, 2024, https://www.archives-foundation.org/documents/g-i-bill-rights/.

All the Presidents' Money

The impact of this bill was felt immediately. In 1947, more than half the students starting college were returning servicemen under the bill. These men, who never would have had the opportunity to go to college, were now able to access higher education. It was transformative—for both the individuals and the country. Between 1940 and 1950, the number of college degrees awarded doubled. From a public policy standpoint, access to education at a reasonable cost was all about the benefits of having a highly educated population.

As a result, all presidents born after this bill walked into a different higher education system. A college degree was almost a prerequisite for social mobility and financial stability. This group included George H. W. Bush, Bill Clinton, George W. Bush, Barack Obama, Donald Trump, and Joe Biden. No longer could you take Lincoln's path of self-education. And as mentioned previously, H. W. Bush is the only president who benefited directly from the GI Bill.

But then two things happened: First, in the late 1950s, student loan programs began, though the loans were quite small due to the cost of tuition. And then the second thing happened—the 1960s. Governor Ronald Reagan took on the University of California system. He had promised in his 1966 campaign to "clean up the mess at Berkeley" and other college campuses. He wanted to cut college budgets. The colleges warned it would cause tuitions to rise. After his election, on January 17, 1967, Reagan addressed this concern in a statement. "This suggestion resulted in the almost hysterical charge that this would deny educational opportunities to those of the most moderate means. This is obviously untrue for two reasons: First, we made it plain that tuition must be accompanied by adequate loans to be paid back after graduation and that scholarships should be available to provide that no deserving students be denied educations due to lack of funds."[111]

Reagan was what I call a "bootstrapper" when it came to paying for his own education—he did it himself. In that era after World War I, it was his most viable option. And perhaps that self-reliance made it hard for him to see how difficult financing an education can be.

---

111 (Archive: January 17, 1967 Statement of Governor Ronald Reagan on Tuition 1967).

Abraham Lincoln Would Like a Library Card Please

RONALD REAGAN BOOTSTRAPS HIS WAY TO A COLLEGE DEGREE

Adams's academic abilities allowed him to get access to a scholarship at Harvard, while other presidents have been able to leverage their athletic abilities for that same purpose. And that brings us to the education of Ronald Reagan, whose education path is a story of athletics and values in the search for tuition money. Born in 1911, Reagan's story reflects the changes that were occurring post–World War I in the United States.

Reagan was one of those people who could consistently find a lucky break when it came to money. But despite his Hollywood image, his early life had challenges due to his father's alcoholism. Jack Reagan's struggle with booze caused tremendous financial instability for the family. One night, when he was eleven, Reagan opened the front door of his family's home to find his father lying drunk on the porch. Yet, Reagan had a lot of compassion for Jack, seeing his alcoholism as a true illness.

As a reaction to this, Reagan found himself consistently drawn to stability, first through his mother, and then through strong male mentors. These two influences would impact how he paid for college. His mother, Nelle, was a pious and emotionally strong woman, and she was extremely charitable, even with the meager Reagan family income. She was described as "a lovely woman who gave of herself in service to others."[112] Also, she often took on small sewing jobs around town to generate extra money for the family.

Nelle connected him with the First Christian Church of Dixon in his hometown of Dixon, Illinois. Reagan met his high school girlfriend, Margaret Cleaver, in church. Reagan himself thought Margaret was the one. He later wrote, "For almost six years of my life I was sure she was going to be my wife."[113]

Reagan and Margaret had dated throughout high school. He was struck not only by her beauty and her intelligence but also by her family life. Unlike his family, Margaret's was the picture of stability. Her father, Ben Cleaver, was a pastor and abhorred drinking to such a degree that he was a proponent of the Eighteenth Amendment.[114] Margaret's sister, Helen,

---

112 (Vaughn 1994) page 9.
113 (R. Reagan 1990) page 40.
114 For more insight into Reverend Ben Cleaver and his influence on Reagan, see Vaughn, Stephen, *The Moral Inheritance of a President: Reagan and the Dixon Disciples of Christ*.

noted that Reagan was always at their house and seemed to see her dad as another father figure.

Reagan, in many ways, became a son to Cleaver, who gently nudged young Ronald to consider college when the time came. Margaret would be following her sisters in enrolling at Eureka College. At the time, for Reagan, going to college did not seem a realistic goal because his family didn't have extra income to pay for college. In fact, when his older brother Neil graduated high school, he went right to work.

Neil explained the predicament that "we came from a poor family, and for years if anybody would have said I was going to college or he was going to college, I would have just laughed. 'No possibility.'"[115]

REAGAN BECOMES A NEEDY STUDENT

As the time drew near for Margaret to leave for college in 1928, Cleaver suggested that Reagan come with them to help move her in. Eureka was a small, picturesque college just ninety miles from Reagan's hometown, with six red-brick buildings sprinkled across green paths and a football stadium in the background. Once Reagan saw the school, he knew he had to stay. The Cleavers encouraged him to go and speak with the dean of admissions. To his surprise, Eureka College was willing to enroll him, even though he had neither the $180 tuition nor the similar amount for room and board.[116]

Fortuitously, the school had a longstanding football program. In fact, the football coach, Ralph McKenzie, had run the program since 1916. The minute he saw 170-lb. Reagan, McKenzie knew he would be a great addition to their offensive line. The dean of the college and McKenzie quickly pulled together a Needy Student Scholarship that covered half of the tuition.[117]

It's hard to imagine a scholarship being created on the spot today, but at the time athletic scholarships were still in their infancy, and the rules were evolving. But one thing Reagan's scholarship had in common with sports scholarships today was that it only paid part of the cost, and the

---

115 (N. Reagan 1981).
116 In the 1920s, it was quite common for room and board to be much more expensive than tuition (Hanson 2022).
117 (Sobota 2018) Jerry Schatz at the childhood home claims that Reagan actually received two scholarships: the Needy Student Scholarship and a swimming scholarship.

balance would have to come from somewhere else. Fortunately, Reagan's impoverished childhood had instilled in him a strong work ethic, and he had managed to save some money. At fourteen, he had worked for a contractor at thirty-five cents an hour and was able to save $200. During the summers, Reagan worked seven days a week as a lifeguard at a local park, earning fifteen dollars weekly. By the time he finished high school, he had wisely saved $400[118] after his church tithing. Reagan paid the balance and was off to college.[119]

After that first year, Reagan had to figure out where the money would come from for the next three years. He had made a good impression on the school and excelled in his classes, and so he was able to renew his scholarship. But he still needed to come up with creative solutions to cover the balance of his costs, so he pledged the Tau Kappa Epsilon (TKE) fraternity, which provided him with board. He took a dishwashing job in the TKE house and worked part-time as a swimming coach to help cover his other expenses.

REAGAN SHARES THE WEALTH OF A COLLEGE EDUCATION

Once Reagan saw how he could craft his education by managing his money a certain way, he wanted to share the wealth. His brother Neil was three years older and working at a cement plant. For the Depression era, Neil was making decent money at $125 a month.[120] Yet Reagan wanted more for Neil, who later said that Ronald "came home at the end of the second year down at Eureka, where he had gotten a scholarship to play football, and he made the announcement that he had it all arranged for me to go to college—a scholarship for football, a job at the girls' dormitory hashing, and then he would see that I was pledged to the fraternity that he was a member of, so that all I'd have to raise was the $10 a month to pay for my room at the fraternity house."[121] Neil felt he was smarter than all those college boys,

---

118 (R. Reagan 1990) page 45.
119 According to the Eureka College student roll call book, in Reagan's freshman year, he paid his entire tuition in the fall in a single lump sum, which took all of his savings. Per discussion with Cassandra Chapman, Curator and Director of Reagan Museum at Eureka College, June 5, 2019.
120 (N. Reagan 1981).
121 (N. Reagan 1981).

and he turned the offer down. But Dixon was a small town, and word of Reagan's offer to his brother got around. Shortly thereafter, Neil arrived at work one day, and his boss's secretary handed him a final paycheck. When Neil asked if he was fired, she told him, "Call it what you want to; Mr. Kennedy says if you're not smart enough to take the good thing your brother has fixed up for you, you're not smart enough to work for him." The next day Neil was at Eureka College with Reagan.

Reagan's financial discipline and commitment paid off. He graduated from Eureka in 1932, and his brother graduated the following year. Upon graduation, Reagan was in an optimal position for both the college income and wealth premiums. He had no debt. He had a college degree. However, unlike today, if Reagan had incurred debt or failed to get a degree, it wouldn't have been the end of his ability to build wealth; it just would have been harder. Further, he could create empowerment for himself in budgeting and piecing together funds from different sources.

And if Reagan reflected the challenges of the generation going to school in the 1920s, his vice president, George H.W. Bush, reflected the change coming out of World War II.

GEORGE H.W. BUSH ISN'T SURE HE WANTS TO GO TO COLLEGE

"Have you read this gov't education Bill? Looks to me like it might be a nice 2 or 3 year rest at college. I'll have saved some money and then they pay you too, it seems," wrote Bush to his parents, Prescott and Dorothy Bush, from his post in the Pacific just a few days after FDR signed the legislation.[122] For most of the servicemen in the US military, this was an unheard-of opportunity. But for Bush, it was merely an interesting development because he was always expected to go to college and his parents had the means to help him financially.

Growing up, the educational path for Bush was laid out for him, much like it was for other young men of his social class and pedigree. He attended Greenwich Day School, then high school at Phillips Exeter Academy, and the next step would be Harvard, Yale, or a similar college. Out of the gate,

---

122 Letter George H.W. Bush to Prescott and Dorothy Bush, dated June 26, 1944.

he was known for his athletic prowess and easy leadership. But something happened on his way to college: war.

Like many of his generation, Bush enlisted, joining the US Navy as a naval aviator. And it was a paying job. Despite his wealth, Bush was a saver. And he had reason to be: he was hoping to marry his girlfriend, Barbara Pierce, when he got back from the Pacific. He was excited that he was able to save the bulk of his $143-a-month salary. It would be seed money to build a life.

A DEFINING MOMENT

During a bombing run in the Pacific, Bush's plane was hit. He was able to parachute safely into the water, but his two crewmen didn't make it out of the plane. Bush was picked up by a US Navy submarine just as he was drifting dangerously close to an enemy-held island. A sailor aboard the submarine actually filmed the rescue and, incredibly, the footage was preserved and can be found on YouTube.

As the end of the war neared, Bush started to ask deeper questions about his path forward. He was deeply affected by the deaths of his crewmen, and because he'd been spared, he was determined not to squander his time.[123] He wrote to his parents, "My mind grasps onto any and every possibility since it's so much fun planning and wondering."[124]

The world was changing. After fighting in the Pacific and seeing all the carnage of war, he wasn't sure if he could go back to the traditional path that had been set out before him. In one letter home to his parents, Bush tossed around three different scenarios: "One thing that would appeal to me, is a job like Pressy's—go to S. America for a year (not much more)… So far I haven't been able to make up my mind on what I want to do… Further education isn't out of my mind by a long shot. If I went to college I'd definitely find plenty to interest me—of that I am sure now. Before, I couldn't see that. It took the war, and the Navy to show me how advantageous a good education can be. I say advantageous and not necessary, for I do feel that would get along with a bit of initiative and honest endeavor

---

[123] (Meacham 2015) page 72. This sense of destiny that Bush felt is emphasized by Meacham throughout his book.
[124] Letter George H.W. Bush to Prescott and Dorothy Bush, dated June 26, 1944.

provided I could get some employer to give me a chance…It would be nice to know I could get a job for sure—a job which would not require me to dig a ditch—merely because I don't have a 'college education.'"¹²⁵

His parents' heads must have been spinning after reading that last part. The idea of going abroad or going straight into the workforce—instead of to college—wasn't what a person of their social class was expected to do.

Bush didn't hear back from them quickly. A little nervous, he wrote again: "Incidentally, Dad I would appreciate it, if you would let me know what you feel I should do after the war. As I have said before, I do think I could get a job—a modest one at first of course, irregardless [*sic*] of my lack of a college education."¹²⁶

Let's just say that didn't go over well in the Bush household back in Connecticut. His father, Prescott Bush, was not only a Yale graduate (class of 1917), but he was on the Yale Corporation, Yale's governing body, and had been since 1944. When Bush published these letters fifty-six years later in 2000, he noted, "*My father definitely did* not *agree with my plan of not going to college.*"¹²⁷

OFF TO YALE—IN A HURRY

Bush returned from war, married Barbara Pierce, and matriculated at Yale, as was expected of him. Naval aviators were well paid, and Bush had saved $3,000 of his salary while overseas. He was happy he did because in 1947, Yale tuition was $1,273, not including room and board. (In today's dollars, it would be close to $17,500, whereas the actual annual tuition at Yale is now almost $60,000—a perfect illustration of how much more expensive college education has become.)¹²⁸ Bush was able to apply his GI Bill benefits, as well as savings.

He and Barbara had their first child, George W., while he was at Yale, and in addition to receiving some credit for his military duty, he worked hard enough that he was able to graduate in two-and-a-half years. Bush

---

125 Letter George H.W. Bush to Prescott and Dorothy Bush, dated July 21, 1944. Pressy is Bush's brother Prescott Bush Jr. who was 4F.
126 Letter George H. W. Bush to Prescott and Dorothy Bush, dated July 31, 1944.
127 (Bush 2000) page 48. Emphasis is Bush's.
128 (Yale Alumni Magazine 2015). For the 2023–2024 year, tuition is $64,700 with room and board bringing it up to $83,880. Yikes!

would later say, "I came back to civilian life feeling that I needed to get my degree and go into the business world as soon as possible. I had a family to support."[129]

Not everybody attends Ivy League colleges or has the family connections that Bush had, but relationships built in college can be critical to one's future success. For example, one of my wealthiest clients was an international student at a college in the Northeast. There weren't many other students from his home country in Africa, but there was one, and that was enough. The two of them connected on campus, and their friendship grew. Once they graduated, they decided to put their degrees to work for them on a haircare product that originated from their home country. For twenty years, they pursued this business—and let me tell you, it was quite the journey. When they finally sold it to a Fortune 500 company in a nine-figure transaction, it was very clear that without the building of the relationship at college, they never would have had the success they did.

EVEN EDUCATION AND PEDIGREE ARE ALLOWED TO TAKE THE PATH LESS TRAVELED

Upon graduation, Bush's career course was laid out for him just as his educational path had been. He would go to Wall Street and work for someone who had been connected to his family for years. But, Bush's parents wanted him to be able to make his own way in life, so they cut him off financially after graduation. Unlike John Kennedy, there would be no family trust fund. Bush's only requirement was to live up to the family mandate: success and service.

Bush knew he could easily use his connections to land a cushy Wall Street job. But as he put it, he wanted "to do something of value and yet I have to and want to make money."[130] He had another option, still through a family connection, but it was a path and industry where no Bush or Walker had tread previously. Dresser Industries made equipment for oil and gas production in Texas, and he was offered a ground-floor position with the company. It was just the professional challenge he was looking for—hard

---

129   (Meacham 2015) page 73.
130   Ibid.

work and some risk but also the potential to earn big bucks—so he moved his family to a tiny duplex rental in Odessa, Texas. He would start at the lowest job on the totem pole—that of an equipment clerk. He would learn the business step by step, even spending nights in the oil fields. He wrote to a friend, "Fortunes can be made in the land end of the oil business, and of course can be lost."[131]

A cynic would say that Bush was born on third base and thought he hit a home run. He may have gotten the Ivy League education, the pedigree of his family and connections, but Bush was able to parlay these advantages and move off of the traditional path. It was important to him that he make his own way—and his own money.

INCOME VERSUS NET WORTH

There are two important concepts to understand when tying education to wealth in the present day. The *College Income Premium* is the extra income earned by a family whose head has a college degree over the income earned by an otherwise similar family member whose head does not have a college degree. Colleges commonly use this number in the modern-day admissions process to explain to prospective students and their parents how they justify their fees. It's a great marketing ploy, but this number is deceptive because it doesn't factor in the debt incurred to get the degree.[132]

That brings us to the second concept of education and wealth building, the *College Wealth Premium*, which considers all your assets and debts to determine what "extra net worth" came from the degree.[133] Or more succinctly, how much more net worth does a college graduate accumulate over their lifetime versus a high school graduate? When we look at John Adams's story under that lens—the mix of a scholarship, his family having assets to use to pay for college, and a reasonable cost of college—he was primed to build wealth when he graduated in 1758.

---

131 Letter George H. W. Bush to Fitzgerald "Gerry" Bemiss, dated January 11, 1949.
132 (Tough 2023).
133 (William R. Emmons 2019) page 297. Also discussed in (Tough 2023).

Abraham Lincoln Would Like a Library Card Please

OBAMA'S TOUGH DECISION

In contrast to John Adams, who went to college before tuition became prohibitively expensive, Barack Obama had to manage his path more diligently due to his student loans (and prior to becoming a senator, he and Michelle did struggle to do that).

He started at Occidental College in the fall of 1979 and had to make tough financial choices throughout his college and graduate careers. Then in the spring of 1988, Obama applied to a number of law schools and was accepted at both Harvard and Northwestern. However, choosing between the two schools was difficult for several reasons. Northwestern Law, a top-twenty law school, was in Chicago, which meant he wouldn't have to move, and Northwestern wanted him. They courted him with the offer of a full-ride scholarship that would enable him to graduate debt-free, and the dean of the school even reached out to him personally.[134]

Choosing Harvard would require a move to Cambridge, Massachusetts, to a school that at the time was experiencing controversy in its academic ranks. More importantly, the offer didn't provide any scholarship. The cost over three years would necessitate taking out loans in the range of $40,000 (this would be $90,000 today). By taking on this debt, he would have to factor in paying it back when he considered jobs upon graduation.

Obama was torn. But he decided to focus on the opportunity set that each path offered.

While taking on the debt could potentially hinder him financially, a Harvard law degree carries a lot of weight in this world. The risk it produced was that he might have to make job choices based on being able to pay off the debt. Obama already had a modest amount of debt coming out of college.[135] He had taken on no debt in the two years at Occidental thanks to a full scholarship, but then he transferred to Columbia, where his

---

[134] It should be noted that in 1970 Bill Clinton faced a similar dilemma. He had attended Georgetown University as an undergrad and his family stretched to pay the $1,200 tuition and $700 room and board fees. When it came to law school, he was torn between University of Arkansas Law School and Yale Law School. He ultimately chose Yale as it seemed to offer more. But it would come with student loans that he paid for years.

[135] (Garrow 2017) page 220. Obama's finances are opaquer than most presidents'. However, Garrow has been able to determine that Obama likely received a Pell Grant as well as the student loans.

$8,620 annual tuition wasn't fully covered. Between that expense and food, housing, and books, he was forced to take out some small student loans to supplement the financial assistance he received from his grandparents.[136]

As tempting as the Northwestern offer must have been, Obama ultimately decided on Harvard, and by the time he graduated, he had taken out $42,753 in loans.[137] He was offered a job at the prestigious firm of Sidley Austen, which would have paid him enough to zero out his debt fairly quickly, but he instead accepted a two-year fellowship at the University of Chicago Law School, where he subsequently taught constitutional law for over a decade while making payments on his loans. At one point, he and Michelle had over $120,000 in student loan debt combined.[138] During a 2012 campaign rally, he noted this and the conundrum many people face: "Michelle and I, we've been in your shoes. Check this out, all right. I'm the president of the United States. We only finished paying off our student loans about eight years ago. That wasn't that long ago. And that wasn't easy—especially because when we had Malia and Sasha, we're supposed to be saving up for their college educations, and we're still paying off our college educations."[139]

Obama's comments at the time reflect the modern-day conundrum that millions of Americans face with student debt: How can you get ahead when you are mired in debt? Yet something unique happened with Obama's story. He wrote a book.

Now publishing a book is not the usual path to wealth. And in 1995, when he sold the book, Obama got a $40,000 advance. The book was a modest success, selling ten thousand copies.[140]

But in 2004, when Obama ran for Senate, the book was reissued as a paperback, and it took off. Obama signed a new contract for the reissue estimated at over $1 million. And when we examine the Obama tax returns from 2004 through 2015 (the last year publicly released), he did quite well financially from the book (as reported on Schedule C):[141]

---

136 (Sweet 2014) Sweet's data on this is from the Obama campaign.
137 (Garrow 2017) page 220.
138 (Stratford 2013).
139 (ABC News 2012) It should be noted that the Obamas funded 529 plans for their daughters Malia and Sasha.
140 (Osnos 2006).
141 The Obamas released their tax returns commencing in 2001 and ending in 2015. They can be found at https://www.efile.com/historic-1040-income-tax-returns-of-us-presidents-and-candidates/.

Abraham Lincoln Would Like a Library Card Please

Tax Year	Schedule C Gross Income
2004	$ -
2005	$1,209,873
2006	$551,240
2007	$4,094,690
2008	$2,603,448
2009	$5,661,666
2010	$1,568,273
2011	$487,928
2012	$273,739
2013	$116,180
2014	$94,889
2015	$60,745
Total Gross Income	**$16,722,671**

Based on the tax returns and his speech in 2012, it appears Obama paid off the loans using the $1.2 million he was paid for the 2004 edition of his book *Dreams from My Father*. And today, as a former two-term president with a blockbuster memoir under his belt and a net worth of $70 million–plus, Obama has exceeded the college wealth premium.

HOW FUTURE PRESIDENTS CAN MAXIMIZE THEIR EDUCATION WEALTH PREMIUM

The common thread with these presidents' stories—Adams, Reagan, Obama, Lincoln, Ike, and Bush—is that education gave them a better opportunity set for financial stability and wealth building. Yet, each man also had to wrestle with tough issues—strategy, finances, and sacrifice—in order to achieve that greater opportunity set. But cost was a key component, and it's a lot easier to make money when you don't have student loan debt.

If we were to take the top ten ranked list of presidents as ranked by historians, it is very easy to see that financial success was not based on ed-

All the Presidents' Money

ucation. But the most modern presidents on this list are Lyndon Johnson (Class of 1930) and John F. Kennedy (Class of 1940).

Rank	President	College Degree	Wealth At Birth	Wealth At Death	Financial Ability
1	Franklin D. Roosevelt	Harvard University	Wealthy	Wealthy	Average
2	Abraham Lincoln	None	Poor	Upper Middle Class/Wealthy	Above Average
3	George Washington	None	Upper Middle Class	Wealthy	Excellent
4	Theodore Roosevelt	Harvard University	Wealthy	Wealthy	Average/Above Average
5	Thomas Jefferson	College of William and Mary	Wealthy	Volatile	Poor
6	Dwight D. Eisenhower	Westpoint	Poor	Upper Middle Class	Excellent
7	Harry S. Truman	None	Poor	Upper Middle Class	Above Average
8	Lyndon B. Johnson	Texas State University	Poor	Upper Class	Excellent
9	John F. Kennedy	Harvard University	Wealthy	Wealthy	Average/Above Average
10	James Madison	Princeton University (The College of NJ)	Upper Middle Class	Volatile	Average/Poor

Clearly the game changed.

I'm not saying we should forgo college and be self-educated—even Lincoln would disagree with that. But there are other options that can help us avoid the burden of student loan debt. For example, a two-year community college track with a transfer to a four-year college for the last two years might be the best way to maximize the wealth premium. Another approach is that taken by a client couple of mine, who decided when their son was born that they were only going to fund part of his education. Over the years, they saved in a 529 plan—with the caveat that their goal was to pay $125,000 of their son's education. (Most of my clients try to fund $250,000 in a 529.) When their son was a junior in high school, we met to review different education options—a state school, a mid-range-cost college, and a private college. With the latter two options, he would spend the entire 529 and still need to take out some loans. But when he reviewed the in-state tuition option, he looked at me and said, "Why wouldn't I do that? I would have money left over for an advanced degree."

He's right. And what we can see is that it was likely easier for them than it is for Americans today. This isn't to say education doesn't give the same opportunity set—it's just harder calculus in paying for it. Or more succinctly: the American dream of education is still alive, but the hurdles to access it are much higher.

Chapter Three

HERBERT HOOVER SAVES THE STANFORD FOOTBALL TEAM
(OR THE ART OF NUMBER CRUNCHING)

A client of mine called me and asked if she could retire. She had just turned fifty-five, so it was a bit on the early side. "I just don't want to work anymore," she said. "In a way, I'm over it. I'm tired of being in these never-ending meetings where we're discussing things that didn't work fifteen years ago. Is there any way I can retire now? I believe I just hit the formula."

After assuring her I would run the numbers, I got to work. After all, we had historically assumed that she would retire at sixty.

Becky was in a unique position. The formula she was referencing was the pension calculation. She was now fifty-five years old with thirty years of service at an old-school, blue-chip company. She qualified for her pension.

When we finally sat down a week later, I laid out the plan for how she could retire, a plan that left no room for error. She had to live on $170,000 net of tax a year or less, grown out for inflation at 3.5 percent.[142] She could draw her pension starting at age sixty-five, so the first ten years relied heavily on her portfolio. If she could make do with $170,000 annually, then yes, she could retire.

---

142 I know this inflation rate might sound aggressive, but when this occurred, inflation was at 2 percent. I have a healthy paranoia with clients making retirement decisions that they really stress test their asset base.

I have to admit I was nervous. $170,000 a year net in the Bay Area can be tight for a high-net-worth individual who is used to a fairly lavish lifestyle. Most of my clients in those areas average between $300,000 and $600,000 net on living expenses. But since that conversation, every January for the past twelve years, I get the prior year's budget and the budget for the year ahead. And every year, she sits there with a grin on her face as it consistently comes in under $170,000, plus inflation.

I'm chalking it up to her budgeting skills. While having a pension and investment accounts are part of the equation, the most important retirement number is how much you spend. If you can't budget, you can't fully assess your financial picture.

HERBERT HOOVER—MODEL BUDGETER

Imagine being orphaned by the age of ten and left with just your older brother and younger sister. You're shuttled between various family members acting as guardians, and a special financial guardian is put in place to manage your parents' estates. Then imagine that to get access to funds to cover your expenses, you're required to submit detailed receipts documenting your costs down to the penny.

That may seem like an odd way to learn about money, but the child who grew up under this system became one of our wealthiest presidents in history: Herbert Hoover. He is widely considered a failure as a president, but when it came to growing wealth, Hoover had the golden touch, perhaps more so than any other president.[143]

I often think of Hoover and his story when clients ask me how to teach their children about money. I make the argument that out of all the skills related to money, the ability to create and follow a budget is most important. I know—incredibly boring, right? Yet, the skill is elusive for many. It's tedious and requires attention to detail.

For anyone who masters it, it's an integral early step in the development of financial skills that can (and should) evolve over time. That evolution enables an individual to make better financial decisions and analysis.

And that is exactly what happened to Hoover. To be honest, I even have a little finance-geek crush on the guy. While a number of Hoover stories relate to money, one in particular highlights the power of budgeting.

---

143 Later on we will discuss how this "golden" touch was literally golden.

Herbert Hoover Saves the Stanford Football Team

A TENSE ELECTION

Herbert Hoover believed his best friend, Lester Hinsdale, was a better candidate for the presidency. The year was not 1928 or 1932, but 1894, and the candidacy was for student body president. Twenty-year-old Hoover was helping his more charismatic friend Hinsdale strategize for the election, which was then the biggest issue on the Stanford campus. In fact, the April 1894 election threatened to upend the entire social order of the school.

Financial inequity drove the divide between the students in the election. While Stanford University did not charge tuition, there was a heavy room and board expense. Students like Hoover and Hinsdale, who came from modest economic backgrounds, worked to afford life in the dormitories. To cover these expenses, Hoover showed early signs of an entrepreneurial ability by generating income, from earning five dollars a week working for the university to starting his own laundry service and paper route.[144]

In sharp contrast, the wealthier students embraced fraternity life. With spare time on their hands and a passion for college athletics, they were responsible for setting up various sporting clubs, including the then-little-known Stanford football team. In 1894, the football team was coming off an undefeated season—having gone 8–0 in just their third season in the Far West College Independents Conference—and with the success, they were now at the center of student life.[145]

Yet the future viability of the program was seriously in question. Corruption and financial mismanagement had forced the team to disband and reestablish itself on virtually an annual basis, and the fraternity system seemed only to encourage this behavior. Stories abounded on campus of sports teams using their ticket money to take unrelated recreational trips and using their game day uniforms for practice.[146] More often than not, the ticket money was unaccounted for and debts accrued. But the success and popularity of the football team caused these issues to come to the forefront.

With the election imminent, it was all that anyone in the "Pioneer Class" (or the first class to graduate after four years) at Stanford University could talk about. The candidates hurled inflammatory charges of favorit-

---

144 Hoover, *Memoirs*, page 17.
145 "1893 Stanford football team," Wikipedia, August 2023, https://en.wikipedia.org/wiki/1893_Stanford_football_team. Coincidentally the tie was against the University of California Golden Bears played on November 30, 1893; they tied at 6-6.
146 (Nash, Herbert Hoover and Stanford University 1988).

ism and improper spending. Even University President David Starr Jordan jumped into the fray, commenting that he was "presiding over young Tammany Hall."[147]

The ticket that was getting the most support from students was one that considered themselves "barbarians" or "barbs." At the head of this ticket was Hinsdale. Chatty and appealing, he seemed a natural fit as president of the student body.

Also on the "Barb" ticket was Herbert Hicks, running for football manager. Hicks was studious and analytical.[148] He also brought strong legal reasoning to the ticket. Together, Hoover believed Hinsdale and Hicks would be a formidable combination to address the woes of the football team. They were members of the law department and saw themselves as promoting the values of the rule of law. But Hinsdale also knew that, for the ticket to succeed, they needed someone with strong financial skills. That's where Hoover would come in.

A very serious student in the geology department and more awkward and quiet than most, "Bert" Hoover had a personality that was the complete opposite of Hinsdale's. The first time they met, it took Hinsdale a good day or so to get the name out of the shy Hoover.[149] They had developed a close friendship since freshman year, and Hinsdale was clear from the moment he decided to run that he thought Hoover would be a good fit for the post of treasurer on Hinsdale's ticket. Hoover agreed.

For Hinsdale, Hicks, and Hoover—the "Three H's"—the election reflected a moral issue about the campus. Years later, Hoover would explain that they "resented the snobbery that accompanied the fraternity system and we suspected favoritism in handling student enterprises and their loose methods of accounting for money. We declared war for reform."[150]

However, in the initial ballot, there was no clear winner for any of the positions, although the "Three H's" were in the lead. After a runoff, the

---

147 Howard Bromberg, "The Early Years," Stanford Law School, https://law.stanford.edu/stanford-lawyer/articles/the-early-years/.

148 Hicks would go on to be a well-respected tax attorney. His life would be cut short by a tragic auto accident.

149 *Tales of Herbert Hoover, His Real Personality And How The Next President and Lester Hinsdale Used To Run College Politics*, Sacramental Union, Volume 213, Number 38, April 7, 1920. https://cdnc.ucr.edu/?a=d&d=SU19200407.2.161&e=-------en--20--1--txt-txIN--------1.

150 Hoover, *Memoirs*, page 22.

result was clear: the Barbs won. Hinsdale, Hicks, and Hoover would enter their senior year as leaders of Stanford. Change was coming.

AN ELECTION WIN AND A RETURN TO THE BASICS

Hoover was elated to be the first treasurer of the Stanford student body and gladly took the role without pay, which was quite a sacrifice on his part, given his limited means. Upon his preliminary review of the books, he realized that the student body was in greater debt than had previously been disclosed. He was aghast of what he perceived to be excess, and he hated waste. In his mind, there was only one course of action: go public with it. Drawing on the financial decision-making process from his Quaker heritage, Hoover knew that if the finances were subject to debate and discussion, the community could make the right decisions and course correct.[151]

Ten years earlier, Hoover's own prospects were as precarious as the football team's. His mother, Hulda Minthorn Hoover, had died rather suddenly after five years of widowhood. Hoover and his two siblings were to be cared for by members of both their late parents' families. This trauma would be one that marked both him and his siblings.

But the Hoover orphans were also given a unique opportunity that would ultimately change how Herbert handled money. Rather than parse out the small Hoover estate among the three guardians of the Hoover children, the Quaker church stepped in. The core values of the church are referred to as the SPICES, which stands for simplicity, peace, integrity, community, equality, and stewardship. In Quaker life, simplicity is defined as an emphasis on the careful use of financial and natural resources, and money is to be used to make life truly better for oneself and others, not for accumulating luxuries. Wealth was to be used for spiritual purposes.[152]

Laurie Tatum, a distinguished Quaker elder, was named guardian of the three Hoover children. Tatum was a unique choice for guardian. Unlike

---

151 While Hoover embraced the Quaker philosophy, he rarely attended Friends Meetings. He was a Quaker throughout his entire life.

152 The other aspects of SPICES were also important. Peace focused on the need to resolve conflict. Integrity meant to treat others with respect and acknowledge interconnectedness. Community emphasized the need to stay connected within the community as well as balancing the needs of the group. Equality focused on the need to respect all different people. Stewardship was social responsibility.

All the Presidents' Money

today, where guardians are chosen for the home they will create for the child, Tatum was chosen for the process and administration he would bring to the young orphans' lives.[153] And while Tatum was the legal guardian, the Hoover children also required physical guardians. The three Hoover children were to be split up among members of both the Hoover and Minthorn families. Hoover was sent to live with his uncle Allan Hoover; older brother Theodore went to live with their uncle Davis Hoover; and younger sister May went to live with their Minthorn grandmother.

Having both legal and physical guardians resulted in a system of checks and balances, with financial decisions discussed and debated. This served to introduce Hoover and his siblings to the world of money at a very early age. Further, it was decided that rather than one pot of funds shared by the three children, each child's share would be managed separately.

This system embraced a "step stool" approach. One leg of the stool was the Hoover child; a second leg was the physical guardian; the third leg was Tatum, the legal guardian. As all parties were educated in Quaker philosophy, they knew the rules and parameters.

For young Hoover, the process was straightforward: Allan Hoover would submit detailed records to Tatum requesting payment. One of the first submissions from Allan Hoover to Tatum stated:

> Springdale, Iowa 8 mo
> Request of Laurie Tatum guardian of Herbert G. Hoover Fourteen 92 Dollars ($14.92) in full for clothing purchased & made for said H.G. Hoover.
> Items of Clothing.
> [Signed] Allan Hoover[154]

Attached to the note was a detailed listing of items purchased, ranging from shoes to a box of collars, all neatly added up.

---

153 Having started out as a schoolteacher, Tatum was well-known in Iowa and a leader in the West Branch Quaker community. His reputation had been further bolstered by his role as an Indian Agent under President Ulysses S. Grant's Peace Policy with the Native American Tribes, working to secure the release of many white captives. His steadiness was an asset, and the combination of his skills provided a unique guardian opportunity for the Hoover children.

154 Letter Allan Hoover to Laurie Tatum, dated April 9, 1884.

Herbert Hoover Saves the Stanford Football Team

Allan Hoover and Tatum kept impeccable records, with every major milestone of Hoover's life documented. From trousers to train tickets to a bottle of croup medicine, all items were annotated by Allan Hoover and reviewed by Tatum, a process replicated for each of the Hoover siblings. By the time Hoover got to Stanford, the process had become a way of life. He couldn't imagine functioning without it.

CHILDREN AND THEIR EARLY MONEY STORIES

Looking at this with modern eyes, it feels like a bit much for a small child. But the truth is, the timing was perfect. Children are usually able to start grasping financial concepts as early as preschool. What's key is to make sure that money is a visible part of daily life while having an eye on the future. For Hoover, he was able to make the connection that by being organized, he had clothing and food. But he was also aware he had to manage his expenses so that he would have enough for tomorrow.

Today, the consensus is that children should be introduced to money early on, and in a consistent manner. The reason is the clear link between the grasp of finance in childhood and financial well-being in adulthood.[155] I see in my own clients how these early "money stories" can impact one's relationship with money. Basically, if done right, the seeds of financial capability can be successfully sown during childhood.

When you think about creating such a space where a child can learn, you need to think in terms of financial socialization guidelines. Parents should "guide and advise rather than direct and dictate," "explain to children what they can and cannot do and the consequences of violating the limits," and "allow children to learn by mistakes and successes."[156] By creating guidelines, we start to move the child away from only emotionally engaging with money to seeing it as a problem set to solve.

The Consumer Financial Protection Bureau has laid out certain age parameters and what a child should have mastery of—and when—to achieve financial capability.[157] When we look at these ages, Hoover was the perfect

---

155 (Bureau 2020) page 3.
156 (Dunrud 2005) page 1.
157 (Bureau 2020) page 7.

test case. For young children both pre-school and early elementary aged (ages three to seven), the goal is to see the child engaging in self-regulation, persistence, and focus. We can see this with things like counting and sorting with young children and learning basic math with currency.[158]

By the time a child is in middle childhood (ages eight to twelve), the measurement goal shifts to the child "begin[ning] to develop a positive attitude toward planning, saving, frugality, and self-control." This is also where the concept of setting goals and planning ahead kicks in.[159] One of the most common techniques used at this level is children doing chores for their allowance.

Finally, as a teenager, the measurement gets more complex as the young adult has to grasp more advanced processes and concepts that are part of financial planning. This is the development of real critical thinking and decision-making when it comes to money.[160] This could include involving the child in the college financing decisions or getting their first job.

Parents today want their children to have strong financial literacy skills. But these skills are learned over years, and kids can make mistakes. Yet for Hoover, these guideposts not only match up to the key moments of his life, but he had to master financial skills in order to survive.

HOOVER SAVES THE DAY

In the October 30, 1894 edition of the *Daily Palo Alto*, Hoover published the "Financial Statement of the Treasurer of the Student Body." For the first time in the school's short history, the finances were open to public review. Hoover's frustration was clear:

"The general student body have known nothing about the way in which debts were being piled up against them year after year…It still remains evident, however, that a debt of $550 has accumulated from the three preceding years, until our credit is bad and the student body have an unenviable reputation for careless financiering."[161]

---

158 (Bureau 2020) page 13.
159 (Bureau 2020) page 18.
160 (Bureau 2020) page 24.
161 "Financial Statement of the Treasurer of the Student Body," *Daily Palo Alto*, Volume V, No. 38, Tuesday, October 30, 1894.

Herbert Hoover Saves the Stanford Football Team

Hoover then went about solving the problem. He made site visits to the various clubs to check supplies and eliminate waste. He put a stop to using game-day uniforms for practice and encouraged the clubs to be frugal with their supplies, while also seeking ways to pay down the debt. He implemented a strict but straightforward voucher system, duly announced and reported in the *Daily Palo Alto*. Vouchers were to be obtained "for expenditures and form the basis of auditing by the various committees."[162] He also required that the voucher carry a certification whereby the individual attested that "to the best of my knowledge and belief, the prices paid were reasonable and just."[163]

In a letter to a friend, Hoover shared the challenges he took on. "Am Treas. Of Student Body you know and it has proved to be a bigger job than I bargained for, taking most of my time…I virtually have control of affairs and am making a hard effort to pay of our old indebtedness of $600.00 & conduct the present foot-ball season successfully."[164]

The initial reaction was negative, and the athletic clubs, including the football team, pushed back. Both coaches and players complained. To some he sounded like a disapproving Quaker elder. But Hoover was firm: no exceptions would be permitted.

His hard work paid off. By January of 1895, Hoover published a financial statement that showed not only that the debt was paid off, but now there was a surplus. The same coaches and players who were initially resistant began to respect his acumen. They saw the benefit of having a strong financial system in place that allowed them to collect tens of thousands of dollars in ticket sales and other revenue.

Hinsdale credited the success of his Stanford student body presidency to what he called the "Hoover influence." Hoover himself was a bit more modest. As he shared with a friend as the year wound down, "We had many

---

162 "Student Body Affairs," *Daily Palo Alto*, Volume V, No 59, Thursday, November 15, 1894.
163 Ibid.
164 Letter Herbert Hoover to Nell May Hill, dated November 7, 1894. Nell May Hill was an older student at Stanford and older than Hoover by six years. Due to poor health and insufficient funds, she could not complete her degree. Hill and Hoover remained friends and corresponded for years.

interesting occurrences in College politics during the year. The barbs won everything and I think things improved all around."[165]

Moreover, Stanford kept the voucher system Hoover developed in place for more than fifty years. It was Hoover's first real public success. Years later, as he rose to national prominence, his classmates would speak to the press about his financial management of Stanford. They all had the same message: Hoover was a success, but it was due to hard work and not just luck.

HOW JAMES MONROE HELPED BUILD THE COUNTRY WHO CAUSED HIS DEBT

Seventy years earlier, a former president was composing a letter that he dreaded writing to his mentor, friend, and neighbor, Thomas Jefferson. James Monroe sat at his desk at his Oak Hill estate and began his appeal. Monroe was gathering receipts to show that the US government owed him money for decades of expenses he incurred during his service to the country. He made a cautious plea to Jefferson to help with the evidence, explaining the trouble he was in. [166] While he had inherited lands as a young man, Monroe had spent most of his adult years focused on government, moving from role to role. He had not cultivated the land and his crops as he should have, nor had he managed his books to weather the financial storm he was in. Now, after a lifetime in government, including eight years as president, he was on the edge of financial ruin.

> My debts abroad were great, and my plantation in Albemarle & here, have added considerably to them every year, so that with accumulated looses [sic], and interest, compound added to simple, they have become immense. This is a true, tho' a melancholy picture of the actual state of my affairs.[167]

As he signed off, he referenced in the postscript that Jefferson himself was in a dire financial situation as well.

---

165 Letter Herbert Hoover to Nell May Hill, dated September 7, 1895.
166 Letter Monroe to Jefferson, February 13, 1826, https://founders.archives.gov/documents/Jefferson/98-01-02-5903.
167 Ibid.

Herbert Hoover Saves the Stanford Football Team

> P.S. I have this moment recievd [*sic*] a paper from Richmond, which gives an account of your application to the legislature, for the grant of a Lottery for the sale of your estate, to relieve you from embarrassment [*sic*]. I cannot express the concern which this view of your affairs has given me, altho' I can readily conceive the causes which have led to it.[168]

But Monroe needn't have worried. A response dispatched from Monticello appeared less than ten days later. Jefferson simply replied:

> Your favor of the 13th was received yesterday. [Y]our use of my letter with the alterations subsequently proposed, needs no apology. [A]nd it will be a gratification to me if it can be of any service to you.[169]

Both men were major Virginia landholders who spent a lifetime managing illiquidity. Through the decades of their relationship, they had both watched the value of their land and crops fluctuate.

Now at sixty-six years of age, Monroe was forced to put together a petition to Congress asking them to reimburse his expenses for his decades of work to help the fledgling nation. But after all of his success, how exactly did he get into such a financial mess?

MONROE—HE'S JUST LIKE THE REST OF US

I have to admit, as much as a financial mess that Monroe got into, he's a pretty likable—and accomplished—fellow. He is modern and relatable, especially in comparison to the other founding fathers.[170] I could see him existing in the present day very easily. His money troubles are similar to those of many other Americans in that some were beyond his control and some were self-inflicted.

---

168 Ibid.
169 Letter Jefferson to Monroe, dated February 22, 1826. https://founders.archives.gov/documents/Jefferson/98-01-02-5927. Jefferson did have him cut one section in the submission.
170 Monroe is often seen as the weakest of the Virginia founders of Washington, Jefferson, and Madison.

Whenever a person is suffering financial misfortune, it's easy to say that they didn't follow the basic building blocks of financial management. Budgeting (or lack thereof) is usually seen as one of the culprits when someone's finances are a mess. But budgeting is a little more complex and nuanced than that, and not all of us get the training Hoover received.

Monroe's financial misadventures start early. Like Hoover, he was orphaned fairly young; however, Monroe's situation was different in one respect. He inherited lands in Virginia that needed to be cultivated in order to turn a profit. Farming was a delicate business and had to be tended to carefully. But he was a very ambitious young man with a lot going on, so he wasn't exactly set up for farming success. And while he did create many budgets over the years, Monroe's budgeting blunders could fill a whole book.

To fully understand how he ended up in so much debt near the end of his life, let's take a look at two incidents: one involving President Washington and the other President Jefferson.

GEORGE WASHINGTON PRESENTS A CHALLENGING OPPORTUNITY SET—1794

Monroe came of age during a time of great revolution and change. He studied at the College of William and Mary before going off to war, fighting under General Washington. He came back to study law under Jefferson and then won a seat in the Virginia House of Burgesses and after that, the US Senate. Based on his experience, the Washington administration wanted to send him to France in 1794 on a diplomatic mission. But there was a catch: Washington gave him an hour to decide if he wanted to go.[171]

Monroe stood at a financial crossroads. On one hand, Paris beckoned—along with potential future glory in establishing the US with its allies. On the other hand, he needed to manage his estate. He had just bought more property in Kentucky. He was still developing a property next to Jefferson's Monticello.[172] He had crops that needed tending.

---

171 (McGrath 2020) page 124.
172 And Jefferson was no help in influencing his budget. Rather, he led Monroe astray at times. And you have to remember, Jefferson was a good fifteen years older than Monroe. This connection with the older man often impacted how Monroe made financial decisions. When Jefferson returned from France in 1789, he wanted Monroe to live closer to his Monticello estate. Jefferson had the wild idea that they could have adjoining properties. (I sort of love this idea of the founding fathers wanting to hang with their friends.)

Herbert Hoover Saves the Stanford Football Team

Trying to manage this from an ocean away would be challenging. And the $9,000 salary offered by Washington wouldn't come close to covering his costs.

He chose Paris—who could blame him, especially given all he had heard from Jefferson about the place? And who says no to President George Washington?

When Monroe arrived in Paris, the city was in a state of transition following the French Revolution. Monroe knew that impressions were important in European diplomacy, and that the United States needed to project gravitas, which in part meant entertaining in the right manner. He wanted his house to be grand enough for that purpose, so he purchased the Folie de la Bouëxière on the rue de Clichy on the Right Bank in Paris. Monroe thought he was getting a deal, and he decided to finance the 73,000 livres[173] personally by taking loans out against his Kentucky land.[174]

Gulp.

Buying the home was a financial stretch, but Monroe wasn't done. He decided to renovate the property "lavishly" and restore the gardens.[175] He and his wife, Elizabeth, bought beautiful French furniture. And then he began entertaining, Jefferson-style, despite the fact that Congress would not be funding that level of diplomacy.[176] The whole time he was in Paris, Monroe kept adding to his debts and avoided taking steps to help his finances.

It took some time but on February 15, 1789, Monroe wrote to Jefferson the good news. "It has always been my wish to acquire property near Monticello. I have lately accomplish'd it by the purchase of Colo. G. Nicholas improvments in Charlotteville and 500 acres of land within a mile, on the road to the R. fish gap. …I shall be so happy as to have you as a neighbour I have not determin'd. In any event it puts it within my reach to be contiguous to you when the fatigue of publick life, should dispose you for retirement."

But again, it was more money than Monroe should be spending. (James Monroe to Thomas Jefferson, dated February 15, 1789.)

173 The purchase price is stated a few different ways due to the fact that France changed its currency in 1795. I have also seen it converted to 350,000 francs. The best way to gauge this value was the house was approximately $70,000.
174 (McGrath 2020) page 145.
175 Ibid.
176 This is a weakness of the early United States. There was no understanding of the costs to have diplomats entertain. Monroe would go on to remedy this in his presidency. Per my discussion with Heidi Stello.

After two years, he was recalled as a diplomat. He sold his Paris house, but unfortunately for Monroe, he had to leave France before he got the final $10,000 he was owed from the sale. He arrived back from his mission in debt and, much to his chagrin, not in Washington's good graces due to Monroe's criticism of the Jay Treaty.[177]

Monroe submitted his other Paris expenses to Congress for repayment, but to no avail. His illiquidity was getting worse and worse. Finally in December 1797, it got so bad that he even borrowed $300 from James Madison to cover some of the furniture shipping costs.[178] Monroe was frustrated and stressed about money, and the experience made him want to move away from governmental roles.

FOOL ME ONCE, FOOL ME TWICE—1803

Monroe was ready to return to his plantation with an eye to getting his debts under control and making his lands profitable.[179] His land holdings were extensive, and he felt he could really make his tobacco crop significant.[180] Running this level of an agricultural enterprise required "considerable business acumen, oversight, personal supervision and innovative judgement."[181]

He had a simple plan: manage his farming enterprise and take up the profession of law. Monroe was well aware that his national stature could grow a strong and profitable legal practice. On the other hand, his potential clients needed to be assured he was done with the pursuit of politics before hiring him. But he had barely gotten his practice up and running when politics pursued him.[182]

Jefferson wrote to Monroe, saying he needed him to return to France immediately to work with Robert Livingston on the purchase of Louisiana

---

177 The Jay Treaty was the 1794 Treaty between Great Britain and the United States that averted war between the two countries. Monroe was not alone in his criticism. In general, the American public also did not like this treaty.
178 Letter James Monroe to James Madison, dated December 10, 1797.
179 Monroe had undertaken a role in the Washington Administration in England and had accrued debt. This debt he had submitted to Congress and was still waiting reimbursement when he got the Jefferson request.
180 (McGrath 2020) page 182.
181 (Gawalt 1993) page 253.
182 In 1799, he became governor and took a further pay cut to a $3,333 salary.

Herbert Hoover Saves the Stanford Football Team

from Napoleon and the French. Jefferson knew Monroe well and how best to motivate him. He was also fifteen years older than Monroe. He wrote that he knew that Monroe was trying to move "into a different line of business" and that taking this new role would be "a great sacrifice on your part."[183] But that ultimately "some men are born for the public nature by fitting them for the service of the human race on a broad scale."[184]

Historians have pointed out that Monroe at times "oscillated between impulse and caution."[185] More importantly, Monroe was the type who could only focus on what was directly in front of him, to the exclusion of everything else, and France beckoned.[186]

Things were dire. Monroe took numerous advances from friends. He struggled to sell his properties in Kentucky and Charlottesville. He was still waiting for the reimbursement to come through from his last diplomatic endeavor in France—six years later. And his loyalty to Jefferson blinded him when it came to negotiating salary terms, despite his experience.

Jefferson and Secretary of State James Madison were concerned that as the three men's friendship "so well known the public will have eagle eyes to watch if we grant you any indulgencies out of the general rule; and on the other hand, the example set in your case will be more cogent on future ones, and produce greater approbation to our conduct."[187] Optically they did not want to be seen as favoring Monroe.

Jefferson then allotted to Monroe the same salary of $9,000 he had received nine years earlier under Washington, plus his voyage expenses and a quarter of a year's salary for his return.[188] This was all as laid out by the government rules.[189]

Monroe knew immediately upon seeing the numbers that it was insufficient to cover his expenses and debt servicing. He might have balked, but Jefferson's request was an urgent appeal to his sense of duty. Monroe

---

183 Letter Jefferson to Monroe, dated January 13, 1803.
184 Ibid.
185 (Cunningham 2003) page 11.
186 (Stello 2023).
187 Ibid.
188 To give some context for this offer, it was roughly the same as a salary today of $300,000. But remember, Monroe would not have an expense budget for entertaining overseas. So the funds had to cover everything.
189 Ibid.

needed to get to France—and quickly. Jefferson wrote, "As to the time of your going, you cannot too much hasten it, as the moment in France is critical.... You should arrange your affairs for an absence of a year at least, perhaps for a long one."[190]

This is a pivotal moment in Monroe's finances. He needed to prioritize his financial commitment, but he was falling into the budget traps of sunk cost fallacy, which is when a person is "reluctan[t] to abandon a strategy or course of action in which one has already invested heavily even when it is clear that abandonment is rationally the correct response." [191] In financial planning, it can be a huge problem.

If Monroe had looked rationally at his financial situation, he would have seen he had a choice. He could have turned down Jefferson's request and focused on his estate. Or he could have decided that in order to prudently manage his finances, he would have had to sell part of his estate to take the job. Monroe did neither. Instead, he sold his furniture and plates from his Oak Hill estate to Madison with the intent of replacing them with finer French goods.

His failure to prioritize, despite all his experience, was his financial undoing. His diplomatic mission was successful, but he arrived back in the United States with more debt than when he had left. However, Monroe was still focused on career building and decided, for the sake of appearances, that he would not submit his open receipts to Congress for reimbursement.

THE BILL IS DUE—1825

While he continued to climb the ladder of success through to the presidency, he bled financially. Monroe could barely service the debt that hung over his head. But he felt he could not seek reimbursement until his political career was over and he no longer had any perceived conflicts of interest.

Finally in 1826, after decades of financial beatings, he found himself $75,000 in debt. ($75,000 has the same purchasing power as $2.3 million in 2024 dollars.) He needed to find a way to survive. His entire retirement depended on it. He was on the precipice of ultimate ruin. It was time to seek reimbursement. So, for the last five years of his life, he focused his

---

190 Ibid.
191 As defined by the Oxford Dictionary.

Herbert Hoover Saves the Stanford Football Team

tunnel vision on getting repaid for what he had spent during a lifetime in government roles.

Unfortunately, Congress was wildly divided politically. Monroe's petitions languished in committee while politicians on both sides chipped away at the $75,000 request. For Monroe, it was agony. He had long imagined a retirement on his estate surrounded by his books, tending to his lands, and visits to friends like Jefferson and Madison. Instead, he had to endure the uncertainty of whether he would be able to survive financially. He felt even more constricted as the Virginia land market was depressed, and he could not get the full value for his properties.

He decided to put his Highland estate up for auction. Jefferson was aghast at this.[192] But much to Monroe's chagrin, the bids were all far too low. He took the property off the market and made the gut-wrenching decision to turn it over to the Bank of the United States, less 707 acres he kept for himself. The bank valued the property at $25,000—less than what Monroe had expected. His debts were still not covered in full.

Monroe continued his wait for Congress to pay. What irked him the most about this process was that he saw the reluctance of Congress as an attack on his integrity. He couldn't understand why Congress didn't appreciate his sacrifices (and Congress certainly didn't appreciate that he had added interest to some of the numbers). When they finally relented, Monroe received only $29,513—an amount too little to pay off all of his debts.

Monroe packed up what was left and moved to New York to live with his daughter. He kept petitioning Congress for his remaining claims, and when he threatened to go public with his story, they grudgingly paid him the remaining $30,000. Just a few months later, on July 4, 1831, Monroe passed away with a small estate to pass on to his heirs. (Yet another founding father who died on the Fourth of July!)

As we look back two hundred years later, we can see that Monroe's contributions to the US were significant—the Louisiana Purchase, the Monroe Doctrine, and the Missouri Compromise. But if he had simply engaged with his budget and avoided detrimental behavior, he may have had the luxury of those accomplishments *and* a wealthy retirement.

---

192   (Cunningham 2003) page 66.

NUMBER CRUNCHERS CAN BE IRRITATING—JUST ASK JANE WYMAN

Decades before he began his political career, Ronald Reagan was a popular B-movie actor, and in 1940, he married fellow film star Jane Wyman. The press has always loved covering Hollywood couples, and because reporters hounded Reagan and Wyman for details of their marital life, we have a few glimpses into the way they handled their finances. According to one account, the Reagans took turns paying the monthly bills. In another interview, Wyman summed up their approach: "As for our finances, Ronnie and I pool ours. There never is the question of whose money buys what."[193]

And later she told another reporter, "Our system is so simple, it doesn't sound like anything. It's just that we save half of everything we make… Every one of our checks was banked away, half in a savings account, half in a checking account."[194] But behind the scenes, it wasn't so idyllic when it came to the Reagan marital finances. The Reagans were part of the patriarchal studio system, so while Reagan was making $10,400 a year, Jane made half of what her husband did.[195]

Both of them came from financially volatile childhoods. Reagan's parents moved in and out of financial resiliency. On one side he had his mother, Nelle, who was industrious and focused on managing money. She kept copious records of her savings in the small bank in town. And she made sure that the savings account was in her name alone.[196] On the other side, he had his father, Jack, a charming shoe salesman who unfortunately had a problem with alcohol. His addiction was such that Reagan's mother asked Jack's employer to give the paychecks directly to her. But women were still treated as second-class citizens at the time, and the store manager refused, thus enabling Jack to squander his paycheck in bars on the walk home from work. At one point, the family had to skip town by train in the middle of the night as a result of Jack spending all of their rent money on a bender.[197]

---

193 (Keavy 1941).
194 (Wood 1941).
195 This would be the equivalent of Reagan making $217,000 and Jane $108,000 in today's dollars.
196 From conversation with Joan at the Reagan Birthplace regarding Nelle's bank book, June 10, 2019.
197 Per Joan Johnson at the Reagan Birthplace.

Herbert Hoover Saves the Stanford Football Team

Jane's childhood was just as financially precarious. She had bounced around in foster care and lived hand to mouth much of the time, so both she and Ronald had experienced childhood financial trauma. When a child is exposed to financial trauma, it can lead to a range of behavioral traits. For some, it means continuing with the chaos in their adult years. They may overspend and not be able to create financial stability. For others, it can trigger hypervigilance and compulsive behaviors where there is a powerful need to maintain tight control over money.

Reagan's trauma manifested itself in his seeking out financial role models and fully committing himself to a rigid system of budgeting. Wyman's reaction was the complete opposite. She overspent as a way to compensate for being deprived in childhood. Her favorite ways of spending her salary were clothing, jewelry, and nights out. Perhaps the couple was an example of the adage "opposites attract" because they were like oil and water when it came to budgeting and spending.

Jane was aware that her money management frustrated her husband. Very early on in their relationship, she realized that Reagan had no tolerance for debt. He had a strict budgeting system that would not allow a single bill to be late. As a result, Wyman had to work very hard to pay off her debt to meet Reagan's exacting standards. As she put it in an interview with a movie magazine, "Ronnie has a phobia about bills."[198]

BUDGETING TO BUY A HOME PLAYS OUT LIKE A MOVIE

While Reagan and Wyman had many wealthy movie star friends, they agreed not to be extravagant in buying a home. They weren't always on the same page regarding what they could and couldn't afford, so Reagan was surprised that Wyman was actually willing to stick to a budget when it came to their house. In fact, he got none of the usual resistance from her regarding budgets. Rather than give up and pay more, Reagan and Wyman kept searching for the perfect construction plan because he wanted to be sure they could afford the house after building it in case they had to take lower-paying jobs.

---

198 (Wood 1941).

All the Presidents' Money

The Reagans had purchased two plots of undeveloped land tucked away in the hills between West Hollywood and Beverly Hills[199] at 9137 Cordell Drive.[200] They loved the location and the fact that they could build a home with a 360-degree view of the city and mountains.

Although Reagan and Wyman socialized with the Hollywood elite, they were earning B-movie star salaries. Carole Lombard and Clark Gable had a twenty-acre ranch in nearby Encino, which they had purchased for $50,000 in 1939.[201] Closer to the Reagans was Bob Hope's Toluca Lake home worth $80,000 in 1940.[202]

Working through the numbers, Reagan and Wyman decided on a budget of $15,000 for construction. They just needed that perfect blueprint and considered a lot of options. They worked with their architect and pored over home magazines. They wanted their dream home but within their budget. The pressure was on.

It ended up playing out in a movie—literally. At the cinema together one evening, they saw the perfect floor plan in the movie *This Thing Called Love*, starring Rosalind Russell and Melvyn Douglas.

In an interview, Jane discussed this aha moment. "As soon as [Rosalind Russell's] house flashed on the screen, both Ronnie and I said at once, 'That's it.' Next morning we dashed over to Columbia and got the plans. We had a miniature house made—it became a regular plaything, with us deciding little changes here and there, and how we'd arrange our furniture to fit."[203]

---

199 Niki Cervantes, "Ronald Reagan, who opposed the Civil Rights acts passed…," United Press International, October 4, 1984, https://www.upi.com/Archives/1984/10/04/Ronald-Reagan-who-opposed-the-Civil-Rights-acts-passed/5331465710400/.

   It should be noted that Reagan and Jane bought six lots in the early 1940s. They built on one and sold two during their marriage. The final three were given to Jane in the divorce, which she immediately sold.

200 "9137 Cordell Drive," Estately, 2024, https://www.estately.com/listings/info/9137-cordell-drive--1. After Reagan's election as president, reporters found that the home had protective covenants in the deed that barred non-Caucasians unless they were servants.

201 Charles Lockwood, "Clark Gable and Carole Lombard's House in California," *Architectural Digest*, August 30, 2016, https://www.architecturaldigest.com/story/clark-gable-carole-lombard-ranch-home-california.

202 Bob Hope's home would sell after his death in 2012 for $27.5 million.

203 (Morella and Epstein 1986) page 45. This story is also recalled in Maynard L. Parker's book *Modern Photography and the American Dream*. However, in Parker's version, Wyman and Reagan wrote to Columbia Pictures asking for the plan.

Herbert Hoover Saves the Stanford Football Team

When their architect first went through the plans, they were well over the $15,000 budget, but they worked through it and made concessions. After numerous revisions, they hit their budget while still being able to afford the luxuries of separate "his and hers" bathrooms, a wine cellar, and a gated private driveway. Jane even agreed to do built-ins in the house—as she noted, "Think of the money I'll save on furniture!"[204]

They had the plan, now they needed to finance it. The couple secured a twenty-year FHA mortgage[205] for $15,000 to build the home with a monthly payment of $125.[206] Adjusted for inflation, today this would be a $256,848 mortgage with a $2,140 monthly payment. It was, and still is, a big financial commitment.

Once they committed to construction, they developed a very tight monthly budget, with each getting twenty-five dollars a week as a personal allowance—not very glamorous for movie stars.

If this were a movie, the credits would roll here, as the two stars moved into their dream house. But this was real life. Could the Reagans stick to the budget? Or would their personal traumas cause the budget to blow up?

FINANCIAL TENSIONS EVENTUALLY COME BACK TO HAUNT THEM

Initially Reagan and Jane stuck to their system. They paid their bills and followed the rules of their budget. But life evolved for them. By 1948, with two children, and with Reagan's Hollywood career stalling and Wyman's cruising—she won an Oscar that year—the marriage began to fall apart. Jane had always bristled under the strictness of how Reagan liked to function, especially when it came to money, and their differences ultimately doomed the marriage. But they did have a happy ending financially. As part of their divorce, they sold the house and profited handsomely. They had approximately $75,000 of community property that they split, and Reagan paid $500 a month in child support.

---

204 (Wood 1941) page 79.
205 Up until the Great Depression, most mortgages were three to five years with no amortization and balloon payments. https://en.wikipedia.org/wiki/Federal_Housing_Administration. FHA mortgages were a key component in the 1940s for helping Americans buy homes.
206 (Morella and Epstein 1986) page 52.

Luckily for Reagan, his next wife, Nancy Davis, seemed to be more amenable toward his budgeting style.

Nancy was willing to stick to the script on budgeting, even to the point of abandoning her dream of a lavish wedding, which he considered a waste of money.[207] Whether it was a matter of having similar financial styles or just Nancy being willing to follow Reagan's lead, the marriage lasted until his passing in 2004.

Oh, and that house at 9137 Cordell Drive? In 2022, it sold again—for $70 million![208]

1 + 1 = 2, EXCEPT WHEN IT DOESN'T

Budgeting for most of us is a pain in the ass. Yet, the crazy thing is that some people actually enjoy budgeting. For Hoover, it allowed him to problem-solve. For Reagan, he was able to manage anxiety and feel in control. I think a good approach to introducing a budget into your life is to figure out why you want to budget—empowerment? anxiety management? connection with a spouse?—and use that as a framing device. And remember, if the word *budgeting* depresses you, adopt the term the wealthy use—*cash flow management*!

---

207 (Tumulty 2021) page 105.
208 (Asch 2022).

Chapter Four

DON'T MESS WITH IKE WHEN IT COMES TO POKER
(OR APPETITE FOR RISK)

"Louise, let's play a cold hand of poker—just the two of us—winner names the stakes."

And so began an article that appeared in newspapers across the country in the early summer of 1965 claiming that President Warren G. Harding had once challenged socialite Louise Cromwell Brooks to a high-stakes game of poker. The article further claimed that when Brooks won the hand, she demanded a set of the White House china, and that a few days later, she was given a set that had belonged to President Benjamin Harrison.[209] The claims made in the article gave rise to the famous rumor that Harding—a heavy drinker—had gambled away *all* of the White House china while soused. The rumor was so prevalent that the curator of the Warren G. Harding Presidential Sites went through all of the White House inventory records from the Harding administration to confirm it wasn't true.[210]

---

209 (Associated Press 1965) The Benjamin Harrison china was heavily influenced by first lady Caroline Harrison. The plate has 44 stars on the border representing the union, a United States Coat of Arms with a cornstalk, and flower edge motif. It is believed that this design was made by the first lady herself. It was a 288-piece set by Tressemanes & Vogt of Limoges. It was ordered through M. W. Beveridge for $732. (Keller 2016).
210 Discussion with Sherry Hall, manager and curator of Harding Presidential Sites, on January 30, 2024.

All the Presidents' Money

While the story does nothing to elevate Harding's reputation, it does highlight a pastime enjoyed by many presidents—poker. You name one, and likely that president played poker: Washington, Grant, and Obama, just to name a few. And it's completely bipartisan as both Democrats and Republicans partake. In fact, presidents love poker so much, there is actually an oil painting series by Andy Thomas showing the presidents sitting around playing poker.

But why poker? And why is it a common pastime for presidents? Poker players are often skilled at managing risk due to the inherent nature of the game. To play poker well, it helps to have some knowledge of probability and statistics, to maintain emotional control, to be able to do risk assessments, and to be adaptable and able to learn from mistakes. The best poker players can make strong decisions with limited information—sort of like what presidents have to do on a regular basis.

So, is there a correlation between playing poker and managing personal finance? If only it were that easy! Every hand in poker has a financial consequence, that's true, but that doesn't mean the decisions made around the hand are good and reliable ones.[211] Unfortunately, just because someone is a good poker player doesn't mean they are automatically good with money. The bigger question is whether they take and manage risk appropriately.[212]

Risk is a fascinating aspect of personal finance. Over my career, I have watched people deal with risk in very different ways. For instance, I work with a lot of corporate executives who worry about the investment risks in a diversified portfolio but not about having 80 percent of their assets in a single stock. I have also seen investors who take on incredible risk in venture capital who barbell (or cut the risk in their portfolio) with high-credit-quality municipal bonds.[213]

---

211 (Duke 2018) pages 27–29.
212 I am extremely indebted to the book *Thinking in Bets: Making Smarter Decisions When You Don't Have All the Facts* by Annie Duke and her explanations about decision-making.
213 In portfolio construction, risk is mitigated by diversifying amount various asset classes. No one position has a high concentration, as that would create risk. That being said, diversification helps grow assets at a reasonable rate of return over the long term. Great wealth is created by concentration, such as a single stock position.

Don't Mess with Ike When It Comes to Poker

What I have found over the years is that, although most risk is pretty controlled (financially speaking), everyone's tolerance for financial risk is different. Life experience has a big impact on that tolerance.

THE EMOTIONAL CONTROL OF IKE

Professionally, Eisenhower was good with risk and judging situations. His part in the planning for D-Day in 1944, which involved weighing risk on a monumental scale with tens of thousands of lives hanging in the balance, was perfectly in keeping with his character. Ike had spent a lifetime judging risk, and this experience allowed him to approach risk with the emotional detachment necessary to make clear-headed decisions.

By all accounts, Ike wasn't motivated by money. He grew up poor (although he never felt that they were). He spent the majority of his career in the army. As we saw earlier, Ike grew up a farm boy. But he also seemed to always have an eye on what he wanted to achieve and how to get the funds to do it.

Still, Ike also had fun as a kid. In Ike's hometown of Abilene, Kansas, there was a local guy in his fifties named Bob Davis. Davis was a bachelor in town who often went out camping on the Smoky Hill River. Ike and other local kids would sometimes tag along with him. Over time, he would teach Ike how to hunt and fish. He also taught him another skill: poker.

Ike would later note that Davis was completely illiterate, but he knew how to calculate the odds in poker. Whenever they were together, Ike recalled that "he dinned percentages into my head night after night around a campfire, using for the lessons a greasy pack of nicked cards that must have been a dozen years old.…Often, he would pick up part of the pack and snap it across my fingers to underscore the classic lesson that in a two-handed game one does not draw to a four-card straight or a four-card flush against a man who has openers."[214]

By 1915, Ike was a second lieutenant stationed in San Antonio, Texas. He was an up-and-comer and had possibilities for where his career could go. He was also a really good-looking guy: five foot ten, blue eyes with strawberry blond hair. We all think of him as bald and in his sixties, but as a young man he was quite dashing. And that's when he met his complete

---

214 (D. D. Eisenhower 1967) pages 88–90.

opposite: a vivacious and wealthy debutante named Mamie Doud. From all accounts, the attraction between the poor farm boy from Kansas and the daughter of a manufacturing executive was electric.

Mamie is one of those underappreciated First Ladies. She was truly a character, known for great bon mots like "every woman over fifty should stay in bed until noon" and "I have but one career and its name is Ike."[215] She knew who she was, and she wasn't afraid to express herself. Could you even imagine our more PR-packaged First Ladies today making these statements? Melania, Jill, and Michelle might feel and think similarly at times, but they aren't going to say so out loud.

When she met Ike at age nineteen, her entire life experience was in being a daughter and a socialite. Her father spoiled her. In one letter to him when she was a young girl, she playfully teased her father for the five dollars he gave her so that she now had seventy dollars in her account. Mamie recalled in her later years how her family was the first family in Denver to have a recreation room that included a victrola, a piano, and a pool table.[216]

As a teenager, she attended Miss Wolcott's finishing school in order to learn the stylings of an upper-class wife among the Denver elite. She was just fancy, and she could have married any suitable man of her social class.

Mamie was drawn to Ike in a way that shook her to the core. Her parents felt it was a speedy courtship. As she recalled years later, her father had a "long talk with her…and pointed out to her that Lieutenant Eisenhower was only making a hundred and forty-seven dollars a month and her life would be very different as an Army wife than it had been at home."[217]

But like any nineteen-year-old girl besotted with her first love, Mamie didn't listen to him. She wanted Ike, regardless of the financial consequences. Both Mamie and Ike felt that her parents' concern was old-fashioned. To them, their courtship reflected the values of the younger generation.[218]

Mamie was willing to give up some of her creature comforts, but she was clear on one thing: Ike was to dote on her.[219] Their relationship quickly

---

215 (West 1973).
216 (S. Eisenhower 1996) pages 11–12.
217 (M. D. Eisenhower 1972) page 5.
218 Ibid.
219 While Mamie was willing to make sacrifices to be with Ike, it was still a shock to her upon her first visit to Ike's family in Abilene after their marriage how different their respective families' financial situations were.

Don't Mess with Ike When It Comes to Poker

grew, and Ike took a step to show the seriousness of his intent. Following the long-standing tradition, Ike gave Mamie a miniature of his West Point ring.[220] The meaning of this was clear to all. Ike intended for Mamie to be his bride.

While Mamie accepted the ring and the marriage proposal it signified, she was quite adamant she also 1wanted two things: Ike's regular-sized West Point ring and a *real* engagement ring.[221] Her heart was set on a ring of diamonds in a platinum setting. It was the type of ring that most socialites received. Ike's salary at the time was $141.67 a month. He was doing okay, but by no means was he flush with cash. She was making a pretty big ask.[222] And to be clear, she wanted to wear the diamond ring on her left hand and Ike's West Point ring on her right.

Ike was not daunted by the task. He borrowed the money from his father. It was a big financial risk to do this. As a young man starting his career, there was no certainty he would make enough to pay the money back. But Ike was not deterred and a ring with a one-and-a-half-carat diamond appeared on her hand. Mamie later shared with her granddaughter, "The diamond must have cost a great deal, but to Ike, the sky was the limit and money never meant much to him except to obtain some specific end."[223]

Ike had what he wanted: a career in the military, the girl of his dreams, and a bright future. But he also had the debt from the ring. He needed to tackle that.

---

220 Today Ike's ring is on display at the library at West Point along with those of Generals MacArthur and Bradley.
221 (S. Eisenhower 1996) page 38. According to Mamie's granddaughter, Mamie also received Ike's full-sized West Point ring that she wore daily except during the 1952 campaign when the ring made her fingers black and blue from shaking so many hands.
222 You can see the ring at "Mamie Eisenhower: Engagement Ring Diamond," Heritage Auctions, 2024, https://historical.ha.com/itm/political/presidential-relics/mamie-eisenhower-engagement-ring-diamond/a/6153-42165.s. However, the ring shown is not her original engagement ring. She gave her diamond to her son John to use for his engagement, and it was remounted into a new setting.
223 (S. Eisenhower 1996) page 66.

IKE TAKES A CALCULATED RISK

Now, I'm sure you are expecting to hear that Ike did the pragmatic thing by saving and budgeting to pay off the debt. Alas, no, the Great Commander of Allied Forces of World War II did not choose to take that path. Instead, he paid off Mamie's ring by playing poker.

Seriously.

Ike had absorbed all the lessons he had received from Bob Davis, and one day in the late fall of 1916, he stumbled across a few of his former classmates who were now in the Aviation Section, which paid twice as much as the rest of the army services. And lo and behold, they were playing poker. The group called out to Ike to join, but Ike played coy. "You fellows don't want me," he said to them. "I've got two silver dollars in my pocket, and that's all. You can't use me in that game."

But the group kept encouraging him to throw the money in and join. Ike finally relented and sat down, taking in the room and getting a good read on the rest of the players. A few hours later, he had turned two dollars into one hundred dollars.[224] He had the girl, and she had the ring, and Ike was debt-free.

Throughout Eisenhower's career, that was his superpower: the ability to assess risk and then execute a plan accordingly.

I'm not advocating that anyone in debt should play poker to pay it off. In fact, if I had worked with Ike, and he shared his strategy, I would have urged him to consider a different path (and he probably would have laughed me off). He was good at poker but not a reckless gambler, later observing that when he saw fellow officers losing more than they could afford, he stopped playing.[225]

Success at poker requires a good poker face, which is about controlling one's emotions in moments of stress. Controlling emotion is also incredibly important in personal finance. If emotion is controlled, then the individual is able to calmly and rationally focus on managing risk—and often times it allows someone to take on higher risk. I was once seated next to a Spanish-speaking world-champion drag racer at a dinner party. I asked him what was his "secret" to being a great car racer at speeds of three hundred

---

224 (D. D. Eisenhower 1967) Ike tells the story in detail in his book, pages 113–114.
225 (D. D. Eisenhower 1967) page 90.

Don't Mess with Ike When It Comes to Poker

miles per hour. He looked at me and said, "In my native language, we call it *frío*." Basically, the man had ice water in his veins. And when it came to the high-level risk assessment required of an officer sending troops into battle, so did Eisenhower.

Empirical data also suggests a correlation between strong poker-playing skills and risk-taking. Over the years, numerous academic studies have looked at traders' success and the types of outside hobbies and activities they engage in. What has been found is that while most pastimes, such as golf and bridge, did nothing for the traders' performance, traders who were regular poker players found that it had increased their edge.[226]

Take, for example, Steve Cohen, the founder of Point72 Asset Management as well as the now-closed SAC Capital Advisors. Cohen got his start as a kid playing poker in Great Neck, New York. For him, poker was a way to look at the world differently. And it was that skill set learned in poker that allowed him to become one of the best traders on Wall Street and principal at one of the most successful hedge funds.

In an interview with *Vanity Fair*, Cohen once stated, "I've always been de-sensitized to money. It was just always there. You know? I didn't think about it." He continued, "It's the same with trading. I think about the risk. I think about the trade. I don't think about the money. Poker—that was the biggest determinant in my learning to take risks."[227]

To some degree, Eisenhower could have made the same statement.

Once they were married and Ike became a breadwinner, his modest pay forced him and Mamie to live frugally. Mamie later said that she often had to "squeeze a dollar until the eagle screamed" during her marriage.[228] But the pair ultimately were able to build considerable wealth, but not until after Ike left the military.

In 1948, he was able to sell the book, film, and magazine rights to his memoirs *Crusade in Europe* for $1 million (or the equivalent of $13 million in 2024 dollars). And just as he had been strategic with poker, he worked hard in developing a tax strategy to mitigate his liability in an era where the top bracket hovered near 80 percent.

---

226 It should be noted that Ike was also a great bridge player.
227 (Burroughs 2010).
228 (S. Eisenhower 1996) page 73.

President Truman had a lot of respect for Ike and connected him with the Treasury Department to seek tax advice on royalties. There Ike learned of a unique loophole in the code: if he was able to hold the copyright for six months, he would be considered an amateur writer and thus only subject to 25 percent capital gains tax versus ordinary tax rates for professional writers.[229] Ike took the advice. He wrote the book, waited eight months to sell it, and then did a deal with Doubleday & Co. The tax savings was $500,000.

It was a well-played hand in building wealth. (And surprisingly, he didn't return the tax favor. Truman paid ordinary income tax for his memoirs during the Eisenhower administration.)

THE SLIDING DOORS OF RICHARD NIXON

Now, let's look at a poker-playing president that didn't quite have the same success with risk.

In the movie *Sliding Doors* from 1998, Gwyneth Paltrow's character is shown making it onto a train but is also shown missing the same train, and that pivotal moment turns out to make a huge difference in the direction her life takes. Well, that's a good analogy for a situation that played out for Richard Nixon and his personal finances. The shape of the twenty-first century might have been very different if this young man had succeeded in his earlier ventures, when Nixon had his own inflection point, or sliding-door moment. Had he ended up the CEO of the Minute Maid Company as was once a possibility, and not our thirty-seventh president, imagine the difference in our nation's trajectory this might have made. How exactly did this moment occur that ended up pushing him on the path to politics and the presidency? And what role did risk play in it?

After an impoverished childhood in Ohio, his father, Frank, was one of many Americans who made their way out West to find their fortune. Frank landed in the aptly named Orange County, California, where the landscape was full of citrus groves. Yet the area was developing rapidly, and Frank realized he had to strike while the iron was hot. As Nixon's brother Edward explained, "My dad decided that they needed to establish a base

---

229 (*New York Times* 1952).

Don't Mess with Ike When It Comes to Poker

that could take advantage of traffic that was bound to grow, as he saw it."[230] That meant settling down in Whittier, California, and opening first a gas station called "Nixon's Service." Eventually, it would grow to a point where they added a grocery on a patch of land halfway between Whittier and La Habra.

Owning a small business in 1920s California was hard on the Nixon family. Besides Richard, his parents had four other sons. The entire family pitched in, and each of the boys focused on a different area of the store. Nixon oversaw produce and would recall a childhood where he would be up at 3 a.m. to help bring in goods from Los Angeles for the store. And at one point, Frank wanted to find a way to make money off the local citrus industry, but he didn't have much luck. Still, even though his entrepreneurial ventures often didn't get off the ground, they made a big impression on young Nixon.

As a teenager, Nixon decided he wanted to get out of Whittier. He was a smart kid and even got into Harvard, but his family couldn't afford it. Instead, he went to Whittier College and lived at home. That meant he could still help out—especially when his older brother struggled with tuberculosis. After graduating, Nixon finally got the opportunity to leave home when he was accepted at Duke Law School. But despite his strong performance in law school, Nixon didn't get a job in either the Wall Street firms or in Washington working for the government. He returned to Whittier, dejected and frustrated. His mother, concerned about her son, asked the local law firm of Wingert & Bewley to hire him, and they did.

But Nixon was ambitious. He wanted more.

Nixon was also a bit unlucky. In his first law case, he made an error in judgment by asking opposing counsel for advice. The advice given caused his client to sue him for malpractice. His law firm settled with the client, but the case raged on for years. All the while, he would hear how well his Duke classmates were doing. It caused Nixon a great deal of frustration. He wanted his golden ticket.

He persisted in his ambition. After a while, he came into his own in practicing law and started earning a good reputation as an attorney in town. He was able to meet a number of influential businessmen. He also met a girl he liked named Pat Ryan. His income had been increasing steadily. In

---

230 (Nixon 2007).

1937, his monthly salary was $75 ($1,600 in 2024 dollars). A year later, he was at $125 a month ($2,700 in 2024 dollars), and it was looking like he might be able to double that.[231] In general, things were good. And then two local businessmen, Ralph Ober and Don Brings, presented a unique opportunity to Nixon.

HE HAD THE RIGHT INTUITION

In the early twentieth century, one of the most important technological developments was the ability to freeze food and transport it to faraway markets. The first breakthrough occurred in 1918, with a technique called cold packing. Cold packing involved the slow freezing of strawberries using ice and salt.[232] Regardless of how long it was frozen, once the strawberries were defrosted, they tasted just as fresh as if they had just been picked. It was revolutionary. If they could do this with a strawberry, what else could be frozen and shipped around the United States?

Names like Birds Eye, Swanson, and Lender's started to dominate the industry.[233] In orange-centric Southern California, entrepreneurs imagined being able to put a fresh-squeezed glass of orange juice on every table in America, and a few citrus producers jumped into the mix trying to find a way to make it work.

As Nixon networked to drum up legal business in Whittier, the frozen orange juice conversation was getting louder, especially in light of a surplus crop in 1938. Ober and Brings had an idea for a company, which they shared with Nixon: they could simply squeeze the juice from oranges, add in a little sugar and gelatin, and then freeze the liquid in a specialized plastic bag. Doing so meant they could ship this new product to cities and towns across the country. It could be revolutionary—and what we would call today an idea that could launch a "unicorn" company.[234]

---

231 (Swift 2014).
232 (Carstensen 1996) page 165. For a great history of frozen food innovation in the United States, I would strongly suggest this article.
233 (Carstensen 1996)
234 A unicorn company is a private start-up with $1 billion valuation or more. The term was coined by Aileen Lee, a US venture capitalist of Cowboy Ventures, in an article in *Tech Crunch* called "Welcome to the Unicorn Club: Learning from Billion-Dollar Startups."

Don't Mess with Ike When It Comes to Poker

Nixon jumped at the chance to be a part of this new business venture. On December 29, 1938, he filled out the requisite paperwork to incorporate the new company.[235] He invested $1,000, which was his entire savings, and Ober and Brings asked young Nixon to be president.

For Nixon, at this moment in his career, it was a unique opportunity. He was young, and due to his work at the family grocery store, he knew citrus. Plus, his father had always given him and his brothers the same advice: "Don't become dependent on anybody if you can avoid it. Otherwise, you'll become weak."[236]

From Nixon's perspective, it seemed like a calculated risk. He had skin in the game—and who would he rather bet on than himself? It's human nature to look at the bright side of any investment. With my clients, however, anytime they're going to take on risk, I guide them to thinking of the negatives. If I were working with Nixon, I would have asked him what he thought the risks were. I'm not sure he thought those through completely.

Ober and Brings were asking an untested twenty-six-year-old attorney to create and grow a business. (I know, it happens every day in Silicon Valley.) Nixon had a day job, and this new role would require many moving parts: he had to purchase the juice, master the science of freezing the juice, create the product, and then ship it across America. This was no easy feat, and, in those days, it wasn't like he had Google at his fingertips.

Nixon was smart and incredibly hardworking. To have the faith of the local businessmen only made him more confident. And then he wouldn't have to network just to bring in more legal work. He was ready to take the leap.

And Citrifrost Corporation was born.[237]

THE JUICE MAY NOT BE WORTH THE SQUEEZE

In capitalizing the company, Nixon and his partners kept it lean. He found a strong manager to drive the day-to-day operations, and the facility construction was done by July 1939. For a start-up, the balance sheet was

---

[235] You can still look up the formation documents on the California Secretary of State website.
[236] (Nixon 2007).
[237] It should be noted that the company is also known as Citra-frost. However, in all the legal documents, the name is listed as Citrifrost.

managed well. By the end of 1939, the shareholder report noted that the Citrifrost facility was producing "21,099 ¼ gallons of orange, lemon, and grapefruit juice, and sold 13,174 ¼ gallons, using approximately 7,000 boxes of fruit, which we feel has proven some of the potential possibilities that we might expect in the future."[238] In the inaugural year, the gross profit was $1,527.09. After expenses, there was a loss of $3,099.49. But Nixon and his stockholders were optimistic that now that they had a real sales program, they could make the product take off.

But then a cascading series of events occurred that undid the business. A delinquency notice arrived at Citrifrost. The claim: failure to file and pay Social Security tax on the Citrifrost employees.[239] Nixon was flummoxed, but the truth is, this was an embarrassing mistake on his part given his legal training. When you are growing a business, you want to mitigate all controllable risks, especially the administrative ones, such as being in compliance with all federal and state laws.

Two employees filed a lawsuit.[240] Right before it was going to court, Nixon and some of the stockholders got together and made loans to the company to pay the employees. Nixon himself loaned $400 at 6 percent a year. The case was settled.

The strain on company finances started to impact other bills that needed to be paid. By December 1940, Nixon was having to make tough choices in regard to paying the electric bill, rent, and vendors. Certain accounts receivable were outstanding. Furthermore, he started to realize that they needed a real bookkeeper to run the books.[241] But as Nixon divulged to his stockholders, the real issues were financial. To make this work, the company needed better capitalization.

Today, when we look at start-ups, we focus on different rounds of funding at different stages of the company—Friends and Family, Seed, Series A, Series B, and Series C. It isn't uncommon to start with Friends and Family who are willing to invest early stage due to the relationship they have with

---

238   (Citrifrost Corporation 1939/1940).
239   (Citrifrost Corporation 1940) The issues regarding Social Security tax delinquency dragged over a couple of years (Internal Revenue Department 1941)
240   (Aitken 1996) page 84. It should be noted that Jonathan Aitken, in his book *Nixon, A Life*, has the most information available on Citrifrost.
241   One of the most fascinating things about the Nixon Library records for Citrifrost is the pages of calculations done by hand by Nixon.

Don't Mess with Ike When It Comes to Poker

the founder or start-up idea. But as the company evolves, Series A, B, and C offer "outside investors the opportunity to invest cash in a growing company in exchange for equity or partial ownership."[242] Each series is a different level in the fundraising.

What Nixon was finding out the hard way was that while he had managed a good Friends and Family seed round, he hadn't thought through how to get the capital to scale.

To make matters worse, it became clear that in structuring the company, Nixon, as the attorney, had made a mistake with its founder, Ober. Ober was the one who had developed the secret formula to preserve the juice while frozen. But his royalty rate was so high, it was eating into the company funds.[243] Nixon frantically tried to get a group of stockholders together to help renegotiate the rate. If Ober couldn't lower his royalty rate, the chances of Citrifrost surviving were slim.

With the company short on cash, Nixon knew he had to pitch in himself on the day-to-day operations. By day, he was a partner in a law firm, and at night, he managed Citrifrost. He worked nonstop. Even his partner Tom Bewley remembered decades later that Nixon "would work like a dog" trying to make the business succeed, which apparently included cutting and squeezing oranges late into the night, still wearing the business attire from his day job.[244]

As Nixon tried to work his way through the financial problems, he was alerted to some manufacturing issues even more serious than the financial ones. The plastic bags that held the juice were faulty, the Citrifrost factory was not sealing them properly, and the company was also getting a lot of complaints that the plastic was affecting the flavor of the juice. Nixon had to solve both internal and external problems—could he turn it all around in time?

And then an event occurred that broke the proverbial camel's back. According to one version, a load of Citrifrost product was on its way to New York by train when the temperature control in the boxcar failed and the frozen juice turned to liquid. As it continued to heat up, the natural sugars

---

242 (Investopedia 2023).
243 Letter Richard Nixon to Harry Hartwell, dated June 17, 1941. It was half a cent per gallon.
244 (Aitken 1996) page 84.

in the juice began to ferment and turn to alcohol, and a resulting explosion wiped out the entire shipment. Another version held that the plastic bags broke and the product leaked, becoming an unusable mess. Either way, Citrifrost was on its way out.[245]

The company shut down in January 1942, and by April they had to declare bankruptcy. Nixon was devastated by the failure but was especially troubled by the impact it would have on the friends, family, and locals who had invested in the company.

What exactly went wrong? It was a good idea that could have worked, but there were two risks that Nixon (and his stockholders) didn't really think through. First, Nixon wasn't a businessman by training. He knew how to draft and file legal documents, but he was learning business on the job. Second, they just didn't invest enough capital. Nixon should have been aware of the various potential risks that might require capital to mitigate. Over the course of Citrifrost, Nixon even invested another $700 of his own money on top of the initial investment to keep the business going.

But he was too proud to admit his own role in the company's demise, as evidenced by the only comments he ever made on the subject: "I experienced my first, and I trust my last, failure in business. Our product was good, the market was there, but we were doomed to fail for reasons beyond our control."[246] He was so embarrassed by the failure that he instructed his secretary not to tell his wife about it.[247]

Citrifrost Corp was declared bankrupt by the US District Court in Southern California on April 14, 1942. Despite the bankruptcy filings, Nixon and his three partners were sued by investors. Nixon was defeated, but you have to respect what he did next. He knew the locals who were adversely impacted by the failure of Citrifrost, so Nixon agreed to assume the debts for the company on his own even though the bankruptcy proceedings shielded him from that liability. He did it because he knew it was the right thing to do.

---

245 Ibid. It should be noted that Aitken interviewed a number of the key people involved with Citrifrost. When I contacted him, he indicated his interview notes had been donated to the Nixon Library. Unfortunately the interview notes appear to be lost.
246 (Aitken 1996) page 84.
247 Interview with Fawn Brodie.

Don't Mess with Ike When It Comes to Poker

When Citrifrost closed its doors in January 1942, Nixon and Pat moved to Washington, DC, where he took a job with the Office of Price Administration in the tire-rationing division. But it wasn't a good fit and after four months, he sought a commission in the US Navy, despite being exempt from military service because of his status as a birthright Quaker. His application was accepted, and Nixon was appointed a lieutenant junior grade in June of that year. After briefly serving at an air station in Iowa, Nixon requested sea duty and eventually ended up as the officer in charge of South Pacific Combat Air Transport Command.

Like Eisenhower, Nixon became a formidable poker player during his time in the military. As his winnings accrued, he would send them back to the United States to pay down the Citrifrost debt. Years later, his brother Edward would recall a conversation their other brother had with Nixon. "Don asked him one time, 'How much did you make on all those poker winnings?' And he said, 'Well, probably $8,000, which was a huge amount of money in 1946, by the time he got out of there.'"[248] Whatever the exact amount, it was enough to clear up his debt and to partially finance his first congressional campaign.

As a postscript to this story, it turned out that Nixon and his investors were on to something. During World War II, a Boston research company developed a high vacuum evaporation process that allowed them to try a technique that had failed previously: boiling the water out of the juice to create concentrate without ruining the flavor. The new vacuum process helped a small Florida company become a player in the citrus beverage industry, and today, Minute Maid owns 24 percent of the $3 billion orange juice market.

That Nixon failed with this business venture is not an unusual story. Entrepreneurs fail all the time—generally early in their careers, and then they learn from those failures and move on (hopefully) to later successes. As for Nixon, he never ran another business again, despite many offers. Losing his first law case combined with the Citrifrost failure made him risk averse, at least when it came to financial matters.

---

248 (Nixon 2007).

OPPORTUNITY SET OF A LIFETIME

Both Eisenhower and Nixon took an approach to risk that was influenced by growing up in households of modest means.

Risk refers to the potential for loss, harm, or negative outcomes that may arise from a particular action, decision, event, or situation. Yet, what if you have so much money, it doesn't matter the risk you take on? For example, I had a client whose net worth was well over $200 million. One day we were on the phone and he started fixating on a $125,000 investment in his friend's start-up. In response, I said, "I appreciate your frustration, but this is a rounding error. Your portfolio goes up more than this in an hour. What's the real risk?" He laughed and admitted that was true.

Quite a few of presidents come from wealth, and one of the more interesting examples was T.R. Roosevelt.

Born in 1858, Roosevelt's life spanned a transformative period in America, from the Civil War to the Gilded Age to the end of World War I. Beginning in the early 1870s, the Gilded Age was a period of tremendous economic growth in the United States, primarily brought about by the advent of the railroad and an immigration boom. It was an exciting time with expansion and possibility around every corner.

While the world was changing for Americans, so was the investment opportunity set. As we discussed earlier, an opportunity set really refers to the range of potential investment options available. The concept of an opportunity set also matches up to a person's risk tolerance as it helps investors make informed decisions and manage their risk effectively. For those with money or smarts or both, the 1870s was ripe for interesting investment. The West was opening up, and suddenly wealthy and ambitious Northeasterners were eyeing the potential wealth that could be made in places as "exotic" as the Dakotas. "New York, Paris, and London newspapers had been reporting a buzz of activity on the northern plains.... Suddenly it was fashionable for aristocrats on both sides of the Atlantic to have a cattle ranch somewhere in those parts of the American West recently wrested from American Indians."[249] Moreover, as the buffalo succumbed to overhunting by European settlers, the plains states were becoming ideal cattle-grazing land.

---

249 (Jenkinson 2006) page 29.

Don't Mess with Ike When It Comes to Poker

Investing in a ranch promised unbelievable riches, often as high as 30 or 40 percent ROI a year.[250] With returns like that, investing in the West became a very popular idea.

A FATHER'S TRUST—AND A TRUST FUND

It was against this backdrop that Roosevelt came of age. He was different than many of our presidents. The third generation of a wealthy family, money was never a concern, and by all accounts he wasn't that interested in making more of it. As a result, T.R. didn't always problem-solve with analytical rigidity. And he could be a bit reckless in managing risk when he got caught up in an idea. But he could afford the luxury of hasty financial decisions, and he could also afford to hone his high-stakes poker skills.

T.R.'s beloved father died at forty-six, after a brief and brutal battle with colon cancer. Buried in the February 17, 1878, edition of the *New York Times* was a small headline that read, "Will of Theodore Roosevelt." Roosevelt Sr.'s estate plan would work very well in today's world. His wife, Mittie, got a third of his estate held in trust for her. She would live on the income and principal of the trust, but at her death, the trust assets would pass to their children. That's pretty normal stuff—and it protected his children in the event Mittie remarried.[251]

His four children would each receive a trust with $60,000 in it—about $1.7 million in today's money. The trust's income would go to the children to use as they saw fit, but the remainder of the estate—and probably the biggest part—would be split into four other trusts for each child. With a patriarchal twist, his two sons could do what they wanted with their respective trusts, but his two daughters would have executors manage their trusts.[252]

---

250 Ibid., page 73.
251 (Will of Theodore Roosevelt 1878). The Qualified Terminable Interest Trust (QTIP Trust) pops up again in presidential estate planning. We saw it earlier with Harding and we will see it again with Washington and Eisenhower.
252 Ibid. Interestingly at the time, the most shocking part of this estate plan was that despite a lifetime of philanthropic endeavors, no charity was contemplated in the estate plan. Further, it should be noted that T.R.'s mother was still alive in 1878. He would likely inherit more when she passed.

THE WEST BECKONS

T.R. grieved intensely for a period, and then he threw himself into his life at school. But the lure of the West was tempting many of the well-to-do young men in his circle, and eventually T.R., who was a passionate lover of nature and the outdoors, succumbed to the extent of investing in a classmate's ranching venture to the tune of $10,000.

Roosevelt's diaries from the period give a clear picture of his lifestyle and spending habits. At the time, the average Harvard student lived on $650 to $850 a year. In comparison, T.R.'s expenses for 1878 totaled a whopping $2,049.45 ($63,500 in 2024 dollars). Perhaps not coincidentally, Roosevelt had met his future bride, Alice Hathaway Lee, that year and commenced a no-expense-spared courtship.[253] When Alice finally relented and agreed to marry him, T.R. bought her $2,500 worth of jewelry ($77,500 in 2024 dollars).

But Roosevelt's undisciplined spending wasn't limited to the demands of his romantic life. A few years later, after the publication of his seminal work *The Naval War of 1812*, T.R.'s newfound appreciation for book publishing led him to offer to buy into the G. P. Putnam partnership for $20,000, despite having only half of that in his bank account.[254] It seemed that in whatever direction his passions took him, his money quickly followed.

Next up was real estate. With Alice by his side, T.R. first purchased sixty-five acres of land in Cove Neck and then three years later snapped up another ninety-five acres. He structured the deal so that he paid $10,000 down and then took a mortgage for $20,000 at a rate of 5 percent.[255] To build his house, he hired the architectural firm Lamb & Rich, who had undertaken other big projects, including Barnard College. This was a huge financial undertaking, but for T.R. it was a calculated risk, partly because

---

253 Diary of Theodore Roosevelt Series 8: Personal Diaries, 1878–1884; Vol. 1, 1878, Jan. 1–Dec. 31; Also discussed in (Morris, *The Rise of Theodore Roosevelt* 1979 updated 2010) page 802.
254 (Morris, *The Rise of Theodore Roosevelt* 1979 updated 2010) page 210.
255 Letter Theodore Roosevelt to Anna Roosevelt, dated August 25, 1883. (Morris, *The Rise of Theodore Roosevelt* 1979 updated 2010) page 185. Morris documents the purchase at $20,000. It has also been documented at a higher amount of $30,000.

Don't Mess with Ike When It Comes to Poker

the real estate was valuable and likely to appreciate and partly because he was investing in the creation of a home for a new generation of Roosevelts.

By 1883, Alice was pregnant and construction of their Oyster Bay home had commenced. Despite Alice's pregnancy, T.R. decided it was time to go see the fabled Wild West for himself and hunt buffalo. He arrived on a train platform in the Dakotas in the middle of the night, without a guide or anyone to meet him, but he soon befriended two ranchers who took him hunting. He loved the fresh air and open spaces and wrote to Alice that "this has been by all odds the pleasantest and most successful trip I have ever made."[256]

We've all been on vacations where we think to ourselves, *Gee, this is great, and I could live here*. But then reason kicks in, and we go home, content with the memories we created.[257] In T.R.'s case, when the hunting trip was over, he told his two new friends, Sylvane Ferris and Bill Merrifield, that he wanted to buy not only a ranch, but the 150 head of cattle the men were tending. Once again, we see his passions take a reckless turn when it comes to risk.

After a negotiation, T.R. handed over a $14,000 check for Maltese Cross Ranch. My favorite part of the story is: when asked if he wanted a receipt, Roosevelt simply replied, "Oh, that's all right."[258]

In addition to satisfying his passion for the outdoors, buying the ranch was also a part of his money management strategy for the trust. As T.R. was still early in his career, he was looking for a passive income stream to help pay for the cost of raising a family. He imagined a life like his father's—a gentleman around town and a supportive husband and father.

But from a risk perspective, handing over the equivalent of $400,000 in 2024 dollars to men he barely knew to cattle ranch, an industry he didn't know, seemed like taking on unnecessary risk.[259]

---

256   Letter Theodore Roosevelt to Alice Lee Roosevelt, dated September 23, 1883.
257   It is this feeling that often gets us to buy timeshares while on vacation, often to regret it over the years.
258   "Sylvane Ferris & Bill Merrifield," National Park Service, https://www.nps.gov/thro/learn/historyculture/sylvane-ferris-and-bill-merrifield.htm. The conversation is also recalled in (Morris, *The Rise of Theodore Roosevelt* 1979 updated 2010) page 209.
259   Interestingly, T.R.'s second wife, Edith, met Ferris and Merrifield and felt while the former was a nice man, the latter gave off an impression that he was not trustworthy.

All the Presidents' Money

Interestingly, Roosevelt actually didn't see it as a risk. He believed he had done the appropriate due diligence. He wrote to Alice, "During these ten days I have also been making up my mind to go into something more important than hunting....I have also carefully examined the country, with reference to its capacity for stock raising; and the more I have looked into the matter—weighing and balancing everything, pro and con, as carefully as I know how—the more convinced I became that there was a chance to make a great deal of money, very safely, in the cattle business."[260] A local Dakota newspaper, *The Bad Lands Cow Boy*, seemed to back up this contention, noting that "it seems to be an undisputed fact that the cattle business yields larger and surer returns than any other business in the world....Everything pays for itself on the ranch. Nothing is a dead loss."[261]

Roosevelt closed the deal and headed home to Alice, but soon after tragedy struck. Two days after giving birth to their first child, on February 14, 1884, Alice died of undiagnosed liver disease, just hours after T.R.'s mother had passed. Roosevelt wrote in his diary, "The light in my life has gone out."[262] Distraught, he decided to move to the Dakotas, leaving his baby daughter in the care of his sister. He managed his grief by tending to his land and cattle. Just a few months later, he wrote his sister to let her know ranching was his "regular business" for the foreseeable future.[263]

On impulse, he bought a second ranch called Elkhorn, and with that much more land and cattle to manage, he came up with what he saw as an elegant solution. He made a deal with two hunting acquaintances from Maine by which he would pay off their $3,000 mortgage, move their families there, *and* also pay them a salary and a percentage of the profit. Most importantly, they wouldn't participate in the losses—T.R. would shoulder that burden alone. By aligning the men's compensation with his goals, Roosevelt felt he was mitigating risk. But he was about to find out that it's the hidden risks that often get you.

---

260   Letter Theodore Roosevelt to Alice Lee Roosevelt, dated September 23, 1883.
261   (Packard 1884).
262   (T. Roosevelt n.d.).
263   Letter Theodore Roosevelt to Anna Roosevelt Cowles, June 17, 1884.

Don't Mess with Ike When It Comes to Poker

THE BLACK SWAN MAKES AN APPEARANCE

The first sign of trouble started just a few months later. The price of beef in the East started to drop in late 1885 and continued dropping into 1886. A dry, hot summer brought fires burning on the range, destroying the grass. It ended with a drought. Ranchers noted that the birds seemed to fly south for the winter earlier and with urgency. Something was brewing. In November, snow fell, and the ground froze, making it hard for the cattle to graze. The cattle "rubbed their faces raw" in an attempt to graze, but to no avail.[264] They began to starve and die. The past twenty years of mild winters were clearly over.[265]

On January 9, 1887, a legendary storm hit: as sixteen inches of snow fell, the winds picked up, and the temperature dropped to below fifty degrees.[266] Whatever cattle had survived now succumbed to the wretched conditions. The event was dubbed "The Great Die-Up."[267]

In today's parlance, this is known as a Black Swan event—an extremely rare and unpredictable event that has a severe impact on financial markets, investment portfolios, or the economy as a whole. Black Swans are characterized by their extreme rarity, their unexpected nature, and their profound consequences, especially for small businesses.

I have a client whose philosophy is to angel-invest in businesses founded by women of color. Now, angel investing is where an individual typically invests in a start-up or a young business in exchange for convertible debt or equity in the company. In 2018, he invested in a travel start-up targeting curated culture tours in Africa. The business was just beginning to take off and was going for another seed round of funding when the COVID-19 pandemic hit. Despite the founder's efforts to keep it going, the business unfortunately failed eighteen months after the pandemic started. While the founder had been building a business under one risk assessment, another unexpected risk annihilated the business.

While investors have weathered Black Swan events (like the Great Recession, Brexit, and of course the COVID-19 pandemic), the likelihood of

---

264 (L. Adams 2014).
265 (Clark 2015).
266 (Clark 2015).
267 (Clark 2015).

these risks is so remote that they are rarely factored in. And that was likely the case with Roosevelt; he may have been a bit financially reckless in assessing how he was managing his money, but it probably never crossed his mind that such a severe winter would annihilate the cattle across the plains. It was a low probability in his mind. Yet, the impact was severe.

T.R., who had just remarried, got word of the storm while on honeymoon with his second wife Edith in Europe. He panicked. Where were the expected returns of 30 to 40 percent? This seemed like financial ruin. He was even concerned about the land he had purchased with Alice in Oyster Bay. He told his sister Anna that he and Edith needed to "think very seriously of closing Sagamore Hill and going to the ranch for a year or two."[268]

When he returned from Europe, he traveled straight to his ranch. Finding the situation worse than he had anticipated, Roosevelt was crestfallen. In early April, he wrote to his sister from out West, "I am bluer than indigo about the cattle….I wish I was sure I would lose no more than half the money ($80,000) I invested out here. I am planning how to get out of it."[269]

From here on out, T.R. was focused on mitigating his losses. Over the next fourteen years, he slowly sold off his interests in the West. Ultimately, his total losses were $125,000—a fortune in those days. While he continued to visit the Dakotas over his lifetime, he never again made a significant investment in the land.

At the same time, his new wife, Edith, took matters into her own hands. She set up a budget for them to live on at Sagamore Hill. She reined in T.R.'s more reckless spending. She kept a monthly account book of all the expenses the family had. T.R. also pitched in by continuing to write, bringing in more income for the family.

The risk that T.R. took in the Dakotas wasn't about making a fortune—he already had one. It was about owning something wild and untamed and growing it into self-sustaining profitability. And although the venture itself ultimately failed, it had not been a complete financial disaster because, as Roosevelt later rationalized, "I have always said I would not have been President had it not been for my experience in North Dakota."[270]

---

268 Letter Theodore Roosevelt to Anna Roosevelt Cowles, dated January 3, 1887.
269 Letter Theodore Roosevelt to Anna Roosevelt Cowles, dated April 16, 1887.
270 (Morris, *The Rise of Theodore Roosevelt* 1979 updated 2010) page 374.

Don't Mess with Ike When It Comes to Poker

THE LESSONS OF RISK

Risk is a key component in all of our financial lives. But our early experiences often impact how we approach it. Our money stories are part of how we choose to engage with risk. As a result, understanding that blueprint can allow us to engage in risk at the right level.

Eisenhower understood that controlling his emotions allowed him to take bigger risks and manage them appropriately. Nixon was willing to take a risk, but when it went sideways, he never went down the path of entrepreneurship again as he was too scared of failure and its consequences. T.R. might have been reckless with money due to his family wealth, but in the end, it wasn't his rashness that led to his investment failure but rather a chain of events that he couldn't possibly have foreseen or planned against.

PART II

Money and Meaning

Chapter Five

GERALD FORD: HATE THE GAME, NOT THE PLAYER
(OR FINANCIAL CONFIDENCE AND ANXIETY)

Over the years that I have been working with wealthy individuals, I've taken numerous late-night calls from anxious clients, and whenever these moments happen, my husband will often look at me and say: "I don't get it. Why are they calling you for that?" He's incredulous as he hears my end of the call, sometimes about a purchase of a home or the considerations of filing for divorce. I try to explain to him that regardless of the size of one's net worth, everyone has financial anxiety. It is easy to look at the situations of the wealthy and feel that they haven't got a care in the world compared to the rest of us. But as we all know, money doesn't necessarily buy happiness, and it certainly doesn't mean the end of financial anxiety.

So, what exactly is financial anxiety? What if I told you that it can't be explained in black-and-white terms but rather in terms of a continuum? From an academic standpoint, how we interact emotionally with our finances is really on a continuum, with anxiety on one side representing when an individual is subject to financial stress and strain.[271] We all know that feeling—that emotion of "will I be able to get by?"[272]

A good definition of financial anxiety that governmental agencies rely on is this: "a condition that is the result of financial and/or economic events

---
271 (Stephen P. Roll 2016) page 1.
272 Ibid.

that create anxiety, worry, or a sense of scarcity, and is accompanied by a physiological stress response."[273]

The other side of the continuum is the holy grail of finances: financial well-being, or as the Consumer Financial Protection Bureau puts it, "a state of being wherein a person can fully meet current and ongoing financial obligations, can feel secure in their financial future, and is able to make choices that allow enjoyment of life."[274] It's the ability to balance security and freedom of choice.[275]

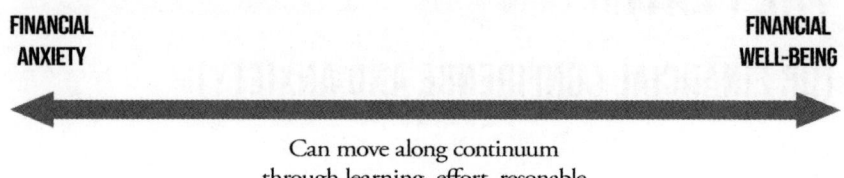

FINANCIAL ANXIETY ←——————————————→ FINANCIAL WELL-BEING

Can move along continuum through learning, effort, resonable opportunity, and support. And also luck.

I can hear you saying that this must be where the rich people are. But this promised land really isn't about income. Rather, it is about being highly satisfied with one's financial condition. And I have to admit, I know a lot of wealthy people who don't feel satisfied. In fact, they feel their finances are quite precarious.

Now, most of us feel that we are stuck on one side, with financial anxiety. Who hasn't gotten up in the middle of the night with their mind racing about money? I will be the first to admit that sometimes at 2 a.m., I want to wake up and talk to my husband about it. But honestly, it's not the best time to think about money.

Back to the continuum. For those of us successful with money, while we may be on the right side of the page, there is always movement on the continuum. Studying the acquisition of financial well-being really comes down to four potential aspects: effort, reasonable opportunity, learning,

---

273 (Martin 2020)
274 (Consumer Financial Protection Bureau 2015) page 18.
275 Ibid., page 19.

Gerald Ford: Hate the Game, Not the Player

and support. And if you think about it, that makes sense. You can work very hard at budgeting, but without any opportunity to earn money, it's all for naught. And the truth is, it just isn't easy to have financial well-being. We can want it, we can work for it, but a lot of forces are unfortunately working against it.

Let's look at the continuum and consider the cases of two presidents that each represent one side. I could pick any number for the anxiety category. But let's start with financial well-being. You see, when it comes to financial well-being and confidence, my pick is quite easy: Gerald Ford. You are probably like, *Really? Ford?* But here's the deal—Ford was a rock star when it came to finances. He navigated financial anxiety like no one's business. And for him, whenever he came to a complex financial crossroads, he just made all the right decisions—or at least pivoted quickly enough to not damage his well-being.

In the process, he changed post-presidential life. Every president after him should say a prayer to Ford as he made it so that no former president should ever struggle (and many have).

On the opposite side of the continuum from Ford is a president who embodied financial anxiety: Harry S. Truman.[276]

Truman and Ford have some similarities, however. Both came to the presidency by being vice president when the president could not serve out his term. Both were practical moderates who made some very tough decisions: Truman with the atomic bomb and Ford pardoning Richard Nixon. Both of them even died the same day, December 26, albeit decades apart.

How they each handled their post-presidential life twenty-five years apart really lays out what I call the Truman–Ford Financial Anxiety Continuum.

Here's what it looks like:

---

[276] One funny fact about Truman is that up until he became president, he never put a period after his middle initial. It was only added when the editors of the *Chicago Manual of Style* contacted him to inform him it was poor grammar not to put a period AND he was being a bad example for young Americans. The Truman Library even has a segment on its website about the issue. https://www.trumanlibrary.gov/education/trivia/use-of-period-after-s-truman-name.

Both men moved around the continuum over the course of their lives. But as we will see, Truman struggled more with financial anxiety and worry than Ford ever did.

THE GOLDEN TOUCH

Now, if we were to look at Ford in retrospect, it seems he had the golden touch. In his post-presidential life, we all got very used to seeing him swinging a golf club in the warm California sun with some celebrity pal or business buddy, looking like he didn't have a care in the world. Yet, the truth is that he spent a lot of time on his financial confidence, especially since he really wasn't a picture of financial well-being when he left the White House. In fact, on the continuum, he was probably all the way to the left as he lost the presidential election in November 1976:

Gerald Ford: Hate the Game, Not the Player

On Tuesday, January 18, 1977, a lot seemed uncertain in Jerry and Betty Ford's financial lives. As the Fords prepared to leave the White House, they were saying goodbye to twenty-five years in the capital. They spent that Tuesday visiting friends and thinking about how they would transition to private life. But as they arrived back at the White House, the Marine Band was there in the portico to surprise them. As the band played "Thanks for the Memories," Ford and Betty danced in the entry of the White House.[277]

In the back of his mind, Ford was aware of the crossroads they had reached. Here he was, about to leave the most powerful role in the world, and he knew their net worth was only a "couple of hundred thousand dollars."[278] He had some peace of mind that at least the small condo they had in Vail, Colorado, was debt-free.[279] Further, he had both a congressional and a presidential pension. But his financial security was always somewhat precarious. Even when he first became president, he was still living paycheck to paycheck—and was anxious enough that he asked someone in the White House when he would be paid.[280]

He was also aware of the choices made by prior presidents. Nixon wrote a book. We saw that Eisenhower had solidified his net worth in the post–World War II years by not only writing a book (and having his royalties declared tax-free by Congress) but by taking the role as president of Columbia University. Johnson, as we'll see later, made his money partly through a family-owned radio station (and dying quickly after leaving office).

But the one issue most on Ford's mind was the challenges faced by Harry S. Truman. He understood Truman on many levels. From his vantage point, he watched Truman struggle in his post-presidential life financially. Ford had even cast a "nay" vote against the 1958 Former Presidents

---

277 (O'Brein 1977) Once the dance ended, they were given a surprise goodbye party by their friends.
278 (P. G. Ford, Ford-Cannon Interview for Ford Presidential Library 1992).
279 (DeFrank 2007) page 78. As DeFrank noted, Ford was cash-strapped but had basically cashed out his life insurance cash value to be debt-free.
280 (Bales 2010) Ford's daughter Susan recalled, "Someone told us the story—I think maybe it was someone who worked with Bill Seidman, but anyway, in his first couple of weeks on the job, maybe less, he asked when he would be getting a paycheck because he had someone going to college and he had several in college at that point and he was literally living paycheck to paycheck."

All the Presidents' Money

Act when he was in Congress.[281] He explained his vote in *Your Washington Review*, his newsletter to constituents, that "I could see no good reason for saddling the taxpayers with another unnecessary burden and setting up for any ex-president a retirement system to which they had made no financial contribution."[282]

Further, even after the pension act passed from what Ford knew, the Trumans lived on a budget.

Ford appreciated Truman's character and especially related to Truman's honesty and integrity.[283] When Ford first assumed the presidency in 1974, he followed tradition to keep portraits of three of his predecessors in his office. The first two he chose were Lincoln and Eisenhower. When the White House curator suggested Andrew Jackson, Ford replied no, he wanted Harry Truman because of his principles.[284]

When Ford prepared to vacate the White House, he also knew one thing: he wasn't going to settle for less than the lifestyle he wanted Betty and his family to enjoy—just as long as it didn't impact his integrity. Ford was also aware that Truman turned down opportunities on the basis that it wasn't appropriate for a president to commercialize his position.[285] But 1977 was a different world than when Truman left the presidency in 1952. Plus, he wasn't going to settle and go back to Michigan. He had changed, and his world had expanded. Both he and Betty wanted to split their time between Rancho Mirage, California, and Vail, Colorado.

Ford's financial situation was not lost on Don Penny, his speechwriter. Looking to help Ford, he suggested that the president be introduced to a contact of his. As Penny described it, "I've got this friend in California named Brokaw who has got a tremendous talent. Mr. President, the bottom

---

281 (House of Representatives 1958) page 10. The resolution passed anyway.
282 (J. Ford August 7, 1958).
283 Interestingly, they both would have something else in common: their dates of death. Truman passed on December 26, 1972, while Ford passed on December 26, 2006.
284 Ford himself recounted this story on May 8, 1976, in his remarks at the dedication of the Harry S. Truman Statue in Independence, Missouri. Speech available at https://www.fordlibrarymuseum.gov/library/document/0122/1252853.pdf.
285 Truman wasn't the only one. Calvin Coolidge also turned down profitable endeavors when he left the White House in 1928.

Gerald Ford: Hate the Game, Not the Player

line is, after you meet with Norman you won't be worth this $300,000 but $9 million, and that's a much better number."[286]

Norman Brokaw was one of the leading talent agents at the William Morris Agency.[287] His clients included Elvis and Marilyn Monroe. And just a few years earlier, Brokaw took Olympic wonder Mark Spitz and made him the first athlete who was a brand beyond his sport.[288]

When Penny initially introduced Brokaw to Ford during the election, the discussion focused on connecting entertainers to the Ford campaign to endorse Ford.[289] Once the reality of his defeat seeped in, Ford sent Brokaw a thank-you for his support. Yet, written in the margins was a curious note. "P.S. You will [be] hearing from me soon or give me a call when you have a comprehensive plan. J."[290]

Comprehensive plan? Sounds like something was in the works. And indeed it was. A few weeks prior to their final dance at the White House, and a month after losing to Jimmy Carter, an entry on the president's calendar on December 13, 1976, appeared right after business for the day was done. It read:

    4:15   Reception Honoring the Secret Service.

               The State Floor.

    5:00   Mr. Richard B. Cheney – The Oval Office.

    5:30   Mr. Norman Brokaw – The Oval Office.

---

286 (Brownstein 1987).
287 Founded in 1898, William Morris Agency is the longest-running talent agency. In 2009, it merged with Endeavor to form WME.
288 It was so revolutionary that Ford himself had written Spitz congratulating him on his memoirs that had been given to him by Brokaw. Letter President Gerald R. Ford to Mark Spitz, dated October 1, 1976. Ford's humor comes through in the letter as he appreciated Spitz sending along his book, *The Mark Spitz Complete Book of Swimming*, as he felt he has "a lot to learn as a swimmer."
289 Memo Jerry Jones to Dick Cheney, dated September 24, 1976. Courtesy of Ford Presidential Library.
290 Letter President Gerald R. Ford to Norman Brokaw, dated November 30, 1976. Courtesy of Ford Presidential Library.

Brokaw presented Ford and his soon-to-be-retired Chief of Staff Bob Barrett with a clear post-presidential plan. Ford was going to build out his business empire. The world would be his oyster if he followed the plan.

WHY A PLAN MAKES A DIFFERENCE

To understand Ford's mindset, you have to go back to his childhood. In the 1920s, American newspapers were full of Horatio Alger stories. They all had a similar plot line: a young, impoverished boy overcomes all odds in front of him to achieve success through hard work and honest living. Like many young boys his age, Ford connected with these stories. He once noted that these stories he read at night during childhood not only "emphasized Horatio Alger books. He wrote God knows how many, but they were all stories about heroes."[291]

Like a character from these stories, Ford understood that hard work would be key. And he wasn't afraid to do it. He worked in the family's paint business. He mowed lawns and bused tables at a restaurant.

When it came time for college, he was easily accepted at the University of Michigan, where he played center for the football team. (He helped them win back-to-back national championships, and his jersey number was later retired.) But like other presidents of his generation like Reagan, Ford had to figure out how to pay the one-hundred-dollar tuition. A small fundraiser was held at his high school to help a little, but it wasn't enough.[292] So what did he do? He devised a game plan to get him over this next hurdle.

Years later, he recalled this financial plan for college. "When I went there, I got a job at the hospital serving interns dining room, cleaning up the nurse's cafeteria. That was a three hour a day job at noon time. And the money got paid I could buy my meals. I didn't get meals. That was my first year. I lived in a third-floor rooming house, the backroom which I shared with a fellow named Don Nichols. He and I paid four dollars a week. He had one bunk and I had the other and the one desk that we shared. My second year, well that first year I had saved enough money to pay my tu-

---

291 (P. G. Ford, Ford-Cannon Interview for Ford Presidential Library 1992).
292 (S. Ford 2011) Ford notes in his interview that when reflecting on his father and money, "He didn't waste money on things. It needed to work, be practical, be usable."

Gerald Ford: Hate the Game, Not the Player

ition which was 100 dollars. Really my only spending money came from an Aunt and Uncle, my step-father's sister and husband, Ray and Ruel Leforge, two dollars a week. That was literally my spending money."[293]

And to top it off, Ford would occasionally donate blood at twenty-five dollars a pop every two months to stay financially afloat.[294] He was embracing this late millennial–Gen Z trend a century before it was a popular way to pay down student loan debt.[295]

Despite needing to work hard to get access to money, Ford displayed a unique attitude. He didn't seem anxious about money. Remember that continuum we talked about? Well, despite no outside training, Ford slowly moved across it in the right direction even as an eighteen-year-old man. And here's the deal with Ford: at every major crossroads in his life financially, he often took a different path.

In February 1935, as a senior in college, Ford got the following letter:

> Gerald Ford   Feb. 11, 1935
> University of Michigan
> Ann Arbor, Michigan
>
> Dear Ford:
>
> While on the Coast you told me you were undecided in regard to playing professional football.
>
> We plan on signing a center for the coming season and will pay you $110.00 per game if you wish to join the "Packers". Our league schedule is not drafted but we usually play fourteen games. We pay in full after each contest and all players are paid whether they play or

---

293 (P. G. Ford, Ford-Cannon Interview for Ford Presidential Library 1992).
294 Ibid.
295 In the current student loan crisis, Kathleen McLaughlin, in her book *Blood Money: The Story of Life, Death and Profit Inside America's Blood Industry*, discusses why so many young Americans are finding blood donation as a method to pay down their student loans.

not and, naturally, all injured players are paid immediately after each game.

Will appreciate an early reply.

With kindest personal regards, I am

Sincerely,

GREEN BAY FOOTBALL CORPORATION

And he got a similar one from the Detroit Lions. Now, today, it would be a no-brainer to take an NFL contract: money, glory, and national recognition. While it wasn't the same in 1935 as it is today, it was an amazing opportunity. Ford, however, viewed it differently. He turned down both offers and took an assistant coaching job at Yale University for $2,400 with the hopes that he might get into their law school.

When asked about it years later, Ford mused, "If I had played pro football, instead of going to Yale as an assistant coach, my whole life would have been totally different…I certainly wouldn't have gone to Yale. I might have gone to Michigan. I probably would have played pro football two or three years, saved enough money, go back [to] law school."[296]

But part of why he was able to also turn it down was that Ford was a good assessor of risk. One way to determine financial well-being is the ability to determine if an opportunity is worthwhile. While he had the football offers, he was also aware that the reason he got the offers was one game in particular that he played well, where the coaches learned of him.[297] Perhaps he simply assessed that he probably couldn't play at that level for a long time—and that it was better to play the long game, even if it was not the obvious choice. And based on the salary, he was still getting security—and choice.

---

296 (P. G. Ford, Ford-Cannon Interview for Ford Presidential Library 1990). To be fair, he was going to get $110 a game in a twelve-game season. The Yale job paid more—and didn't put his body in a bad situation where he could be injured.
297 Ibid.

Gerald Ford: Hate the Game, Not the Player

ESTABLISHMENT OF A FINANCIAL PLAN

But back to Norman Brokaw and the post-election appointment on Ford's schedule. For Ford, the plan's goal was pretty clear-cut. He wanted to build an asset base for his family, so he no longer had to live paycheck to paycheck. Further, it had to ensure he would have no debt. And that is one thing to know about Ford financially: he hated debt.

Brokaw and Ford's chief of staff, Bob Barrett, felt Ford had three avenues for earning income: publishing a book, speaking engagements, and entrepreneurial endeavors to be determined. Forty-nine days after Carter's inauguration, dueling articles appeared in newspapers around the country: Ford and Betty were signing a first-of-its-kind contract to write their memoirs "separately but equally," which earned them a joint $1 million.[298]

At the same time, Ford announced he was building a 6,500-square-foot hacienda in Palm Springs that would be done by Christmas.[299] The house was on the thirteenth fairway on the prestigious Thunderbird Country Club in Rancho Mirage. They had hired the same architects that had built the iconic Capitol Records building in Los Angeles. Betty was able to hire a decorator, and she chose a highly sought-after Beverly Hills specialist named Laura Mako to do a modern seventies aesthetic in lime green and faux bamboo. Clearly, they were feeling flush.[300]

The plan was in motion. He and Betty would use their memoir earnings as a way to pay down their new home in the desert. But Ford also knew he had a bit of a timing issue with the sequence of events. No reason to wait until the memoirs were in the bookstore for construction to begin. Ford took out a building loan while he wrote his book *A Time to Heal*. By the time it was published, the mortgage was already in his rearview mirror.[301]

And it should be noted, you couldn't even argue leverage with him. His daughter Susan tried. In an interview, she discussed her father's views on mortgages: "You would say, 'But Dad, that's the only tax write-off you can

---

298 (New York Times News Services 1978).
299 (Associated Press 1978).
300 As a side note, after Betty's death, the house was sold and refurbished. The renovation was done in light of the Fords' former residency and can be seen in the June 2, 2019, edition of *Town and Country* magazine. https://www.townandcountrymag.com/style/home-decor/a27547641/inside-gerald-ford-betty-ford-house/.
301 (Bales 2010)

get. You don't want to have any debt.' Well, to him, credit cards were useless because you pay for everything in cash, you weren't to have a mortgage and to him you were to pay that mortgage off as fast as you possibly could."[302] Ultimately, she gave up. It just wasn't in his character.

Now you must be thinking, *Of course he's financially confident.* Anyone would be as an ex-president who had everything going according to plan. In fact, on the continuum, he's doing as well as anyone could want to do. He's satisfied with where he is financially. He's debt-free and living the lifestyle he aspired to. Through his opportunities and efforts, he has broken through to financial well-being. Ford is the face of financial well-being.

We can even move him over on the continuum.

He has that golden touch—that is of course, until he doesn't.

FINANCIAL
ANXIETY

FINANCIAL
WELL-BEING

A TACKY MISSTEP

Whenever we have financial success, it makes us more confident in our decision-making and keeps us on the continuum of financial well-being. Using the book to finance the new house did that for Ford. Unfortunately, sometimes financial confidence can mask risks you didn't consider.

To understand where Ford made some missteps on his financial journey, you have to go back a few years to when he was president. The biggest national event was going to occur under his watch: the Bicentennial of 1976. There were going to be ceremonies, performances, and parades.

---

302   Ibid. Susan is referencing that the mortgage write-off is one of the few tax deductions available to high earners. You often hear wealthy individuals keeping mortgages due to the fact on an after-tax basis, it isn't costing them a lot.

Gerald Ford: Hate the Game, Not the Player

Memorabilia appeared on store shelves across the country. Everyone wanted a piece—or had a piece to sell—of American history. And what could be more American than profiting off of the Bicentennial?

Enter the Franklin Mint. Today, the Franklin Mint is seen as the purveyor of collectible kitsch, but it wasn't always that way. While the Franklin Mint had been founded as a private mint in 1964 in Pennsylvania, by 1968, it had established itself as a key maker of American collectibles. With the Bicentennial only eight years away, the Mint knew it needed to create products that would appeal to patriotic Americans.[303] Some of their Bicentennial strategy included launching a multi-year commemorative medal collection, silver plates showing Thomas Jefferson drafting the Declaration of Independence, and even a national competition for a medal design that was later adopted by thirty-seven states.[304] Further, they partnered with the Daughters of the American Revolution, the Bicentennial Council of the Thirteen Original States, and even the White House.

The bottom line to all this: Their profits were up 40 percent in 1976 to sales of $306 million.[305] And they were key in working with the Ford White House to commemorate the event. Both Ford and Betty sent numerous thank-you notes to the Mint for all the charitable donations they made during the celebrations.

But fast forward two years later, and things weren't so rosy for the Mint. Fatigue and inflation had set in on the American consumer. While revenue had been doubling on an annual basis, post-Bicentennial collecting seemed to be in the toilet. Further, most of their "collectibles" did not increase in value. In fact, it was found that they often got only 20 to 40 percent of their original value upon resale. The impact was devastating for the company. The Franklin Mint was the worst-performing stock of 1977.[306]

In comparison, Ford's future seemed rosy as he considered all the opportunities that lay in front of him. The sale of his memoirs had been brisk, and he continued to consider other offers that were put in front of him. And unlike the presidents who had retired before him, he was in a different situation, so he was open to considering a lot of different opportunities.

---
303 (Dekom 1976).
304 Ibid. See also (Franklin Mint 1976).
305 Ibid. Further this was up from 1967 sales of $2.6 million.
306 (Moscowitz 1978).

All the Presidents' Money

The Franklin Mint approached Ford and Brokaw with a very simple pitch. They wanted to launch what they saw as a definitive study of the presidency with an educational medallic book. To add the right level of gravitas, they wanted to hire Ford to use his presidential influence to endorse a series of medals from the Mint that depicted the one hundred most important events of the American presidency. It would culminate in a medal of him speaking on the Bicentennial in 1976.[307] He wouldn't be shilling it; rather Ford would make his imprint by helping choose these moments of history and edit the text. What could be more presidential than that?

When some of his team looked back in retrospect, they thought that Ford was, well, he was a bit naïve about the money that would surround him as he left the White House.[308] In fact, some thought that "he was pretty much brainwashed to think that he should expect and deserve everything" from the agents who were helping him.[309] Ford himself saw it a bit more along the lines of how he handled the NFL decision years ago—paving a new path.

Out went a letter with the salutation, "To My Fellow Americans" signed by Ford. The ads for the coins showed him in profile, serious and contemplative. This was a serious man and a serious project. Purchasers had only until March 15 to commit to either a solid silver set for $1,950 or 24-karat gold over sterling silver for $2,750.[310] In 1978, this was also a serious amount of money. Each set came authenticated and signed by him.

For all their planning, neither Ford nor Brokaw really thought through the optics of this move. That was a huge misstep. A collective gasp occurred when the ads started to appear in papers nationwide in February 1978. The vultures pounced. Their charge: the commercialization of the presidency.

"There is but one word for Mr. Ford's latest venture: Tacky," wrote the *Corpus Christi Caller*.[311]

The *Miami Herald* sneered, "For all we know there's even a medallion depicting Jerry Ford signing a contract with The Franklin Mint…here

---

307 (Grey 1978).
308 (Circle 2008). Circle was Ford's chief of staff after Bob Barrett. She was incredibly protective of Ford.
309 Ibid.
310 (*New York Times* 1978).
311 (The Corpus Christi Caller 1978).

Gerald Ford: Hate the Game, Not the Player

we see Ford assuming a hi-there-I'm-Jerry-Ford-and-I-heartily-endorse-this-Medallion-pose."[312]

"A Huckster with a capital 'H,'" said the *Philadelphia Daily News*.[313]

The *Baltimore Sun* was even more snarky. While pointing out that publishers only wanted Ford because he was president, he needed to remember where he came from. "Had Mr. Ford remained minority leader his memoirs would have been worth practically nothing."[314]

Ouch.

A lot of other personalities would have taken the criticism hard. They would have questioned what they were doing. Perhaps the plan wasn't working. I mean, could you see any of the other presidents shilling random products? Well, other than you-know-who?

But that's the thing about financial confidence. You have to know when to change course. Or simply don't panic and make the adjustment to get to the next right spot. While he didn't cancel his agreement with the Franklin Mint, Ford recognized that this type of endorsement could easily become quicksand from which his post-presidential career might not recover.

With his golden touch slightly tarnished, he completed his contract and finished with the Franklin Mint. And good thing, too—just a few months later, *60 Minutes* did an exposé on how the collectibles from the Mint were really not that collectible. Today, the medal collection Ford endorsed can still be found on eBay valued at pretty much the same price as it was in 1978.

FORD MASTERS THE PIVOT

The Franklin Mint agreement was a misstep, but Ford took steps to pivot—which is why he never completely lost his golden touch. In financial wellness, this is key. And he learned his lessons. He made some thoughtful movements. Rather than just go for lucrative payouts, he joined the American Enterprise Institute. He traveled the country speaking at college campuses. Once he decided not to run in 1980, he turned his attention to

---

312 (Meeder 1978).
313 (Philadelphia Daily News 1978).
314 (Lippman Jr. 1978).

corporate boards.[315] But unlike the Franklin Mint engagement, for the boards, he did a lot of analysis—first in deciding to join, then in the work he did.

He continued to be criticized. But this work was different than an endorsement. It was real work. CEOs like Sandy Weill of Citigroup found that the experience and integrity Ford brought to the board was priceless.[316]

Ford always remained quite touchy on the criticism he received. "First place, I've turned down for every business opportunity I've had, I've turned down nine for every one I have accepted. I've been very discriminating, and when you look at the list of the people I've been associated with, they are all first class."[317]

Ultimately, his confidence and ability to work through difficult financial moments was a game changer. He is the model for modern post-presidency life. And in financial planning, he is a model for financial well-being. If he was anxious about money, he sure didn't show it. And when he died, his net worth was estimated to be between $7 and $8 million—just shy of Brokaw's original prediction.

THE "FRAILTY" OF HARRY TRUMAN'S MONEY

Twenty-five years before Ford and Betty danced their way out of the White House, another former president was making a journey into his own post-presidential financial situation: Harry S. Truman. Truman is one of those presidents that people adore. He's also one of those presidents who is always on lists ranking him as one of the poorest presidents. That myth—and it is a myth—is so persistent that even fellow presidents like Ford believed it.

Truman's story is a little more complicated than that. In fact, out of all the presidents, his financial life is probably the one that most of us can relate to. He's the ultimate everyman. He had been a farmer, an oil man, a soldier, and even a haberdasher. When it comes to the continuum, he's like the rest of us—filled with financial anxiety. When you hear the story,

---

315   He wasn't the first president who considered board work. As we will see, Calvin Coolidge had offers.
316   (Weill 2011).
317   (P. G. Ford, Ford-Cannon Interview for Ford Presidential Library 1992).

Gerald Ford: Hate the Game, Not the Player

you will understand why. Remember, however, this is Truman—and he is always one to rise to great challenges.

Let's go back to early 1953. Twelve days before Truman passed the presidency off to Eisenhower, an article appeared in the *Sacramento Bee* titled "The Forgotten Man—An ExPresident." Writer Gladstone Williams lamented that one of the biggest challenges facing former presidents is that "men who have served for years in an office with the greatest source of power on earth are thus cast off and left to their own resources…and no provision is made for their remaining years whatsoever."[318]

Gladstone had a good point. At that time, there wasn't a pension for a president to rely on. Most presidents, upon leaving office, usually followed the pattern of going back to their prior profession, like being a lawyer. Others took on interesting roles for the government, like Taft becoming Supreme Court chief justice. Others quite honestly died quickly, like Washington or Coolidge. In fact, when Truman was leaving office, the only other surviving former president was Herbert Hoover. And as we know, Hoover wasn't hurting for money.

But Truman was different. He went into politics to get away from a career filled with more failures than successes. In fact, he had weathered financial precariousness throughout his life. As a former president, the only reliable income he had was his World War I pension of $112.56 a month. Clearly, that wasn't enough to survive on, much less enough to begin building a presidential library.

His return to his hometown of Independence, Missouri, confirmed he was a financial everyman. He was spotted on the train platform buying a newspaper and claimed he was just like everyone else. But crowds met him along the way, cheering for him.

Truman had a secret in those post-presidential days. He wasn't the same poor old Harry he had been when he entered the White House. Truman had assets and a legitimate net worth. He and his wife had financial security. But while he might be in a good financial position for the first time ever, these circumstances weren't going to change him. Nor was he going to divulge it. In fact, while most Americans believed he was in a financially precarious situation, the truth was that he was already on his way to financial confidence.

---

318 (G. Williams 1953) Williams also pointed out that security was not provided even though there are "intrusions into their private lives by crackpots."

He was, finally after sixty-plus years, moving along the continuum in the favorable direction.

A HISTORY OF FINANCIAL INSTABILITY

One of the weird things about financial anxiety is that sometimes it is generational. The Trumans, for example, as a family line, had a long history of achieving financial security only to have it taken away in a single stroke. And that creates something even worse than financial anxiety—it creates real financial trauma.

Truman's grandparents had helped settle the West and had acquired twenty thousand acres of very valuable, fertile farmland in Missouri. Over time, the farmland got chopped up, and by the time Truman was born, the working farm was down to six hundred acres. The family's finances went up and down during Truman's childhood because his father, John, was impulsive and made some bad business decisions.[319] Although primarily a trader in livestock, John was also a part-time inventor. He patented a staple-puller and a wire-stretcher that brought in an occasional check for twenty dollars, but his most potentially lucrative invention was an automatic railroad switch.[320] The Missouri Pacific Railroad offered him $2,000 a year in royalties, but he decided to test the market instead. He got the Chicago and Alton Railroad to offer $2,500 a year, but rather than accept it, he tried to get both railroads to pay him a combined $5,000 a year. Apparently wise

---

319 (Slaughter 1984).
320 These patents and the small amount of money earned on them are found in Truman's sister Mary Jane Truman's Papers held at the Truman Library.

to his game, they both retracted their offers and John ended up with nothing, thus depriving the family of what would have been a decent revenue stream. But instead of learning his lesson, John decided to try his hand at speculating on wheat futures using all of his family's assets. In an instant, $40,000 in assets and farmland were gone, including the funds for Truman's college education.

This is an absolutely devastating turn of events. Truman was about to graduate from high school and, despite being salutatorian of his class, gave up his dream of college and went to work on the railroad, then as a cashier in a bank, and finally at home on the family farm.

Losing financial stability is overwhelming for anyone. But the risks Truman's father took shifted a potentially vulnerable household to one at extreme financial risk. And that is one facet of financial anxiety that is often overlooked: lower-income households suffer more from financial anxiety due to the stress and strain of managing their money. In today's world, this has become more pronounced due to wages not keeping up with the cost of living. The shift for the Trumans was abrupt and unexpected. By all accounts, John never recovered from losing all their money. Their farming neighbor noted that they were always strapped for money, almost inexplicably so.[321]

---

321 (Slaughter 1984). Eight years after his father lost everything, another calamity struck the family farm. In 1909, Truman's maternal grandmother, Harriet Young, passed away. Harriett had been married to Truman's grandfather, and he had died intestate. She inherited everything. Upon her death, her will was read. Of her seven children, only two—Truman's namesake, Harrison, and his mother, Martha Ellen—were to inherit the farm and its assets. Harriet left only five dollars to each of her other five children.

Why Harriet disinherited them is not clear. Decades later, Truman's cousin Mary Ethel Noland described Harriet as "a very quiet woman...but a woman of fine judgement and fine principles." Clearly, she felt Harrison and Martha Ellen were more deserving of the inheritance, especially since neighbors saw her other children as irresponsible and often gambling and drinking. In contrast, Harrison and Martha Ellen took care of their mother.

The disinherited children banded together and sued to contest the will. The litigation took five years. When it was all said and done, the will dispute was settled in 1914. While Harrison and Martha Ellen won, they still had to pay a settlement of $9,500 to their other siblings, plus $3,000 in attorney fees. But while they had assets, Martha Ellen was cash poor. She didn't have the liquidity necessary. She decided the best thing to do was to take a mortgage against the farm for $7,500.

This might seem like an innocent financial move, but Martha Ellen was committing herself to the debt. The farm was supporting Martha Ellen, Truman's two siblings, and Truman himself. It was a lot of mouths to feed. And unlike today, taking

Further, the Trumans, at times, didn't manage the farm the right way. Other farmers felt that they had a great piece of land. But the choices the Trumans made in managing it caused it to not do well. For instance, they often had three or four hired hands helping the family. In comparison, other farms of similar size made do with one. The Trumans also had great pastureland, yet they had no cows. When asked why, Truman's sister often explained that the whole family hated milking cows. They created high overhead for themselves and made poor decisions on maximizing the land, thus pushing their finances into a more dire position.

AN AFFINITY FOR THE GET-RICH-QUICK SCHEME

The family's money woes left their mark on Truman, who developed an obsession with "get-rich-quick" schemes as a way to make his fortune. A "get-rich-quick" scheme is a plan or strategy set up to make a quick return on an investment. People are drawn to them for any number of reasons. One common theme is a lack of financial knowledge, which means an individual may not fully be able to understand the risks involved or the potential for losses and be swayed easily by the promise of high return.

Between his father's impulsiveness and the loss of the family's money, it's no surprise Truman embraced capriciousness when it came to financial matters; this is not uncommon with individuals who have experienced such instability. And unfortunately for Truman, he only made it worse.

Truman had no interest in farming, so he had to find some other way of earning a living. And with no college education, he would have to rely on his grit and ambition to make money. He was also feeling the need to make something happen sooner than later because he was courting Bess Wallace, who was from a well-off family and wasn't thrilled at the idea of a penurious life on the farm. So, she made him wait.

---

on a mortgage for a farm was a precarious decision. Some years were going to be better than others whether it was weather, labor, or just the general market. There was a strong likelihood that the mortgage payments might be missed. In comparison, today's farmers have been enjoying greater government protections since the passage of the Agricultural Adjustment Act of 1933 that provided programs with price and supply controls. Further, technology has mitigated other risks that previously came with a labor-intensive industry as well, and the United States has fewer farms today, yet on average they are larger. (Dimitri, Effland and Conklin June 2005) page 2-9. The pieces of this story are recounted in both (Noland 1965) and (Slaughter 1984).

Gerald Ford: Hate the Game, Not the Player

In February 1916, he wrote Bess of his frustration: "I am getting very impatient of my slow progress at home. You know my prospects there were of the brightest at the outset and one disaster after another has almost put me to the bad.…You know I am most anxious to do that for the most excellent reason that I am crazy to marry you. In the last year my finances have seemed to put me farther from that happy event rather than closer to it… then I think of all the debts I'm saddled with and of my present inability even to buy you a decent ring."[322]

Truman hatched a plan to open a zinc mine in Oklahoma. He partnered with two men named Culbertson and Hughes, and the TCH Mining Company was created. Getting into mining, which was wild and unregulated at the time, was no easy task. When Truman first arrived, he had to hire a mill expert to tell him how much to spend on the mine. As Truman explained to Bess, the company would have to spend $1,500 for the mill, but then they would be able to find about $4,000 in waste ore lying around to help with the financing.[323]

Letter after letter to Bess over the course of 1916 illustrated the precariousness of setting up the zinc mine. Truman struggled to pay invoices and workers. He was constantly in pursuit of more capital, and at one point he became so desperate to cut costs that he gave up his fifty-cent-a-night accommodation and slept at the zinc plant, which would also save the $2.50 a night he was paying for a watchman.[324]

At one point he lamented to Bess, "I have only gone in the hole on this hole about $11,000. Do you suppose I'll ever catch up?"[325] Yet, whenever he started to truly despair, he focused on what a "win" would be. "All my debts paid…a city home, a country home, some automobiles and flying machines—and who knows but maybe a yat [yacht? what?], and you to boss the whole layout."[326]

Ultimately, the illiquidity struggle was too much in the face of the risk. TCH was just always short of cash. Along with the cutthroat nature of the business and the partners not always being aligned, by November 1916, the TCH Mining Company ceased operations.

---

322 Letter Harry S. Truman to Bess Wallace, dated February 1916.
323 Letter Harry S. Truman to Bess Wallace, dated March 5, 1916.
324 Letter Harry S. Truman to Bess Wallace, date illegible.
325 Letter Harry S. Truman to Bess Wallace, dated August 5, 1916.
326 Letter Harry S. Truman to Bess Wallace, dated August 19, 1916.

All the Presidents' Money

It was a setback, but he quickly turned his attention to another classic get-rich-quick scheme: drilling for oil. He had learned his lesson from the zinc mines, and he wasn't going to struggle with illiquidity this time. So, he sought out Friends and Family financing, which included a contribution from Bess. But despite managing liquidity better this time, hitting oil proved elusive, and he was forced to sell his share in the well. Beaten down and frustrated, Truman himself noted, "I seem to have a grand and admirable ability for calling tails when heads come up. My luck should surely change. Sometime I should win."[327] Sometime, but not this time: just a couple of months later, the well that Truman sold struck oil. He had just missed getting rich quick.

A few years later, after World War I, Truman set up the famous haberdashery with his friend Eddie Jacobson. This time, he had worked through all the issues that had hurt him previously: he had liquidity, a strong partner, and support from his fellow war veterans who came to the shop. But Truman was dealt one last financial blow. The post-war recession led to deflation that caused the haberdashery's inventory to fall in value from $35,000 to $12,000. They became saddled with debts—including a long-term lease. The shop failed, and Truman's partner declared bankruptcy, but Truman refused to follow suit. He held onto the debt and did not pay off the last of it until 1935. But Truman was finally done with entrepreneurship, and he used the contacts he'd made in the military to become a county court judge, which launched his political career.

A PRESIDENTIAL WINDFALL

When Truman took office, the presidency paid $75,000 annually. This was no small amount and made Truman one of the highest earners in the country. However, one rule that all presidents must follow in the White House is that they need to pay for their own living and food expenses.

At first glance, this might not seem like such a big deal. But the truth is, the White House staff will provide the family with *anything* they want. Seventy years after the Trumans left the White House, Michelle Obama lamented this in an interview with Jimmy Kimmel. "They let you get whatever you want. Like, if you say you want some exotic fruit—then you get the bill for a peach, and you're like, 'That was a five-hundred-dollar peach!'"

---

327 Letter Harry S. Truman to Bess Wallace, dated May 27, 1917.

Gerald Ford: Hate the Game, Not the Player

Michelle said. "I used to tell Barack, 'Barack, do not express pleasure for anything unless I know how much it costs.'"[328]

Truman and Bess were accustomed to not having much money, and $6,250 a month pretax was an unbelievable sum. Even after taxes, they netted $48,000 annually and could save a significant amount.[329]

And then two things even more unbelievable happened for the Trumans financially. Congress increased the president's salary to $100,000. Given the hosting duties of the First Family, they also did something else that was a bit controversial. They gave the president a $50,000 tax-free stipend for entertaining. Congress justified the increase in the president's compensation by pointing out that the salary had not been raised in years. Further, the committee report supporting the increase made it clear that Congress wanted financial well-being for the president. "We want the president to have something left besides his rubbers when he leaves office."[330]

Despite Congress's understanding of the president's finances, most presidents would probably spend the whole stipend and more. Entertaining world leaders doesn't come cheap, but Truman was spared that expense because the White House was falling apart. A young congressman named Jerry Ford was part of a group given a tour by Truman of the building, and he noted some features. From "the hole in the floor in [his daughter] Margaret's sitting room" to "the huge crystal chandelier that almost crashed down in the middle of an East Room reception" to the ceiling of the state dining room that was "only held up by force of habit," no one could deny the White House was in a bad state, and Congress approved a $5.4 million renovation. The Trumans were moved across the street to Blair House, and thus, White House entertaining temporarily came to a halt.[331] But the Trumans still received the tax-free $50,000 stipend and simply saved it.[332] This

---

328 Obama appeared on *The Jimmy Kimmel Show* to promote her book *Becoming* on November 16, 2018. The full interview is at https://youtu.be/AktU2gettoU.
329 (Lawrence 1949) The president did get other items completely paid for from housing to transportation. These items are not factored into his income.
330 (Shoop 1948) The article cited the committee's report.
331 Ford himself recounted this story on May 8, 1976, in his remarks at the dedication of the Harry S. Truman Statue in Independence, Missouri. Speech available at https://www.fordlibrarymuseum.gov/library/document/0122/1252853.pdf.
332 Truman himself noted this in a letter he wrote to Bess that he included with his 1953 will. The letter can be found at the Truman Library in Bess W. Truman Papers, Financial Affairs File, 1953: Will.

was an opportunity unlike no other. It wasn't far from Truman's mind that just a few years earlier, a loan his mother had taken on the farm property had forced the land into foreclosure. The family had to buy it back in an auction.

After decades of never catching a financial break, suddenly Truman was making money hand over fist—and some of it tax-free. But his financial PTSD never went away, and he remained hypervigilant about money, scrimping and saving every penny into government bonds. He was also aware after all the prior financial failures that this window of opportunity might not last.

And he was right. After two years, Congress changed the rules. The stipend must be accounted for. Yet, two years was all he needed to build a nest egg. When Truman left the White House, he drafted a will, including a net worth statement that read:

> Land: $250,000
> Bonds: $250,000
> Cash: $150,000
> Book: $100,000[333]

Truman was worth $750,000. In 2024 dollars, this would be over $8.4 million. What's more interesting is that despite being worldly, Truman stuck to very conservative investments. He even noted to Bess that he had cash hidden in a safe when they were in the White House.

Despite this building of wealth, Truman had difficulty reconciling this windfall with his previous financial issues. He didn't want to lose the image of "good ole Harry" that the public knew.

And I see this with clients. So much of their identity is tied up with a certain image that it's hard to layer in the money. Think of the guy who hits the lottery who you find hasn't changed: he still drives the same car he always did and lives in the same house.

In recent years, some commentators have painted a picture of nefarious behavior committed by Truman. One article even noted that "the supposedly difficult post-presidential economic situation faced by Harry Truman was a complete fabrication created by Truman himself via what can only be characterized as a series of shockingly dishonest and radically misleading

---

333   Bess W. Truman Papers, Financial Affairs File, 1953: Will.

Gerald Ford: Hate the Game, Not the Player

statements to Congress and the public."[334] But in my eyes, Truman was a guy who financially struggled throughout his life, and those who are accusing him don't come from a financial background to understand what might really be happening.

Truman may have also been struggling with something we see in financial planning with successful individuals—and more often women—called *bag lady syndrome*. Bag lady syndrome is a fear (whether rational or not) that one will outlast their money and literally become a bag lady on the street. It is extreme anxiety over finances, and it can be absolutely debilitating. Numerous studies show that this level of anxiety impacts more Americans especially in light of increased longevity, the elimination of workplace pensions, and increased costs of living.[335]

I worked with an incredibly successful female executive for years. She was worth well over $60 million. Yet we would spend most meetings grinding numbers to ensure that there was no way she would be a "bag lady." She wanted to be in complete control of what she spent and how much income her asset base generated. There were times I wished she could enjoy her financial success more.

While we will never know if this level of anxiety consumed Truman, it could account for his need for secrecy about the level of his asset base post-presidency. After a lifetime of financial instability, the fear of losing it all—and negatively impacting his beloved wife, Bess, and daughter, Margaret—likely increased his anxiety. And unlike today, he had few to discuss with.

Today we use financial planning discussions to work through this type of anxiety. In Truman's case it would have been helpful if he could have spoken to some of his predecessors as other presidents were more fortunate to have. Two months before Woodrow Wilson's inauguration, on January 6, 1913, William Howard Taft sent a letter to the president-elect. In it he noted:

"You will find, as I have occasion to say publicly, that Congress is very generous to the President. You have all your transportation paid for, and all servants in the White House except such valet and maid as you and Mrs.

---

334 (Campos 2002) page 4.
335 Over the past fifteen years, this issue is studied regularly. For more information see (American Psychological Assocation 2015) and (Gailey May 8, 2023).

Wilson chooses to employ. Your flowers for entertainments and otherwise are furnished from the conservancy…Altogether, you can calculate that your expenses are only those of furnishing food to a large boarding house of servants and to your family, and your own personal expenses of clothing, etc. This of course makes the salary of $75,000, with $25,000 for traveling expenses, very much more than is generally supposed."

And then Taft lets Wilson into his own personal finances:

"I have been able to save from my four years about $100,000. I give you these personal details because I am afraid I shall not have an opportunity, in view of your engagements, to meet you under conditions that will enable me to have a long talk with you, and I feel as if I would have liked the same kind of information when I came in."[336]

Wilson took the advice to heart. Over his two-term presidency, he was able to save $250,000.

If Truman knew this, I often wonder if he would have felt less anxious about the public finding out he had made money during his years as president.

THE CONTINUUM ALWAYS CONTINUES

Financial anxiety and financial well-being run hand in hand with each other. What makes the Ford and Truman stories compelling is that it wasn't easy for either of them to gain well-being. In many ways, it is surprising how simplistic both of them were in approaching money.

For Ford, his strength was in decision-making and being unafraid to go a different path. But in order to do that and to achieve financial well-being, he had to master the pivot when things went wrong.

For Truman, he had failed so much that he felt that when well-being found him, he couldn't be open about it. It was like he was too afraid it would disappear if he mentioned it to others.

---

336   Letter William Howard Taft to Woodrow Wilson, dated January 6, 1913. This letter gives more personal information on life in the White House. Taft might not have known how much he could have saved as his predecessor was Theodore Roosevelt, who not only had outside means but had six children and a very lively White House. I am indebted to Walter Stahr for finding and sharing this letter with me. In 1913, $100,000 had the buying power in 2024 of $3 million.

Gerald Ford: Hate the Game, Not the Player

But Ford did something else: he revolutionized post-presidency finance. As long as you won the presidency, you won the golden ticket to wealth, regardless of financial skills or education.

President	College Degree/ Grad Degree	Wealth At Birth	Current Wealth/ Wealth at Death	Financial Ability
Richard Nixon	Whittier/Duke Law	Poor	Wealthy	Above Average
Gerald Ford	University of Michigan/ Yale Law	Poor	Wealthy	Excellent
James Carter	Georgia Institute Tech/ US Naval Academy	Middle Class	Wealthy	Excellent
Ronald Reagan	Dixon	Poor	Wealthy	Excellent
George H.W. Bush	Yale University	Wealthy	Wealthy	Excellent
William J. Clinton	Georgetown/Yale Law	Lower Middle Class	Wealthy	Above Average
George W. Bush	Yale University/ Harvard Business School	Wealthy	Wealthy	Above Average
Barack Obama	Columbia University/ Harvard Law	Lower Middle Class	Wealthy	Above Average
Donald J. Trump	U Penn / Wharton	Wealthy	Wealthy	Excellent
Joseph Biden	University of Delaware/ Syracuse Law Delaware	Lower Middle Class	Wealthy	Average

(Nixon is included as he benefited from Ford's actions.)

Chapter Six

CALVIN COOLIDGE IS RATHER THRIFTY
(OR THE VALUES OF MONEY)

If you asked me to name the smartest thing that the wealthy do with their money, I would probably tell you that they seek help with managing their personal finances. In the realm of personal finance, a lot of the basics are straightforward and can be learned simply by reading books on the subject. But the numbers are the easy part. The reason the wealthy really seek help is quite simple: money is emotion.

Every individual has a wide range of emotions about money due to different religious, financial, or educational backgrounds. As a result, everyone puts their own *values* on money. In personal finance, your values are defined as your beliefs and principles that impact your relationship with money. These values often evolve over the course of one's life as different experiences shape your outlook.

As a result, when meeting with clients, we may be going over the nuts and bolts of finance—taxes, investments, or cash flow—but the theoretical question we are working with is: *Are my values reflected in how I live my financial life?* The best way to answer that question is to work through the problems that come up with money. Debating and looking at issues from different angles allows you to land on the right solution for you and your values.

What you find, in my experience, is that the people who understand their values and stick to them are often more satisfied with their financial life. And remember that the values that are important to one person might not be important to another.

CALVIN COOLIDGE HAS A STRONG MORAL CODE

If there was one president whose financial behavior was values-driven, it would have to be Calvin Coolidge.[337] Now, this was a man who had a firm money philosophy. And if Coolidge had been asked to define that philosophy, he would probably sum it up with one word: "thrifty." Over the course of his life, this philosophy had a big impact on his major financial decisions—and not all to his benefit.

Coolidge focused on every penny to such an extent that when he got married in 1905, he and his wife, Grace, lived in a rundown hotel/boardinghouse called the Norwood Hotel. They loved it. They even got lunch there for fifty cents a day. When it closed down, Coolidge and Grace bought all the bed and table linens from the owner for a pittance even though it had "Norwood Hotel" embroidered on it.[338]

An inside peek into the White House and its occupants was published by the former housekeeper, Elizabeth Jaffray. Jaffray had worked for four presidents (Taft, Wilson, Harding, and Coolidge), and in her tell-all book, the most scandalous thing she could say about Coolidge was that he "save[d] the most money." To her chagrin, he was a little too engaged in the household management and spending, going so far as to complain to her that "six hams…seems an awful lot" for a sixty-guest dinner at the White House.[339]

His thriftiness centered on moral values of humility, community, and self-control. Coolidge historian Amity Shlaes emphasized that in order to understand Coolidge, you had to see that fundamentally, he was a missionary.[340] It always makes me chuckle that he was Warren G. Harding's vice president. The two men could not have been any different.

BUILDING THE VALUES

Unlike a lot of presidents, Coolidge didn't grow up poor. The Coolidge family owned a lot of land in Vermont. And in the village where he grew

---

337 In fact, he was even thrifty with words. Coolidge's memoirs are one of the shortest sets of presidential memoirs coming in at a crisp 247 pages. When it came out in 1929, it made the bestsellers list.
338 (Shlaes 2014) pages 90–91.
339 (Jaffray 1926) pages 4, 105.
340 Conversation with Amity Shlaes on June 30, 2023.

up, his family was one of the most financially successful.[341] Despite this financial stability, biographers have noted that the loss of his mother and sister caused his childhood to be filled with great sadness and loneliness.

He grew up in a household of self-imposed austerity and was taught to work and save. Self-sufficiency was seen as a virtue. Coolidge's father kept budgets in a small notebook; it was a way of managing thrift.[342] His father would tell him cautionary tales of family members who failed to budget and manage their finances well.

He also taught him a powerful lesson about compounding early on. Coolidge would recount it years later when discussing his education. He was fortunate to attend Black River Academy for secondary school, where the tuition was $150 a year ($5,000 in 2024 dollars), which his father paid. Coolidge had earned money selling popcorn and apples at local town meetings, but his father insisted that he put that money in the bank. "He wished me to be informed of the value of money at interest. He thought money invested in that way led to a self-respecting independence that was one of the foundations of good character."[343]

Warren Buffett would be very pleased to hear this advice indeed.

Coolidge trained as an attorney, and fairly early on he realized he wanted to be in the public arena as a way of giving back. He decided that in order to remain clean in his pursuit of public office, he would simply have to just accrue less wealth and live on what he had. He would be thrifty. For him, thriftiness was a choice, and he would attain it through self-control.

But Coolidge also knew something else: he was going to inherit property from his father. Due to the deaths of both his sister and mother, there was no one else. He could be thrifty, but if he ran into trouble, he could get help from time to time. Luckily for Coolidge, his father had no problem giving him an allowance. And he would, until Coolidge was forty years old. Letter after letter between the two was filled with requests from Coolidge for money to live off of. Thrift was a much easier money philosophy with such a backstop.

Coolidge passed the bar in 1897 and set up his own practice in 1898 in Northampton, Massachusetts. He was known for being efficient in bring-

---

341 (Gilbert 2005) page 87.
342 (Shlaes 2014) pages 16–17.
343 (Coolidge, *The Autobiography of Calvin Coolidge* 1929) page 43.

ing clients' issues to resolution, and he didn't charge high legal fees. In fact, his peers would berate him for his low fees and out-of-court settlements. For them, he was a little too thrifty.

Here's where all this thriftiness converges in an interesting way regarding Coolidge's financial planning. While starting out, he decided to rent. Initially, he rented because he wanted to save money for marriage. But even after he became successful and married his wife, Grace, he still rented. And it's not like Coolidge didn't understand the fundamentals of owning a home. In his law career, he had a lot of exposure to it. But perhaps that is one of the reasons he avoided purchasing a home.

In 1899, a small mutual savings bank was going to be opened in Northampton called Nonotuck Savings Bank.[344] By coincidence, it was in the same building where Coolidge was practicing law. Northampton was a small city where locals knew each other, so it was only logical that the bank's treasurer called on Coolidge; they requested that Coolidge not only take on some of the legal work but be one of the original corporators when it officially opened.

Coolidge worked closely with the bank, and he soon joined the board of trustees.[345] He handled mortgages and did title work. This complemented his law practice; he even managed real estate.[346]

At the time he was in banking and considering real estate, a change was going on across the country that was encouraging more Americans to buy homes. And leading the charge was the *Ladies' Home Journal*,[347] a publication that had a circulation of more than 1.6 million readers at the time, making it the biggest magazine in the country.

A special home-building article in the *Ladies' Home Journal* caused a debate between Coolidge and Grace. The article espoused the idea that having a mortgage was a virtue, as it was forced savings.[348] It's forced savings

---

344 A mutual savings bank is a financial institution chartered by a central or regional government, without capital stock, owned by its members who subscribe to a common fund (courtesy of Wikipedia). The bank was eventually acquired by TD Bank.
345 (Whitbeck 2020 (reprinted) original 1921)
346 (Coolidge, *The Autobiography of Calvin Coolidge* 1929) pages 86–88.
347 (Roth 1991) page 187. The driving force of this was one man: Edward Bok, who was the executive editor of the *Ladies' Home Journal*. For over thirty years, he influenced not just home buying but interior and exterior design of American homes.
348 (Shlaes 2014) page 86.

Calvin Coolidge Is Rather Thrifty

because the payments build equity in the home that can be unlocked when the property is sold.

The math on a home at that time was reasonable. In the magazine, there were often homes shown ranging from $1,500 to $7,500. The Coolidges could have afforded one on the lower end of the range. But both of them waffled in their courage to actually move forward on a purchase. The difference in home buying at the turn of the twentieth century was that it was typically the equivalent of a year's salary. In comparison to today, that seems like a pretty good deal.[349]

But renting can be a mistake in wealth building. While I have seen numerous clients build wealth through houses over the years, I can share a personal story. Just out of law school, my then-husband and I decided to buy a home in Hoboken, New Jersey. The price was $292,000. We scrimped together 10 percent of the down payment and did an 80-10-10. That is 10 percent down, 80 percent first mortgage, and 10 percent second.

Unbeknownst to us, we were lucky on timing and lucky that our condo came with a garage parking spot (in a city, that's a big deal). Two years later, when Goldman Sachs moved me to California, we sold. In that short time period, the condo had appreciated. We sold it for $600,000. Not a bad return on invested capital. It gave us the down payment for a home in California. If only Coolidge had had the courage to buy a home, he could have built wealth.

Despite his experience and the social knowledge of home ownership, the Coolidges remained renters for the next twenty-four years. 21 Massasoit Street in Northampton was a modest house, but it boasted a porch that Coolidge loved.[350]

That begs the question, given his experience and career, why didn't he buy a house? In his era, home ownership was a logical financial step for someone of his economic background. In studying Coolidge's thriftiness, there are two underlying reasons that held him back. The first is one we can all relate to: anxiety. The second was how he wished to be viewed politically.

First, after working in the banking system and experiencing several of the panics that occurred as the US financial system expanded, renting a

---

349 (Roth 1991) pages 189–191.
350 The house still exists today. You can see pictures at https://clui.org/ludb/site/calvin-coolidge-northampton-home.

home provided protection. In particular, he was in a senior role at the bank during the Panic of 1907 (it was like living through the Great Recession of 2007–2009).[351] Prior to the establishment of the Federal Reserve, regional banks had more vulnerability. Given his cautious nature, and seeing how banks worked, it might have made him uncomfortable, much like the experience of Millennials a century later.

Coolidge even noted his anxiety years later in his *Autobiography*. He wrote, "I know very well what it means to awake in the night and realize that the rent is coming due, wondering where the money is coming from with which to pay it. The only way I know of escape from that constant tragedy is to keep running expenses low enough so that something may be saved to meet the day when earnings may be small."[352]

For him, this anxiety was paralyzing, as he was unable to evolve his financial life. It was far easier to label himself "thrifty" than to acknowledge the fear he had. Like we saw with Joe Biden and financial trauma, the behaviors we see Coolidge engage in—rigidity, fastidious focus on moral values, perfectionism—are so extreme financially, it suggests that some other psychological factor might have been at play. I can only speculate on what it might have been, but in working with clients with these behaviors, it is not uncommon to involve a therapist at some point to help. Staying rigid appears to have helped him feel safe financially and in control.

There was also another reason behind his behavior. He believed it was imperative to remain pure financially or "stay clean." He was concerned that by doing business while being tied to one bank, he could be seen as lacking objectivity.

At that time, there weren't national mortgages. The mortgage industry was far more local, and the terms didn't function like they do today. Rather than thirty-year mortgages, the terms were much shorter, typically five or six years. You would pay interest and then there would be a balloon payment at the end. The trade-off was that buying a house wasn't as expensive as it is today, given it usually was the price of a year's salary. So hopefully the homeowner could pay it off in the end.

---

351 For more insight into the Panic of 1907 and its similarities with the Great Recession of 2007–2009, see (The Federal Reserve 2015).
352 (Coolidge, *The Autobiography of Calvin Coolidge* 1929) page 94.

Calvin Coolidge Is Rather Thrifty

Coolidge wanted to remain independent and not beholden to anyone. He eschewed the idea of having a favored banker just because he chose to have a mortgage somewhere. And Coolidge was incredibly cautious. This was a man who had a lot of life insurance on him as he was convinced that he would die young. Part of that came from traumatic stress in his childhood. Losing his mother and sister and the repressed manner in which he dealt with it may have caused unresolved grief. It can be argued that his grief in turn created an insecurity in him that made him fearful about taking on a home purchase.[353]

But while he didn't want to buy a home, he understood the importance of building relationships with others where both sides benefited in an up-front and clean way. He deposited money at multiple banks in town.[354] It allowed him to work with different people, but at the same time, he mitigated risk. In the time prior to the FDIC protections on banks, he would rather have saved small amounts at multiple banks versus a high balance at one bank so that he could be protected in a bank crash.[355]

Yet by staying clean, Coolidge was also making a choice about money. His thriftiness didn't always allow him to enjoy money. There is a darker side of thriftiness: by not engaging in some of the more routine parts of financial life, he could retain a moral superiority over others.

COOLIDGE FINALLY BUYS A HOME

The Coolidges put off buying a home for some time. He became governor, vice president, and president without owning a house. But when Coolidge left the White House in 1928, his presidency had been a time of booming finance. He may have been austere in his financials, but the rest of the country had been having quite a time. Cheap money led to significant market speculation.

At the time, one man was quite concerned about where the country was going: Charles Merrill. Today, we know the name Merrill as one of the founders of Merrill Lynch. But back then he was a flamboyant guy who not only helped create an investment firm but also provided investment

---

353 (Gilbert 2005) page 90.
354 (Shlaes 2014) page 90.
355 And it did in the 1929 crash.

banking services for the merger of Safeway Supermarkets, which was the beginning of chain stores in retail.[356]

Merrill had a very bad feeling about all the speculation that was occurring. The market had been rising, and no financial intervention from the Federal Reserve could cool the momentum. He reached out to Coolidge.

Coolidge and Merrill agreed that either interest rates had to come down or the market had to cool. Merrill offered a grand plan to Coolidge: come join the board of directors at Merrill Lynch. He would be able to use that platform to help guide the business as well as make statements to help manage the market. The offer from Merrill was rich: $100,000.[357] That would be the same purchasing power as $1.8 million today.

But Coolidge declined. He felt he didn't know enough about banking and investing to be involved as a director.[358] Merrill would continue to ask Coolidge to get engaged in the markets even post market crash. Finally, in November 1929, Coolidge sent him a tersely worded note, stating, "I am not now in a position to get information concerning business conditions and so could not speak of them anyway and besides I have retired from office and feel that if any statement out to be made it should be made by those who are now in office or in a position to know what conditions are."[359]

As Coolidge passed on Merrill's offer, another one came in. Richard H. Waldo, the editor and publisher of the McClure Newspaper Syndicate, reached out to him. What if Coolidge was to write a column for McClure?

Due to the syndicated nature of the newspaper, there was a way to make this a very attractive opportunity for him: McClure would syndicate the column to papers nationwide that wanted to carry it. Then McClure and Coolidge could split the revenue with 40 percent to McClure and 60 percent to Coolidge. Plus, McClure would guarantee $3,000-a-week minimum payment.[360]

---

356 (Nocera 1998).
357 (Farlin 2008) page 6.
358 As an interesting footnote, Merrill was so convinced in February 1929 of an impending crash, he liquidated his firm's portfolio. When the crash occurred in October, he became legendary.
359 (Coolidge, Letter Calvin Coolidge to Charles Merrill Dated November 29, 1929 n.d.).
360 (Waldo 1935).

Calvin Coolidge Is Rather Thrifty

It was a pretty sweet deal, yet Coolidge declined. Unlike the Merrill offer, Waldo would later recall that "his declination was put in such a way that the door was left open."[361]

A SHOCKING HEADLINE

Five months after Black Tuesday hit Wall Street, wiping out $14 billion in stock market value in a single day, a headline appeared in the April 2, 1930, edition of the *New York Times*. The public was taken aback:

> "Coolidge Buys A $45,000 Estate"[362]

Was this really the Coolidge they knew so well? He was always after them to go on a financial diet. When he was gifted lion cubs as president, he named them "Budget Bureau" and "Tax Reduction." And now, with the markets and the economy in a free fall, the purchase of a sixteen-room home with a swimming pool seemed a little tone deaf, especially when the average home cost in the range of $6,000.

But just a few days after the *New York Times* announced his home purchase in April 1930, Coolidge reached out to Waldo again after almost two years. Was that opportunity still available? It was, and they quickly came to terms. He would have the freedom to write whatever he wanted to. Coolidge decided how he would approach it—at 150 to 200 words daily.

When the word got out about the *Calvin Coolidge Says* column, newspapers went wild. Years later, Waldo noted that "The New York *Herald Tribune* headed the list at $900 weekly. Eight Hearst newspapers paid $2,000 a week collectively. The extra monthly settlements came to $47,045; making today of $203,045 for fifty-two weeks' work."[363] It was only after a couple of years of writing the column that Coolidge shared something with Waldo that explains why he took the job and why he finally bought a house.

When the Coolidges left the White House for Northampton, they found they really couldn't stay in their old place because it had become a

---

361   Ibid.
362   (The New York Times 1930) This would be akin to buying a $1 million home today in a small town. It was a big number.
363   Ibid. Interestingly, Coolidge had one firm rule: he would not write anything that had to do with the problems of government as he said, "I refuse to be Deputy President."

magnet for curiosity seekers who wanted to see the president. People were showing up night and day. It became a nuisance not just for Coolidge and Grace, but for their neighbors as well. They had to find a solution and they hoped it would be in Northampton, the town they loved.

They didn't have to look far. Right up the street, Coolidge and Grace found the perfect home. The house they bought had not only a pool and a wine room but something that would help protect their privacy: gates.

Before Coolidge bought the house, he talked to his wealth manager at JP Morgan & Company, where he had moved his accounts to when he left office in 1929.[364] As with any major purchase, he wanted to confirm it was a good financial decision with an objective adviser.

Waldo shared that Coolidge told him that "the leading banking house in New York—his most trusted advisers—had told him that the depression was over, and he would have the advantage of the rising tide of prosperity if he waited."[365] This thinking appealed to Coolidge's financial values. Buying at a low could be a thrifty way to enter the housing market finally.

Coolidge felt it was fair advice and bought the new house. He sold three thousand shares of Standard just after the dividend was paid on April 3, 1930, for $74,430—enough for the purchase but also to take on a loss.[366]

Yet, the Depression did not get better. It was then that Coolidge reached out to Waldo about the syndication column again. In 1932, he told Waldo about the advice from JP Morgan regarding the Depression ending in 1930 by simply saying, "They seem to have been mistaken."[367]

Coolidge taking on a writing job to generate income was likely a way to manage his anxiety in making large financial decisions during a precarious time in the country. Controlling the controllables is a key tenet in wealth building to help manage the stress. Like Hoover and Reagan with their budgets, generating income was a way to help relieve the pressure.

Finally, at fifty-seven years of age, Coolidge achieved true wealth building. If Coolidge had been my client, I would have worked at trying to get

---

364 (Ball 2021) page 11. Even after the job offer from Charles Merrill, Coolidge chose JP Morgan to manage his money. I would suspect the reason was that he felt Merrill was catastrophizing the crash and that it wasn't necessary to get out of the market.
365 (Waldo 1935).
366 (Ball 2021) pages 11–12. Coolidge put money to work in September 1929—right before the crash. He purchased three thousand shares of Standard Brands Incorporated for a total of $96,000 on September 5, 1929.
367 (Waldo 1935).

him to see that home ownership and a mortgage when just starting out was not as precarious as he thought it was. We would have had to work through the financial rigidness he imposed to get him to feel safe in a financial decision. Yet, when he finally jumped into homeownership, he had less than three years to enjoy it. At age sixty, he passed away suddenly from a coronary thrombosis.

Thriftiness is both a blessing and a curse. Coolidge's thriftiness allowed him to be a great political candidate, and he never lost his humility. But thriftiness can be a slippery slope. It clearly helped him live within his means, but it may also have been a way to manage anxiety. As a result, he never really *enjoyed* money or the fruits of his labor the way most of us would want to. Coolidge would have been better served financially if he had a touch of self-interest.

THE VALUES OF THE SUMMER OF 1946

In a sixty-seven-day period in 1946, three of our most charismatic modern presidents were born: Donald Trump on June 14, 1946, George W. Bush on July 6, 1946, and finally William Jefferson Clinton on August 19, 1946. It seems statistically unlikely for three presidents to be born so close together.

Actually, it wasn't the stars aligning as much as a US military operation called Operation Magic Carpet that commenced on September 6, 1945, and lasted for 360 days, bringing home over eight million Americans from the European, Pacific, and Asian World War II theatres. Both Bush and Clinton had fathers who fought in the war and returned home during that period to start families, so 1946 was a banner year for childbirth in the US—the Baby Boom had officially begun.[368]

While they all were born the same year, you couldn't have three more different individuals. All three are beloved by some, polarizing to others. Yet what they had in common is one thing: the ability to grow their wealth.

Using a mix of money, charm, and relationship building, Bush became part of a group that acquired the Texas Rangers in 1989 for $83 million ($207 million in 2024 dollars). In truth, he didn't have a lot of money as he

---

368 (The Menke Group n.d.). It should be noted that Donald Trump was the fourth of five children that were born from 1937 to 1948. His birth was not related to Operation Magic Carpet.

only put in 0.6 percent of the purchase price of $500,000.[369] But another key factor was that he wanted to create something of his own and not just be seen as George H.W. Bush's kid. Part of the Bush family philosophy is that each generation must strike out on their own.

W himself noted that "I was also the person that aggressively sought the deal. I was a pit bull on the pant leg of opportunity. I wouldn't let go."[370] For Bush, it was the additional value of tenacity that made the difference.

If you are going to rely on knowing the right people to make money, you also need to have strong due diligence skills. When it comes to financial matters, due diligence can be defined as "an investigation, audit, or review performed to confirm facts or details of a matter under consideration."[371] What I am really getting at is that when you are handed an opportunity, you need to ask a lot of questions.

And guess who is really good at this?

Donald Trump.

Love him or hate him, he does have certain financial skills that are good for wealth building. There is no question that Trump's charisma, along with his family wealth, has enabled him to build relationships that have helped him create a real estate empire. He is always working the phones and taking on big risks (often in a theatrical way).

When it comes to Trump, his money values are focused using charm, relationships, and negotiation to create scale. Everything with him is BIG. And he can get away with it as he is incredibly sophisticated about money and isn't afraid to say it.

These financial values were very much on display when Trump's show *The Apprentice* launched on January 8, 2004, along with the sound of The O'Jays singing "For The Love of Money." In the opening minutes, he charismatically gives what he sees as the secret sauce to wealth building: "*I used my brain, used my negotiating skills and I worked it all out.*"

And that sounds good in a television opening, but there is a lot more to it. If we had to distill down what Trump does that can be added to all

---

369 Bush financed his $500,000 by obtaining a loan from Midland Bank where he was on the board of directors. His collateral was Harlan Stock, an oil company that he was also on the board of.
370 (Pooley and Gwynne 1999).
371 (Chen 2024).

of our financial planning: he asks a lot of questions. On *The Apprentice*, he even shows you how he does due diligence on a sophisticated level. He calls his top two executives, George and Carolyn, his "eyes and ears" (and in later seasons they are replaced with his kids). Like a family office operation, Trump wants to handle the parts he enjoys—the relationships and the negotiation—but leaves the tough part of due diligence to those who are going to look at the transaction with unemotional eyes. They will lack bias and will focus on the pure mechanics of process.

Trump learned the importance of questions early in his career. When he was twenty-three years old, he became an investor in a Broadway show called *Paris Is Out*. He put up half of the $140,000 needed to produce the show (the equivalent of $1.1 million in 2024 dollars). The producer he partnered with, David Black, recalled to the *New York Times* decades later that Trump "took him to the private Metropolitan Club, peppered him with questions on the ins and outs of the theatre business," adding, "He had done his homework, and that was unusual."[372]

But it was not unusual for Trump, given that his mantra is essentially *trust no one completely and ask questions*. After all, he has found that diligence often protects his interests.

CLINTON VERSUS TRUMP

Now, the value of not trusting others might seem like an odd one, but the inverse of this is that one can be too trusting when it comes to money.

The ability to turn down a deal might have served another president born in the summer of 1946. Bill Clinton's values include the power of charisma and relationships. But one of Clinton's most well-known financial transactions went off the rails due to his overvaluing relationships when he lacked financial sophistication in his early thirties. In many ways, he is the opposite of Trump when it comes to trust—he's simply too trusting. His money values center on believing in the connection he's made.

One night back in 1978, two couples ran into each other while waiting for a table at the family-run Black Eye Pea restaurant in Little Rock, Arkansas. They were old friends with a shared professional history going back ten years. Jim and Susan McDougal had known Bill and Hillary Clinton

---

372 (Paulson 2016).

for years, and over dinner, the McDougals mentioned that they had just agreed to buy and develop a vacation home community in the Ozarks. Six local businessmen had formed 101 River Development and acquired a 3,200-acre property that could be developed to create an ideal retirement community. The group packaged the lots to sell to developers, including the McDougals. At first glance, it seemed like a no-brainer. With the local real estate boom in full swing, what could possibly go wrong? Even the name of the property in question had a tantalizing sound to it: Whitewater.

At the time, Bill Clinton was the recently elected Attorney General, and Hillary was starting her legal career at the Rose Law Firm. Building wealth was part of their ambitious plans, and they both felt they had bright professional futures ahead of them. Still, as Hillary later put it, she was concerned that "because politics is an inherently unstable profession, we needed to build up a nest egg. I had never given much thought to savings or investments until I realized that if our growing family were going to have any financial cushion, it would be mostly my responsibility."[373]

But while Hillary had the more prestigious and better paying job, it was Bill who brought a unique currency to the equation. Clinton was a public servant with a political job paying $26,000 a year ($123,000 in 2024 dollars). Yet he has always been a charmer with charisma to spare. The common takeaway from those who engage with him is that he has a way of connecting with you so that you feel like you're the only person in the room. (Interestingly, the same is often said of Trump.)

Yet for all that, Bill Clinton had a challenging relationship with money. He had seen his mother struggle to support the family along with his two stepfathers. But while he didn't get a great education in personal finance, he did learn the power of connecting with people. To him, connection was a way to create wealth.

Bill met Jim McDougal while he was working for Senator Fulbright in 1967. The two built a friendship, but in many ways, it was like an older brother–younger brother connection. To the then young and unsophisticated Clinton, McDougal was trustworthy and wise.

Fast forward to 1978. In the years since he had met Clinton, McDougal had gone from congressional aide to real estate developer. He had had some success, and the deal he pitched that night sounded intriguing. In

---

373 (H. Clinton 2003).

Calvin Coolidge Is Rather Thrifty

terms of numbers, the deal was straightforward. It was $203,000 for 230 acres of land. But there was one issue: the Clintons really did not have the money to embark on such an investment. To give context, it would be like deciding to purchase a stretch of property in today's dollars in the range of $1,400,000.

If I were advising the Clintons at the time, I would have asked three key questions that help in financial decision-making.

"First, Bill and Hillary, what due diligence have you performed?"

In his Whitewater testimony, Bill answered that question by referencing a previous investment just a year earlier in 1977 where McDougal "asked me if I wanted to invest a small amount of money in one in Pulaski County. And I did, I invested, as I recall, about $2,800 for about a year and a half, and I liquidated the investment and made about $5,000. So I had a profit of $2,100, it was a nice profit."[374] (This profit is the equivalent of $10,750 in 2024 dollars).

His response basically translates to, "I invested with a friend because I thought he knew what he was doing based on a previous transaction with him." The problem is investment pitches from friends tend to highlight the potential upside and under-promote the overall risks. The idea that a simple land investment would create great riches sounds wonderful. But that should have alerted them that something didn't seem right.

Friends know our strengths—and weaknesses—and McDougal knew Clinton's. Clinton wasn't interested in business and investing, so he knew very little about either subject. And on the surface, it seemed like a fair exchange: the Clintons got a good real estate deal and in return, McDougal got to say that the gubernatorial candidate and his wife were investors. It gave the project "cachet."

So basically, Clinton was an easy mark, given his philosophy on money. Clients like this are challenging, and sometimes you are just trying to keep them from harming themselves.

So that leads us to question #2.

---

374 Deposition of William Jefferson Clinton as Defense Witness, *US v. McDougal*, taped April 28, 1996. https://www.pbs.org/wgbh/pages/frontline/shows/arkansas/docs/clintondepo.html.

All the Presidents' Money

"What are all the potential risks and what can go wrong here?"

One of the striking details of the Whitewater land purchase came from the banker who helped finance the property. When the Clintons came into the bank to sign the documents on the loan, the banker, Frank Burge, noted that they were "uninquisitive." McDougal himself even felt that money "never got [Clinton] excited" and that his decision to do Whitewater was similar to his deciding to buy a potted plant.[375]

After twenty years of working with clients, I can tell you the reason they were "uninquisitive"—they didn't understand the deal, and they didn't want to look stupid asking questions, which is a pretty common mistake in personal finance. Instead, they relied on McDougal.

I suspect if they had questioned McDougal, he would have mentioned that the biggest risk was that they couldn't sell the land and they would be carrying the note. There were other risks too, but McDougal likely would not have mentioned big economic issues like stagflation and rising interest rates. Furthermore, a full infrastructure needed to be developed and put in place—who was going to pay for that?

There is a psychological term that describes what happened in this moment with the Clintons: "irrational exuberance." It's a great phrase that was used in the 1990s by Clinton's own Federal Reserve chair, Alan Greenspan. It's a common phenomenon where basically an investor believes the past performance is indicative of future performance and thus the market is likely to keep going up.

And that leads us to the third question I would ask them.

"Finally, in the event this is ever on the front page of the *Wall Street Journal*, what will the optics be like?" (I actually use this question a lot to get my clients to really think through what this could look like to an outside party.)

The thing about this purchase was that it was taking place while Clinton was running for governor, so the transaction could be seen as capitalizing on his public office. Together with the McDougals, the Clintons formed

---

375 Ibid., page 148, 151.

Calvin Coolidge Is Rather Thrifty

a corporation called Whitewater to borrow $183,000 from the bank. The McDougals actually had financial assets, and they acted as guarantor. And since each couple had to pony up another $20,000 for the down payment, the Clintons went to another bank for that loan. Basically, the Clintons added even more risk to an already risky investment. And once the land was purchased, the deal went pear shaped fairly quickly. Interest rates skyrocketed. The idea of retirement homes in the Ozarks wasn't gaining traction. As a result, the land dropped in value.

It's possible that if these three questions had been asked, they may still have done the deal. But they would have been better educated about the risks and wouldn't have been so trusting. I really wish I had been at that diner back in 1978. I could have saved them from a lot of heartache and big investment losses. And even if they had been made fully aware of the risks and decided to go forward with the purchase anyway, I would have insisted on building protections into the structure of this deal to help on the downside risk.

What the wealthy will tell you is that you can never overlook the importance of due diligence as a money value. It's a way to ensure you avoid pitfalls that can undo your wealth. It is also a method to ensure that when an investment goes right, it can't just be chalked up to luck. So regardless of how you feel about Clinton or Trump, the advice here is to cultivate relationships like Clinton, but kick the tires before you buy like Trump.

EXTERNAL VERSUS INTERNAL

Thriftiness was an internal value that Coolidge placed on himself. W's values include upholding family ideals. Both Trump and Clinton value relationships when it comes to money—although both have different feelings on due diligence. All of these values are based on one's life experience.

Studies have shown that as an individual gets wealthier, their overall empathy can diminish, and their entitlement increases. Further, money can be a corrupting influence. At UC Berkeley, researchers studied driving patterns at busy intersections and found that upper-class drivers (based on vehicle status) were four times more likely to cut off vehicles at busy intersections and three times more likely to cut off pedestrians at crosswalks.[376]

---

376 (Piff, et al. 2012)

Through their extensive research, they determined that due to their resources, wealthy individuals can demonstrate greater unethical behavior as they have more favorable attitudes toward greed.[377]

One of the biggest stories in America's history of greed and personal finance is that of slavery. It is a story where one group's greed for wealth and power puts another group in chains. And there is no better example of this than our eleventh president, James K. Polk.

AN INTERESTING LEGACY

When presidential legacies are rated, a lot of envy occurs over Polk's impact on the United States. Now, we don't talk about Polk much these days, and if you're struggling to remember what he looked like, he's the one with the mullet hairstyle.[378]

But the reason other presidents and historians are fascinated by Polk's legacy is that he was our expansionist president. In his one-term presidency, he grew the United States by over one million square miles through the Mexican War and a treaty with Great Britain all under the banner of Manifest Destiny.

And that's probably all you learned about him in school before you moved along to Zachary Taylor and his unfortunate encounter with a bowl of cherries. But Polk consistently ranks in the top third of presidents.

A RETIREMENT PLAN, A WILL, AND A PURCHASE

In the winter of 1849, Polk was very busy organizing his financial affairs. One of his pledges when he ran as a Democrat in 1845 was that he promised to serve one term. It had been a productive term, in large part due to his energy and work ethic. It was noted he had taken only twenty-seven days of vacation while president.[379] Now, as his term neared its conclusion, he was very focused on the future.

---

377   Ibid.
378   Presidents with mullets apparently became a thing in the world of 2023 memes. AI-generated images made everyone curious as to how different presidents would look. Even Newsweek and CNN did stories on it. You can check it out at https://www.newsweek.com/what-us-presidents-would-look-like-mullet-ai-1784814.
379   (Price 2023).

Calvin Coolidge Is Rather Thrifty

The presidency had been profitable for Polk. He had gone from making $2,000 as governor of Tennessee to $25,000 as the chief executive. In his first year as president, he had worked hard to pay down his campaign debts of $16,000. It was hard initially as all additional cash flow went to debt. He even noted to a friend that "I find that my present position is a no money-making affair."[380]

But once his debt was gone, things shifted financially for Polk. He was flush with cash. Despite the cost of entertaining in the White House, Polk would ultimately save over $40,000 of the $100,000 earned in his four years as president. By 1849, he felt firm in financial security.

Polk was aware that he and his wife, Sarah, were retiring as one of the youngest presidents and First Ladies at age fifty-three and forty-six, respectively. And he had quite a vision of retirement.

During his presidency, he and Sarah visited Mount Vernon. He was taken with the estate and how George Washington had built it. His hope was that he and Sarah would have such an estate in retirement to entertain and enjoy.

By 1847, he had found the property he was hoping for: an 1818 home previously owned by the man who had taken Polk on as a young attorney. Polk made an offer of $7,000 to the man's estate, and the home was his.[381] At the time, it was considered one of the grandest homes in Nashville. But by the time Polk acquired it, the house was in no shape for a president. The Polks worked with architects to redesign the property. By the time they completed the renovation, they had easily sunk another $12,000 into the property.[382] They renamed it Polk Place.

A DARK, PASSIVE INCOME STREAM

Along with finishing up the home, Polk was planning ahead to finance his retirement. With his excess salary, he had saved $11,000, which he had placed in Treasurys yielding 6 percent. And of course, there was no presi-

---

380 Letter James K. Polk to Samuel P. Walker, dated September 24, 1845.
381 (Armistead Jr 1956) page 136.
382 It should be noted that when the renovation was about to begin, a unique situation arose. A building used to store gunpowder near the Polk's new home was struck by lightning. The ensuing explosion caused two of the walls of the Polk house, along with the windows, to explode.

dential pension yet. But Polk knew he had a passive income stream to rely on. He had been developing this income stream for almost two decades, as he was acutely aware of the ups and downs of political life. And the source of that stream was slave trading.

Polk was born to a slaveholding family. Previous generations on both sides had owned slaves, as did generations of his wife Sarah's Childress relatives. The Polk family legacy was the inheritance and continued enslavement of human beings.[383]

Think about that. Today, wealthy families hand over businesses, stocks, art, and other valuable assets through wealth transfer. It's hard to imagine that just 140 years ago, that type of financial transfer also included slaves. And as we will discuss later, it was common for estate plans to include these provisions.

Sadly, Polk was not unique among our presidents in that regard. Twelve of our presidents were slaveholders—basically, a quarter of all our presidents. Nor was he alone in understanding slavery was morally wrong. All of them knew. And despite that awareness, they could be alarmingly proprietary about it; Washington himself not only owned slaves, but also when one named Ona Judge escaped from Mount Vernon, he placed weekly ads in newspapers, hired people to try tracking her down, and even misused his presidential authority to seek her return. (He was unsuccessful, and Ms. Judge remained free for the rest of her life.) So, in the cases of our slaveholding presidents, their financial stories are always overshadowed by the fact that they made their money using enslaved people as free labor.

Owning slaves and owning land in the South often went hand in hand. Polk, like other presidents, was often focused on land speculation. But in addition to benefiting financially from using free labor by turning a profit as a plantation owner, Polk supplemented that income by engaging in slave trading—buying and selling slaves for profit.[384]

As we noted, he initially inherited slaves first from his father and then from his brothers. When he married his wife, she brought with her ten

---

[383] Polk had inherited nine slaves from his father and his deceased brothers. (Dusinberre 2003) page 13. Dusinberre noted that Polk's father had fifty-three slaves at his death that he passed through his estate plan to his widow and ten surviving children.

[384] Technically, slave trading consisted of capturing, selling, and buying slaves. Polk typically bought and held.

slaves.[385] When he bought his first plantation in 1831, he immediately acquired three slaves for $930 to help with the growing and harvesting of cotton. The better his crop, the more excess money, which he would use to acquire more slaves.[386]

And he hired an agent to do his bidding. From Polk's letters to his agent, these purchases were often discussed just like the purchases he made of mules and other plantation animals.

What is important to note is that when the value of his slaves went up, that impacted his overall return on the plantation (which I'll get to in a moment). He wasn't successful at first. Yet after the Panic of 1837, his plantation consistently generated income. As Polk's political career grew, those profits often subsidized his living expenses.

When a person is willing to enslave human beings to turn a profit, it is, among other things, a measure of how greedy they are. And Polk's greed was about to get worse.

A DEFINED VISION TOWARD BUILDING WEALTH

In the election of 1844, Polk was between a rock and a hard place. In a bid to win the presidency, he had to appear electable to both slave-owning Southerners and anti-slavery Northerners. Polk was able to appeal to both sides by making the argument that while he did own slaves, he had inherited approximately twelve to fifteen of them and was not "a large slaveholder."[387] Apart from the fact that this was a barefaced lie, it's hard to imagine how claiming that you were only a slave owner by birth and didn't keep all that many could have placated the anti-slavery portion of the electorate, but apparently it satisfied enough of them to put Polk in the White House.

Meanwhile, Texas was about to be annexed, and all that land would be available for growing crops, which in turn meant the demand for slave labor would drive up their value. By 1846, the price of slaves had increased 30 percent, and Polk's net worth increased accordingly.[388]

---

385 (Marsh 1977) page 7.
386 In the 1830s, Polk's correspondence, both to him and from him, detail these transactions. I am indebted to Richard Marsh's research in 1977, which details these transactions in-depth.
387 Polk's ally Gideon Pillow had created this defense. The Southerners loved it.
388 (Dusinberre 2003) page 53.

All the Presidents' Money

As his debts were paid off due to his higher income, he had excess cash flow. His strategy was straightforward. First, in order to hide the true number of slaves he owned, he needed an agent who would be discreet. He found one in Robert Campbell. Campbell also helped oversee his plantation. Campbell and Polk devised a shorthand to discuss his purchases, and they made sure the purchases were in Campbell's name, not Polk's. In many of their communications, it was not uncommon for Polk to write, "I need scarcely repeat to you my former request that as my *private business* does not concern the public, you will keep it to yourself."[389] Secrecy was key.

We can see this early in his presidency in 1846. A slew of these cryptic messages was sent to Campbell. "Majr Childress informs me that he made you fully acquainted with my wishes and of the description of the property which I want. He informed you also of the reasons why, it should not be known to anyone but him and yourself that you were making the purchases for me. There is nothing wrong [in] it, but still the public have no interest in knowing it, and in my situation it is best they should not."[390] The "property" in question was five teenage slaves that he acquired for $2,347.[391]

That they were teenagers is further evidence of Polk's greed because young slaves would eventually have children, which meant he would also own them—a built-in return on invested capital as more slaves to work the plantation and more cotton to sell.

On another occasion, Polk bought a twelve-year-old slave boy for $392. His agent then quickly resold the boy at $450.[392]

In the years he was president, he was generating at least $2,700 a year in excess profit. He reinvested the money into the plantation by buying more slaves. Nineteen new slaves were acquired. But here's the most bizarre part of all of this: while he was flush with cash, he wanted to use only the money from the plantation profit to buy slaves. He was okay buying, selling, and using people for free labor against their will, yet he felt it was improper to use the funds coming from his presidential salary to buy slaves—definitely

---

389 Letter James K. Polk to Robert Campbell Jr., dated January 23, 1847.
390 Letter James K. Polk to Robert Campbell Jr., dated August 15, 1846. Brackets in original.
391 Letter Robert Campbell to James K. Polk, dated August 27, 1846.
392 (Dusinberre 2003) page 18. Dusinberre does a phenomenal job of working through Polk's papers. In his footnotes, he mentions that in studying the papers, he can determine the age of the slave based on the price.

one of the most nauseating cases of selective morality I've ever come across.[393]

FITTINGLY, JUST REWARDS

As Polk finalized his plans for his retirement in 1849, he also went to work on his estate plan. In the event of his death, he wanted to protect his asset base and make sure his wife was protected after his death.

But Polk did something interesting. A provision at the end of his will stated, "Should I survive her, unless influenced by circumstances which I do not now foresee, it is my intention to emancipate all of my slaves, and I have full confidence, that if at her death she shall deem it proper, she will emancipate them."[394]

At first glance, it appears he frees his slaves. It would be easy to assume that finally he sees that owning slaves is not morally right.

But upon closer reading, it's not that clear if that is what he is really mandating.

Polk says he would have freed his slaves *if he survived her*—but the truth is, that is mere conjecture. As for the direction to his wife, he merely lets her decide if it is proper.

Don't forget, Polk was a lawyer. If he really wanted her to free the slaves at her death, he could have put in much more restrictive and prescriptive language to have her do so. He was probably very aware that history may judge him. Under that light, he would want to look magnanimous versus greedy and self-interested. As we will see with George Washington, a manumission clause in the will might soften the harm done to the historical record by owning slaves.

Polk didn't get much time to enjoy his retirement income stream—117 days, to be exact. He ended up catching cholera after leaving office on a farewell tour of the South. He died on June 15, 1849. But Polk was successful in creating that retirement income stream. His wife, Sarah, enjoyed it for fifty-two years after his death.

---

393   Ibid., page 205.
394   Will of James K. Polk, dated February 28, 1849. Full text of the will can be found in (Armistead Jr 1956) on pages 137–139.

All the Presidents' Money

And as for their slaves, the Civil War intervened, and their slaves were freed under the Thirteenth Amendment of the Constitution. We will never know if Sarah would have freed their slaves of her own accord.

History has given Polk the ultimate comeuppance to his greed and self-interest. Polk kept copious records that included his slave purchases. He didn't expect to die young and pretty much as soon as he left the White House. If he had lived, it's likely he would have destroyed the correspondence that detailed these transactions. We wouldn't have known he behaved in this manner. Instead, the historical record is so detailed and clear that we know exactly what he did.

Chapter Seven

FDR AND ELVIS GET THE WORLD ALL SHOOK UP
(OR CHARITABLE INTENT)

The year 1956 was the year of Elvis Presley. Teenagers across the nation couldn't get enough of "Hound Dog," "Don't Be Cruel," and "Heartbreak Hotel." There were over 110 tour stops across the country.[395] Girls screamed his name, and boys dressed like him. And now as November neared, a new opportunity arose for Elvis—starring in the film *Love Me Tender*.

It was quite a whirlwind for this young man from Tupelo, Mississippi. Then Colonel Tom Parker, Elvis's manager, got a call from the US government who needed a favor: Would Elvis be willing to get the polio vaccine publicly? It would be quite a statement to the teenagers of America if the man with the swiveling hips could help them fight a disease of paralysis.

In today's world, we're pretty used to seeing celebrities as the face of a vaccine. But in 1956, this was revolutionary. The US government was in trouble. Despite Jonas Salk's discovery of the polio vaccine, Americans—and especially those aged fourteen to eighteen—weren't rushing to their doctors to get it.

---

395 Official Blog of Graceland available at https://www.graceland.com/blog/posts/elvis-presleys-tour-dates-in-1956#:~:text=Fans%20heard%20his%20music%20on,110%20tour%20stops%20in%201956.

The request resonated with Elvis who said, "Whatever I do, I always want to do my best for the teenagers. I certainly never wanna do anything that would be a wrong influence."[396]

On October 28, 1956, Elvis got the vaccine backstage at the *Ed Sullivan Show*. The impact was immediate: teenagers went from a vaccine rate of 0.6 percent to 80 percent. Even the *New York Times* approved, noting that he "is a polite, personable, quick-witted and charming young man."[397]

While this is an interesting historical tidbit regarding Elvis, it also is the culmination of one president's charitable focus. But before we explore that story, it is important to understand the role of charitable planning when it comes to wealth.

THE FUNDAMENTALS OF WEALTH AND CHARITY

Modern-day wealth is focused on access. Access can be to the right schools, the right career path, or the right investments. It can also provide access to a whole area of wealth: the world of charity. While all of us can be charitable, for those with means, it is a different personal finance experience.

There is a moment when a person starts to make money that the technical aspects of personal finance gives way to a discussion of values. In my practice, it usually comes during a tax-planning discussion. Given there is little available to high-net-worth taxpayers in terms of mitigating tax, the one deduction available is charitable donations.

While most Americans may give to charity, it is when you have means that you can start to have a more focused approach to giving. The *2023 Bank of America Study of Philanthropy* found that 85.1 percent of high-net-worth households of $1 million or more in the United States give to charity with an average donation by these households in 2022 of $34,917. Yet, even among high-net-worth households, there was some disparity. For those in this group who considered themselves "experts" at giving, their average was $43,838. Further, on average, high-net-worth households gave to seven charities.[398]

---

396 (O'Brien 2021) Elvis can be heard making this statement in a video produced by the Ed Sullivan YouTube Channel to promote vaccines for the Covid-19 epidemic.
397 (Presley Receives A City Polio Shot 1956).
398 (Bank of America 2023).

FDR and Elvis Get the World All Shook Up

Having a defined charitable strategy also gives wealthy individuals a feeling of "this is what having wealth means." It is typical that when you start to have significant assets, so much of it focuses on maintaining the asset base, mitigating taxes, and being private about your personal finances, as it can be an uncomfortable topic with friends and family. But donating to charity can be a freeing and creative experience. It's a way of expressing yourself with money that reflects who you really are.

High-net-worth donors have evolved over the years and have become a core tenant in wealth management.

And that brings up the three-part equation of high-net-worth giving:

Intent + Donation = Impact

Donor intent (also known as charitable intent) can have a pretty broad meaning, but it generally is what is expressed in the words, actions, beliefs, and giving practices of the donor. Usually there is a personal feeling in what creates this intent. In modern-day philanthropy, it's not uncommon for wealthy families to spend months working through a mission statement that captures this type of intent so that the money does make a difference.

Donations are quite straightforward: it is a gift of cash or other appreciated property to a nonprofit organization to help achieve its goals. But this is where the IRS has a heavy hand in how we shape them. Understanding and documenting the value of donations can be arduous and technical. Further, donors often want to focus on getting the maximum donation and are willing to work through different timing and valuation strategies.

Finally, there is impact. It used to be that impact was measured on whether it benefited the charity. But as donors have become more sophisticated and make larger donations, they are more focused on what we call "high-impact philanthropy." This is linking donations not just to helping a charity, but what social impact it will have to get the best bang for the buck. Think of the Gates Foundation trying to eradicate malaria. They want to solve problems—and they want to put metrics around those donations to understand how deeply it is addressing those problems.

The presidents also capture these elements in their charitable donations. Millard Fillmore was not a successful president, but post-presidency he focused on his charitable intent. Richard Nixon was all about the tax deduction. And finally, FDR is an example of creating high-impact philanthropy that can be measured by the difference it makes.

THE INTENT OF MILLARD FILLMORE

Today, we require our modern presidents to be charitable. They all have foundations and initiatives tied to the goals of their presidencies. But then again, they all monetize their endeavors post-presidency (thanks, Jerry Ford!), which makes being aware of their optics key. They have to ensure that others see them giving back to society for the unique opportunity set they have been given.

This idea isn't limited to modern-day presidencies. History has seen a lot of great charitable presidents. John F. Kennedy believed that donating his $100,000 presidential salary was the right thing to do given his family's wealth. The charities he supported included the Boy Scouts, the Girl Scouts, and the United Negro College Fund.[399]

Jimmy Carter was still building houses for Habitat for Humanity well into his mid-nineties (true!). And, yes, Washington did gift one hundred shares of James River Canal Company stock to Liberty Hall Academy. In appreciation, they renamed the school Washington Academy, and sixty years later it became Washington and Lee University.

But I think it's important to look at our more obscure presidents to find someone who was charitable but in a unique way.

And that leads us to Millard Fillmore.

Yes, Fillmore.

I know you are wracking your brain trying to figure out where he falls in the mix. The thing about Fillmore is that, not only does he typically rank in the bottom quartile of presidents,[400] but his legacy is so bad it is a stain on our country's history.

The Fugitive Slave Act of 1850 was enacted during his presidency. This act stated that if a slave escaped and was caught, they were required to be returned to their owner, regardless of whether they were in a free state or not.

---

399 (United Press International 1962).
400 Interestingly, Fillmore consistently ranks as the seventh worst president from C-SPAN, US News, Siena College's Presidential Experts Poll, and the Presidential Greatness Survey. https://www.usnews.com/news/special-reports/the-worst-presidents/slideshows/the-10-worst-presidents.

Fillmore not only signed this into law, but he vigorously enforced it. Hence the bad reputation. That law was as egregious and horrifying as it sounds.

I'm not here to redeem him. It's pretty much impossible not to think of the pain, brutality, and cruelty that Fillmore's endorsement of the Fugitive Slave Act caused many people.[401] But his post-presidential life is pretty interesting when it comes to charitable intent. Let me explain.

LAYERS OF CHARITABLE INTENT

Fillmore's life in brief is the makings of a great American story: the second-poorest president at birth, he was raised in the harsh frontier and suffered incredible hardship. After a brief apprenticeship to a wool dresser, he found his way into studying law, became a lawyer, and grew a successful practice. He was then thrust into politics, ultimately becoming the president of the United States due to Zachary Taylor dying after consuming iced milk and cherries over the Fourth of July.

It's the stuff of Horatio Alger—or even his contemporary Abraham Lincoln.[402] And it would be as compelling a rags-to-riches story as Lincoln's but for the aforementioned involvement in the Fugitive Slave Act.[403] What made Fillmore's involvement in the act so surprising was that he wasn't a Southerner. Rather he was from Buffalo, New York.

Buffalo had been a key part of the Underground Railroad for many slaves seeking freedom, as it shared a border with Canada and the Niagara Frontier. Slavery was abhorrent to the majority of its residents, some of whom included very well-known abolitionists.

---

401 It should be noted that even at the time of his death, his contemporaries were well aware of the tragedy of the Fugitive Slave Act and its impact on Fillmore's legacy. But as he was a living person that they had interacted with, they saw his actions more nuanced.

402 It should be noted that a lot of the newspaper articles at his death in 1874 noted how he was such a great American story rising from poverty to be president. Interestingly, Fillmore and Lincoln had a professional relationship that culminated in 1861 when Lincoln came to Buffalo and stayed as a guest of Fillmore. Ultimately, they differed on slavery and severed ties. However, Fillmore led the Buffalo delegation to view the Lincoln funeral procession in 1865.

403 The act also included provisions that admitted California as a free state, and the territories of Utah and New Mexico could vote on whether or not they would allow slavery.

All the Presidents' Money

In 1850, when the act was being considered, Fillmore's first wife, Abigail, had given him a startling prophecy: if he signed it, he would never be able to recover his reputation politically. But he felt he had no choice.

Fillmore signed it, and she was right. He didn't recover his political reputation.[404] He returned to Buffalo in 1853 after being easily defeated by Franklin Pierce. He also didn't recover his reputation in general. The stain of the act hung over him. The people of Buffalo strongly disapproved of his signing—and enforcing—the act. For many, it was shocking that the Fugitive Slave Act came from one of their own.

Almost immediately, there were repercussions in Buffalo. The reputation that had taken fifty years to build gave way practically overnight.

The first shot across the bow came from within the Unitarian Church that he himself had been a charter member of twenty years prior, since 1831. Days before Fillmore signed the Fugitive Slave Act in September 1850, Reverend Dr. George Washington Hosmer, himself a declared abolitionist, received a letter from a female congregant, Sallie Holley, discussing her support of the spiritual life she had inside the Unitarian Church:

"Yet nevertheless, I think I cannot consent that my name shall stand on the books of a church which will countenance voting for any pro-slavery presidential candidate. Think of a woman-whipper and a baby-stealer being countenanced as a Christian! My anti-slavery sympathies burn stronger and stronger."[405]

She doesn't beat around the bush in terms of how she sees Fillmore. She's comparing him morally to someone who beats women and steals children. Further, she's criticizing the president of the United States to a top Buffalo religious leader as a woman in 1850. Now, Holley was an outspoken abolitionist who fought against slavery throughout her whole life. Yet, she was bold in writing these words. It is not unreasonable to suppose that her words reflected the feelings of other church members. Fillmore was beginning to have his reputation undone in Buffalo, and he still was in the White House.

---

404 Interestingly, he wasn't in favor of slavery. When he signed the act, he wrote to Daniel Webster, "God knows I detest slavery, but…we must endure it and give it such protection as is guaranteed by the Constitution till we can get rid of it without destroying the last hope of free government in the world."

405 (Holley 1899) page 69. Letter Sallie Holley to Rev. Dr. G. Hosmer, dated September 16, 1850.

But it got worse from there for Fillmore. Buffalo's pride in the president being a local boy had been strong.[406] Even those who were proud started to turn away.

Writing almost fifty years after the act was signed, local Buffalo historian Frank Severance described the scene that awaited Fillmore. "Mr. Fillmore was denounced in the most intemperate terms. In his home city of Buffalo, some of whom had hitherto prided themselves on his distinguished acquaintance, estranged themselves from him, and on his return to Buffalo, he found cold and formal treatment from people whom he had formerly greeted as friends. Insults were offered to him; and the changed demeanor of many of his townsmen showed itself even in the church which he attended. Certain ardent souls there were who refused any longer to worship where he did."[407]

In a world where the church was often the center of spiritual and social life, Fillmore was now persona non grata. It was a devastating blow to him. Further, he already knew the experience of not belonging. He had experienced that as an impoverished boy who had to hope for the grace and kindness of society to help him succeed.

FEW PAPERS BUT MANY CHARITABLE ACTS

Tragically, Abigail died one month after he left office in 1853. Fillmore was left adrift upon his return to Buffalo. Most historians are quick to note that throughout Fillmore's life, he was deeply insecure and struggled with personal uncertainty.[408] And suddenly he was alone, in a town that had severely judged him. He was not able to focus his time. He himself noted that he couldn't go back to the law as it wouldn't be fair for anyone up against a former president.[409] In his correspondence with Dorothea Dix, Fillmore expressed how adrift he was after his wife's death and that he often spent time at his son's law office daily as a form of amusement. Finally, in 1858, he was remarried—to a wealthy widow.

---

406 It should be noted that he was Buffalo's first president. Thirty years later, Grover Cleveland, who hailed from Buffalo, would serve two separate terms as president.
407 (Severance 1899) pages 269–270.
408 (Finkelman 2011) Finkelman also discusses this in his speech for Buffalo and Erie County Historical Society in Buffalo, New York, on June 23, 2011. It can be found at C-SPAN at https://www.c-span.org/video/?301493-1/millard-fillmore.
409 (Snyder 1975) page 163.

Before going any further in his story, I should tell you this about Fillmore: his life is a bit mysterious because, unlike other presidents, he didn't leave copious records. Additionally, a badly worded provision in his estate plan convinced his son Powers to destroy his papers.

As a result, historians have been limited to a few of his papers that survived as well as responses to Fillmore's letters. In biographies written about Fillmore, his last twenty years are basically a listing of all the charities he established or supported in Buffalo. It's as though Fillmore decided his best course of action was simply to bear the shuns and act honorably.

He spent his post-presidency as a "one-man progressive movement" and became a civic leader for Buffalo.[410] He became chancellor of the newly established University of Buffalo. He helped organize and became the vice president of the local Society for the Prevention of Cruelty to Animals, the second of its kind in the nation,[411] and the Buffalo Young Men's Association. The list went on and on.

SEEKING REDEMPTION THROUGH CHARITY

This brings us back to donor intent and why someone donates their money (as well as time and reputation to a cause). In studies on why high-net-worth individuals donate, the top five reasons donors give come down to belief in the charitable mission, belief in making a difference, personal fulfillment or enjoyment, seeking to remedy an issue that you are close to, and to give back.[412] Yet, in working with these individuals, it is more common that it is a mix of all of these reasons.

One family I work with gives to charities focused on helping foster youths. While there are numerous charities for this issue, the requirements they look for in donating include keeping the money local and having a personal engagement with the organization to make a difference. These parameters are very important to them—especially given the size of the donations they make.

In a similar vein, Fillmore's charitable endeavors are multi-layered. Here is where we have to use a little historical speculation, along with reason, to

---

410 Interview with Cynthia Van Ness, Director of Library and Archives, Buffalo History Museum, January 18, 2023.
411 (Organization of the Society for The Prevention Of Cruelty to Animals 1867).
412 (Bank of America 2023) page 20.

determine what his intent was by his actions. First and foremost, Fillmore had an appreciation for Buffalo and the opportunities the city had provided him. Buffalo and Fillmore grew in sync together over the course of his lifetime. As the town grew, so did Fillmore's involvement in civic duty. His charitable intent was an act of appreciation to a city that had given him opportunities beyond what a poor boy could have imagined.

Further, there is a social aspect to being civically engaged. Prior to Ford, there was no clear-cut path. Being charitably focused literally gave him something to do with his time.

Finally, there may have been something deeper with his charitable intent. Fillmore may have been seeking *redemption* for the actions he took as president in that the good acts he took on negated some of the bad acts he engaged in. What can be more American than that? Think about it—we are so accustomed in our news cycle to tear down our public figures and then have them redeem themselves. Of course, not all public figures who have broken the law or otherwise stumbled morally or ethically have successful redemption stories.

I've mentioned a few of Fillmore's charitable endeavors, but one in particular made a big splash in Buffalo: the founding of the Buffalo Fine Arts Academy. At the inaugural event, where the "youth, beauty and fashion" of the town attended, Fillmore was front and center as master of ceremonies.[413] "Thirteen gentlemen of this city have loaned to the Academy each the sum of five hundred dollars making a fund of six thousand and five hundred dollars, which has been used in the purchase of paintings, or have been loaned without interest, to compensate the owners of the valuable works temporarily secured for exhibition."[414]

From a contemporary perspective, this doesn't feel like a large charitable donation. But $500 in 1865 was the average US salary. And it established Buffalo as just the third city in the country, after Boston and Philadelphia, to have a permanent art museum. He was making a significant impact.

While Fillmore was the MC and the local Union Cornet Band played, "an impressive and eloquent prayer by Rev. Dr. Hosmer followed."[415]

---

413 (The Art Gallery Inauguration Last Evening 1865).
414 Ibid.
415 Ibid.

Yes, *that* Reverend Dr. Hosmer—the same abolitionist preacher of the Unitarian Church whose own church members shunned Fillmore. I can't imagine it was comfortable for them to interact in society all the time. But at least when they did, it was Fillmore acting for the benefit of Buffalo.

It was one chance to rehabilitate his image among his Buffalo peers for the horrifying thing he did by signing and endorsing the Fugitive Slave Act. I'm not saying he wouldn't have done many of the same civic engagements without signing the act, but the impact that it had on his reputation would have been a motivating factor to be such a leader in Buffalo.

And to some degree, it worked—at least for a while. Upon his death, Buffalo led the nation in mourning our last Whig president. Fillmore even made one last gift to the city he loved with a $1,000 bequest ($25,000 in 2024 dollars) in his will to the Buffalo Orphan Asylum.[416] Within every obituary would be the listing of the charities and civic organizations he advocated and founded. And then there would also be a passage with the following judgment against him: "[Fillmore] was responsible for much of the legislation which cursed the country and made her a bye-word and a reproach among the nations."[417]

RICHARD NIXON AND THE POWER OF THE TAX DEDUCTION

While Fillmore's charitable intent is more in line with most donors, there are other donors who may be a bit more pragmatic about charity. It is all about the monetary value that the tax deduction provides.

The charitable deduction has been in the US tax code since 1917. The Revenue Act of 1917 established that a taxpayer can take a deduction for a donation made to a tax-exempt organization. The impetus for this was quite clear: tax rates had been rising in order to fund the World War I effort, and Congress wanted to encourage taxpayers to give to charity.[418]

Ever since that time, taxpayers have given to charity to lower their tax bill and have gotten savvy with this deduction. After all, most people hate paying taxes. Given where the tax code is today, charity is often one of the few levers you have to lower your tax liability.

---

416 (Collins and Weaver 1976) pages 104–106.
417 (Fillmore and His Times 1874).
418 (Paul Arnsberger 2008) page 3.

FDR and Elvis Get the World All Shook Up

I have a client whose son was recruited onto his college's baseball team. One day, he got a call from their development office and was asked to donate to help renovate the baseball field. The suggested donation was $500,000 to be funded over five years.

In fact, we spend a lot of our time working through different tax scenarios on an annual basis. But in years his income is significant, we often frontload his charity into a vehicle called a donor-advised fund or a DAF. A DAF is where the donor can open an account at a brokerage firm under a charitable organization that is a 501(c)(3). The donor moves cash or appreciated securities into the account and gets a tax deduction in that year.

But here's the unique catch: there is no requirement that the money has to be given away. Donations basically can be invested, and when the donor is ready, they are then given to charity. Of course, one of the biggest critiques of these vehicles is that often the money sits in the DAFs for years growing—and not going to charity.

In this case, we did a "bunching" strategy where we made a large donation in a big income year and then gave the money away over time. The good news was that the year he was asked to pledge a donation for the baseball field was a big income year. He funded the DAF with $500,000 but only gave it to the school over five years. That way he benefited, too, and the money had a chance to grow.

TRICKY DICK DOES A DONATION

When I think of presidents who are transactional when it comes to charity, I think of Richard Nixon. When Nixon left the vice presidency in 1960, he took a lucrative path and joined a top-tier law firm as a senior partner. After years in public office, Nixon was making money.

Ah, but with making money comes taxes. Nixon, like others in his position, wanted to lower his tax bill. And that's where the charitable deduction comes in for Nixon.

Prior to Ford, it was hard for those in the top tier of government to monetize. But Nixon had an illustrious career—taking on Alger Hiss on TV and being Eisenhower's vice president. He had something of value: his personal papers.

You might not think anyone would care about that. However, the personal papers of a president (and vice president) were seen as private property since the US started. Trust me, several presidents from the eighteenth and nineteenth centuries have few papers to research, as certain presidential papers have been lost or destroyed (Chester Arthur, I'm looking at you). But once FDR signed into law the legislation creating presidential libraries, which was later bolstered by the Presidential Libraries Act of 1955, presidential (and vice presidential) papers became even more valuable.[419]

In February 2023, a 1787 letter from George Washington was put up for auction and expected to sell for $50,000. The letter in question is an interesting one as it relates to Washington's personal finances. The contents of the letter reveal that Washington was trying to sell 1,644 acres of land in Pennsylvania to Israel Shreve to help with liquidity issues.[420] A lot of Washington's cash flow issues would have been solved if he could have sold his papers!

Back in December 1968, newly elected President Nixon decided to donate his personal papers and take a tax deduction. He had gotten this advice from none other than LBJ himself.[421] So, as the year drew to a close, Nixon donated some of his papers and booked an $80,000 tax deduction. A few months later, on March 27, 1969, he made another donation. This time the donation was $576,000.[422]

To be clear, when charitable donations pass a certain amount, a qualified appraisal is required. That was the rule then, and it is still the rule today. Back then, however, the value of the donation could be equal to the *full appreciated value* of the papers. For instance, the papers and notes for the famous "Checkers" speech would have a much higher value than, say, a memo issued during his vice presidency. In effect, the donor could "zero out" their tax liability. This rule gave the presidents a lot of power when it came to value.[423]

---

419 After the law went into effect, Truman, Eisenhower, and LBJ all made donations to the National Archives.
420 (Barrish 2023).
421 And in true tax talk, the value of the papers was not considered income to the presidents—another tax benefit.
422 (Thorndike, Tax History: Did the IRS Drop the Ball When Auditing Nixon's Tax Returns? 2023) Thorndike's study on this tax case even notes that Johnson's advice included the name of an appraiser.
423 This is not the case today with charitable donations, which are not only limited by the percentage of one's AGI, but the percentage is impacted if it is cash or the type of non-cash donation made.

So, this was all completely legal and within the law. Nixon's 1969 donation was so large that he couldn't even use it all. It carried over to 1970 and 1971.

All seemed fine until Jack White, a reporter with the *Providence Journal*, did an investigation on Nixon and found out something rather shocking: the Nixons were on the "zero taxpayers list."[424]

White reported that in 1970 and 1971, while Nixon was drawing a $200,000 presidential salary, he had paid a total of $1,670.84 in income tax and received $131,503.84 in tax refunds.[425]

The low amount paid in taxes was more of a political optics one regarding the timing of the donation.[426] Between when Nixon made his first donation in 1968 and his second, not only had he been sworn in as president, but the tax law changed.

Greater scrutiny was put in place and limited the donation of personal papers to the physical value of the papers at the time of creation.[427] Thus, the donation of papers that had more historical significance versus other documents would be equally weighted prior to the law change. The demarcation time between the two tax laws was that all donations under the previous law would have had to occur prior to July 25, 1969.

Nixon claimed he made the charitable gift on March 27, 1969.

IN TAX, THE DETAILS MATTER

Thus began the investigation as to whether Nixon's charitable deduction was legitimate.

The issue was brought before the Joint Committee on Internal Revenue Taxation. As we mentioned, an appraisal is needed for the amount concerned. But given the historical significance, the moment the charitable gift is made does matter. What taxing authorities focus on is that moment when a donor relinquishes control.

Nixon had a deed of gift dated March 27, 1969. However, the papers were not submitted to the National Archives until April 10, 1970. The deed

---

424 (White 1973) As a side note, White's investigative journalism won him the 1974 Pulitzer Prize for National Reporting.
425 Ibid. Nixon himself would acknowledge that these liabilities were nominal.
426 Akin to Trump's $750 tax bill.
427 (Thorndike, Tax History: Did the IRS Drop the Ball When AuditingNixon's Tax Returns? 2023).

wasn't even signed by Nixon but rather the White House deputy counsel to the president. Plus, for all of you tax geeks like me out there, some of the gift was restricted to a later date. It was the gift of a future interest and thus not deductible until that time.[428]

As a result, the gift was made after July 25, 1969. The deduction was disallowed.[429] Nixon paid the liabilities for tax years 1970 through 1972 with interest.[430]

Do I think that Nixon was focused on charitable intent and giving when he made his donations? No, not at all. But I can completely attest to the fact that donations are often made to lower a tax bill. He wanted to pay less in taxes. Not everyone is searching to change the world with charity. But in Nixon's case, he just didn't follow the rules. And in tax, regardless of the charitable intent, following the rules is key to getting the financial benefits.

FDR GOES SOUTH IN SEARCH OF A CURE

Three individuals arrived at a small rural train station in Georgia on a warm summer day in 1924: Franklin Delano Roosevelt, his wife Eleanor, and his devoted assistant, Missy LeHand.[431] FDR's sunny optimism contrasted against the poverty around them as they made their way over the rough, ten-mile car trip to the forty-six-room Meriwether Inn. Eleanor was uncomfortable with staying in the ramshackle green-and-yellow cottage on the grounds of the inn. It was "too poor and too ugly" for her to bear.[432]

They headed there on the advice of George Peabody, a friend and native Georgian. Peabody had recently acquired a co-ownership interest in the inn and had been raving to FDR about the therapeutic benefits of the springs around the inn, called Warm Springs. The selling point for FDR

---

428   (Thorndike, JCT Investigation of Nixon's Tax Returns 2016).
429   Also at issue with Nixon's tax return was the sale of property in San Clemente, sale of his New York residence, and use of government aircraft by family and friends.
430   (Joint Committee on Taxation Staff 2019).
431   It should be noted that when FDR first arrived, the town was called Bullochville. However, FDR eventually changed the name to Warm Springs in order to attract more visitors. For our purposes and to avoid confusion, we will call the town by its current name of Warm Springs.
432   (E. Roosevelt 1949) page 27. In her memoirs, Eleanor respected that her husband loved Warm Springs but to her it was not an enjoyable place. She noted her reaction of their first trip where "the first house we lived in and my surprise that I could look through the cracks and see daylight."

to make this trip south was a story Peabody had shared with him: a young boy with polio, described as "practically helpless,"[433] who, over three years of summers swimming in the springs, "found he could move his limbs in the water and by persistent effort and exercise so increased their strength that by the end of the third summer he was able to walk once more without braces and with the aid of one cane."[434]

While these claims regarding the springs may have seemed fantastical, FDR was desperate to find a cure for this disease he would call a "great scourge." He would go anywhere and listen to anyone if he felt it was on the path to an answer.[435]

In the three years he suffered from polio, FDR himself had become an expert on treatments and in particular, the impact that exercise in water had on polio patients.[436] FDR shared his insights with one of his doctors who initially diagnosed him. "In the summer of 1922 I began swimming and found that this exercise seemed better adapted than any other because all weight was removed from the legs and I was able to move the legs in the water far better than I had expected."[437]

He headed to Georgia to see for himself if Peabody was right that the unique waters of Warm Springs would help him walk again.[438]

---

433 *Warm Springs Brochure 1931,* page 5, https://dlg.galileo.usg.edu/warm/pdfs/brochurec1931.pdf.

434 Ibid.

435 In the FDR Archives, there are numerous letters from 1922 and 1923 with various therapies and machines for him to try. He considered light therapy as well as the use of a moto-chair. Usually once he explored, the practicality of these options faded.

436 Letter FDR to Dr. William Egleston, MD, dated October 11, 1924. In this letter, FDR not only explains his medical history with polio, but lays out a series of "Don'ts" for patients, including "Don't use heavy massage but use light massage rubbing always towards the heart," "Don't let the patient feel cold, especially the legs, feet or any other part affected. Progress stops entirely when the legs or feet are cold," and "Don't let the patient get too fat."

437 Ibid.

438 Interestingly, after he heard about Warm Springs, he was contacted about a similar type of spring in Tennessee. The FDR Library Archives has a letter to FDR from William A. Millikin, dated July 31, 1924, espousing the benefits of Tate Springs near Knoxville, Tennessee. FDR replies on August 5, indicating he has just recently decided to check out a spring in Georgia. No record exists if FDR ever went to the Tennessee springs.

Eleanor left after the first day as she couldn't bear the environment. But the next day, FDR and Missy went to the springs. To his surprise and delight, he could move his legs underwater for hours on end.[439]

The days he spent in Warm Springs became his big aha moment. Excitedly, he wrote to Eleanor, "The legs are really improving a great deal.... This is really a discovery of a place and there is no doubt that I've got to do it some more."[440]

FDR decided to stay on at Warm Springs for a bit longer, along with Missy, as he mentioned to his mother, "it takes three weeks to show the effects."[441] He would spend the days in the water.[442] He "swims, dives, uses the swinging rings and horizontal bar over the water, and finally crawls out on the concrete pier for a sun bath that lasts another hour. Then he dresses, has lunch, rests a bit on a delightfully shady porch, and spends the afternoon driving over the surrounding country, in which he is intensely interested."[443]

FDR's realization was based on science. The water's temperature was eighty-eight degrees Fahrenheit and reached the surface at a rate of eight hundred gallons per minute.[444] Most people would find the temperature too high and could only bear to be in the water for a few minutes. Yet for those with polio, their limited circulation allowed them to stay in the water

---

439   This was no surprise that FDR was open to the idea that specialized waters could treat his polio. As a child, his father had been ill with heart issues. To help, nine-year-old FDR accompanied his mother, Sara, and his ill father, James, to the warm mineral baths in Bad Nauheim, Germany, for three years in a row as these waters were thought to be beneficial for heart patients.

    As a side note, I find it interesting that FDR spent significant time in Germany as a child—more than he did in Britain and France. He went to German school there and spoke the language. In a letter to his cousins, he wrote, "I go to the public school with a lot of little mickies and we have German reading, German dictation, the history of Siegfried, and arithmetic, in which I am to 14 x 11."

440   Letter FDR to Eleanor Roosevelt, dated October 1924.

441   Letter FDR to Sara Delano Roosevelt, dated October 1924.

442   In 2017, Missy LeHand's family donated to the FDR Library numerous home videos she took from 1932 to 1941. Included in them is a video of FDR walking around the pool and swimming in Warm Springs. Unless you were aware of his affliction, he looks like he has normal use of his legs. The library has set these videos up on a YouTube channel at https://www.youtube.com/watch?v=hUaQqMW40Eo&list=PLnYXL2y-0SAPEHz67IEGAqRd3ZBsfZz330&index=2.

443   (Cleburne 1924).

444   (E. Roosevelt 1948) page 569.

for two to three hours at a time.[445] The temperature and mineral quality of the water helped paralyzed muscles. Combined with the exercises he had developed, FDR was convinced that progress was at hand.[446]

FDR'S VISION EVOLVES TO CHARITABLE INTENT

We all know the end of the story: FDR conquers his polio, becomes president, ends the Depression, and saves the world in World War II. But you see, back in the mid-1920s, that future seemed a long way away for him. He was struggling with despair as his whole world had changed. What got him out of bed in the morning was the conviction that if he could walk again, he could become president.

However, this struggle with polio created a deep empathy within FDR that he had lacked prior to contracting polio. And that empathy, combined with his great charisma, gave him the ability to transform things.

Empathy is an important trait in charitable intent. When studying donor intent, researchers have found that often individuals support a charity because they empathize with those suffering. This empathy is heightened when donors feel that those suffering are powerless against their affliction. In plainer terms, a charity like the Susan G. Komen Breast Cancer Foundation resonates as cancer is not self-inflicted. In comparison, charities that fight obesity, drug abuse, and alcoholism are harder for donors to relate to. Why? Because all of these can be seen as self-inflicted—even if they truly aren't.[447]

But FDR's empathy had a unique edge to it; he was wealthy. He could take on projects that he wanted to, simply because he could pay for them. Plus, the concept of philanthropy had changed over the course of FDR's lifetime. While FDR was growing up, Andrew Carnegie had put together thoughts on charity that came to be known as *The Gospel of Wealth*. While

---

445 Swimming and water rehabilitation was seen as an option to help polio victims. But as FDR noted to his mother in an August 26, 1925, letter when he was undergoing swimming rehabilitation in Massachusetts, the big differential with Warm Springs is that other places, "the water being much colder [that] I cannot stay so long."

446 Many commentators have noted that this first trip was probably the high point of his treatment in the springs. Yet it didn't deter him.

447 Of course, an exception was the amazing Betty Ford who, after treatment helped her through her alcoholism, established a nonprofit hospital for treatment of those addicted to alcohol and drugs.

FDR was never going to embrace Carnegie's saying that "the man who dies thus rich dies disgraced," the idea that those with money could help solve long-term problems had greater resonance.[448]

During those first few visits to Warm Springs, Missy and FDR would spend time with Peabody's co-owner, Tom Loyless, a former journalist. Loyless and Peabody wanted to transform the Meriweather Inn into a high-end resort spa like the ones in Europe (and like the one FDR visited in Germany with his parents). Over long drives in the country followed by evening cocktails, Loyless and FDR would discuss what this resort would look like and the types of well-heeled individuals it would attract.[449] There would be beautiful cottages, a golf course, and of course, pools to access the springs. As the nights passed, FDR started to incorporate into that vision the idea of the springs helping those with polio as well. He started to convince himself that this could be quite a profitable idea.

Dreaming up schemes was not exactly foreign to FDR. Wealthy since birth, FDR had a nonchalance with money that only comes to those who have never had to worry about it. And unlike many others who were wealthy, his was not new money. The Roosevelts had generational wealth that had been passed down over the centuries.[450]

But the vision he had of Warm Springs was about to change all of that.

A NEWSPAPER ARTICLE LAUNCHES AN ENTREPRENEURIAL VENTURE

Like a lot of FDR's business ventures, his vision might have languished a bit longer or even faded away if something unique hadn't happened. As Peabody had hoped, the presence of FDR in rural Georgia piqued a lot of curiosity. A journalist named Cleburne Gregory of the *Atlanta Journal* reached out to see if he would be interested in a profile on his time in Warm Springs.

Like any good politician in search of favorable publicity, FDR quickly assented. Unlike many stricken with polio, he had the resources to get the best possible care. He was aware that his political aspirations were depen-

---

448 (Carnegie 1889).
449 (E. Roosevelt 1948) page 565.
450 (E. Roosevelt 1949) page 16. While he never really articulated his feelings on money, interestingly, in her memoirs after his death, Eleanor gave insight that FDR didn't want his children to be dependent on him for money but rather to "be allowed to make their own decisions and their own mistakes."

dent upon his being seen as conquering his disease. He consistently told his fellow Democrats that he would not run "until I can throw away my props; not until I can stand upon my own legs."[451]

And with all the FDR charm at play, he spent the day with Gregory. He took Gregory to the springs and swam. He posed by the pool. He opined that "I am deriving wonderful benefit from my stay here. This place is great. See that right leg? It's the first time I have been able to move it at all in three years."[452]

Roosevelt continued to celebrate the springs' benefits, saying, "The best infantile paralysis specialist in New York told me that the only way to overcome the effects of the disease was to swim as much as possible, and bask in the sunlight. Conditions here are ideal for both prescriptions. The water in some way relaxes muscles drawn taut by the disease, and gives the limbs much greater action. The sunshine has curative effects, I understand." [453]

Now, today his interview seems innocuous—something that would have made the pages of *People* magazine as a human interest story. But in 1925, it had a very different impact. It went viral across the country. You see, polio was frightening to the American public. Those who were afflicted led a difficult life—often shut away from others, they were dependent for the most basic life functions. But FDR was well-known as the former vice-presidential candidate and fifth cousin of President Theodore Roosevelt. More importantly, he was known for being wealthy. His comments on polio treatment carried weight because he had seen the best treatments possible. If this was working for him, then it could work for others.

Fellow polio sufferers wrote FDR directly asking for help to get to Warm Springs. More surprisingly, calls would come in from the small Warm Springs train station. Polio sufferers were simply arriving and looking for the inn for treatment.

In modern times, turning the inn into a treatment center could take years. There would be medical and legal issues to work through. Equipment would be needed and accommodation would have to be put in for all the wheelchairs. But FDR understood the anguish and hopelessness these

---

451 (Daniels 1932) page 80.
452 (Cleburne 1924).
453 Ibid.

people faced and sprang into action to get the site ready. His passion helped accelerate the process.

But unlike centers that existed for polio sufferers, FDR turned this into one with a camp-like atmosphere. A set schedule included exercises and swimming sessions in the water. There were group mealtimes and game playing. And the fellow afflicted surrounded FDR—or "Dr. Roosevelt" as he called himself—for wisdom, motivation, and most importantly, hope.

The nights of envisioning a special place for treatment now moved into a reality. In the fall of 1924, his mother, Sara, received an uplifting letter from her son—and one that laid out the initial vision. "I am going to have a long talk with Mr. George Foster Peabody who is really the controlling interest in the property. I feel that a great '*cure*' for infantile paralysis and kindred diseases could well be established here."[454]

While Sara wasn't excited about her son's potential venture, she was witnessing a change in him. After four years of struggle, FDR had something to focus his life on. She bantered back, via letters, and showed support for the son who had always been the center of her world. But privately, she worried. After all, she had seen previous ventures—like the boat he owned in Key Largo—fall into disrepair and sold at a steep discount.

In turn, FDR felt it could be a family venture. He wanted his mother's involvement and even felt that her insight and influence could "not only do a great deal of good but will prove financially successful."[455] Of course he had to make this argument to her as she was the trustee of his trusts. He had to make sure his mother would not worry that her son would bankrupt the trust.[456]

Eleanor was also leery of the concept. After almost twenty years of marriage, she had experienced his entrepreneurial side before and had seen money simply disappear. She wrote a friend that FDR "never went anywhere in the world that he didn't want to buy something and stay there."[457]

---

454 Letter FDR to Sara Delano Roosevelt, dated Autumn 1925. Reprinted in *Roosevelt*, 1948, page 568. Also cited in Oshinsky, page 35. Loyless did have an ownership interest but much smaller than Peabody. "Cure" is FDR's emphasis.
455 FDR to Sara Delano Roosevelt, dated March 7, 1926.
456 (E. Roosevelt 1948) page 602. Over the years, he would consistently tell Sara the goal was to make sure "every step is being planned either to pay for itself or make a profit on." Letter FDR to SDR, dated October 13, 1926.
457 (Gallagher 1999) page 43.

FDR and Elvis Get the World All Shook Up

She didn't want to directly stop him, but she put up some resistance. Back and forth they went via letters in a marital dance. What about the children? Private school education? Their homes? The servants?

"Ma will always see the children through," he breezily replied.[458]

She bantered back, "I know you love creative work my only feeling is that Georgia is somewhat distant for you to keep in touch with what is really a big undertaking…It is just I couldn't do it."

FDR simply ignored her entreaties.

But eventually she too was resigned to Warm Springs. As she wrote to her close friend Marion Dickerman, "he feels that he's trying to do a big thing which may be a financial success & a medical and philanthropic opportunity…."[459]

Negotiations began in earnest in February 1926.[460] As FDR rallied his nearest and dearest to his dream, one man was aghast: his law partner and friend Basil O'Connor. Upon word of the impending purchase, he wired back seven words: "Don't do anything. Am taking the train."[461]

Once on the ground in Georgia, he took one look around the inn and saw a crumbling enterprise and a money pit. He would recall in later years that "squirrels ran in and out of the holes in the roof. The place was a miserable mess."[462]

O'Connor was a practical businessman. He couldn't fathom why FDR would want to be here. The price was outrageous. He had much to achieve politically. He pointed out to FDR that Warm Springs would be an expensive distraction. But his reasoning could not dampen FDR's enthusiasm.

I totally get where O'Connor is coming from. When you are in that role, all you see are the risks and negatives. But here's the deal: sometimes you just have to go with the passion. I'll give you a quick story. Clients of mine had been having some cash flow challenges. We had been working

---

458 Ibid.
459 Ibid.
460 From FDR's log on his boat, dated February 24, 1926. He had been frustrated since late 1925 that Peabody had not shared what the plans were for Warm Springs. In a letter, FDR notes to a friend that Peabody will give no indication at all if he is willing to sell the property. Letter FDR to Hon. Mark G. Dubois, dated September 29, 1925.
461 (Gallagher 1999) page 43.
462 (Whitman 1972).

on these liquidity issues, when one day they shared that they had made a pledge to their local hospital. It was a multi-year commitment that would mean we would have to donate $50,000 a year for five years. It was completely not in the budget. It wasn't impossible, but they should wait.

But after my initial objections, they explained why it was so important for them. They had moved into their community a few years back and were one of the few families of color. But as the community grew, they wanted to invest in the hospital so that they could feel comfortable aging there. They knew their donation was part of a larger plan to help with the hospital's diversity. And I completely respect that.

Back and forth FDR went with Peabody in the negotiation.[463] Like his prior attitudes with money, FDR didn't care what the cost was. He had to have the Meriweather Inn. FDR and Peabody finally agreed to a price: $201,667.83, a sum almost three times more than Peabody had paid just a few years earlier.[464] Shockingly, the inn had fallen into further disrepair during Peabody's ownership. That it had actually gone up in value was difficult to believe. But the deal closed on April 29, 1926.[465] Warm Springs was now FDR's.

What was $201,667.83 to FDR? In today's numbers, it doesn't seem like much. To give context, in 2024 values, it is around $3.4 million.[466] Further, it was two-thirds of his inheritance. This was a substantial purchase, and one that would require investment to grow it. It was clear why Eleanor was so concerned.

---

463 Loyless was dying of cancer and was not very involved at this point. One of the surprising elements of the FDR-Peabody transaction is that Peabody was incredibly philanthropic—yet he chose to charge FDR more than he paid.
464 The property included the springs, the hotel, and the cottages, along with 1,200 acres of land. See Roosevelt, 1948, page 609.
465 One interesting aspect of how FDR focused all of his time in and on Warm Springs can be found in the correspondence regarding his 1926 tax return. He was delayed in filing and blamed it on his brother's sudden passing and the temporary loss of his files from his time returning from the South. However, in the correspondence with the auditor, FDR makes clear he is consistently in Georgia at Warm Springs and needs more time to meet with the auditor. See *FDR Financial Records, FDR Library, 1926 Income Tax Return and Correspondence.*
466 (Oshinsky 2006).

Immediately, he retitled the property legally as the Warm Springs Foundation. But it wasn't a charity. He was still focused on growing the inn to be profitable.[467]

He charged patients forty-two dollars a day to stay there. The price included everything—room, board, treatment, and medical supervision. Privately, he admitted that the forty-two dollars was below cost for what they were providing and wasn't sufficient to cover costs.[468] Given the needs of the patients, the property required a staff of 110.[469] Additionally, the increasing number of polio patients that appeared at the inn caused a sharp drop in regular tourists.

FDR had used his own money to buy the property, but to grow it, he needed to come up with a different solution. FDR knew it was necessary to make Warm Springs a legitimate cause for those to rally around and create donors. He worked with the American Orthopedic Association to provide a study on Warm Springs' viability as a treatment center, which eventually turned into an official designation in 1927.

With legitimate medical approval in hand, FDR now turned to O'Connor. FDR needed to fund the project, and he knew a lot of people who could help. O'Connor had different intentions. He wanted FDR to come back to the firm and be a figurehead. More importantly, he wanted him to focus on his political career.

That was the challenge—FDR wasn't willing to go back to the law and to politics unless his Warm Springs project was financially stable.

Thus began the Warm Springs Foundation as a charity. O'Connor filed the requisite paperwork to turn the ownership into that of a charity. FDR made a loan to the organization to buy the property from him.[470] A board of trustees was established, and they capitalized the organization at

---

467 On June 30, 1926, a small notice appeared in *The News Journal* in Wilmington, Delaware, announcing a new corporation called Georgia Warm Springs Foundation Inc., with an initial value of $450,000 (New Corporations 1926).
468 Letter FDR to Lyman Ward, dated February 4, 1928. It should be noted that some polio sufferers could not cover the costs. FDR covered their costs.
469 (E. Roosevelt 1948) pages 623–625.
470 The note from this transaction can be seen in Eleanor Roosevelt's book, *This I Remember*.

$75,000.[471] The organization could now receive charitable gifts and grants. Its financial stability could be established.

THE CHARITABLE INTENT EVOLVES

FDR developed empathy and established the Warm Springs Foundation, but that doesn't mean he suddenly became quite good at handling money. Like the system he grew up under, with his mother as trustee, FDR knew that he needed a good steward to manage the foundation. He chose O'Connor.

O'Connor led the foundation and the day-to-day management. FDR could get on with what he did best—politicking and mixing with the electorate. But this time, it wasn't political gains he sought but funds for the foundation.

He urged his mother to hold dinners to raise funds with wealthy friends and family, but only a few wrote checks.[472] He realized that to make an impact he couldn't rely on simply asking his wealthy friends.

BUILDING A LEGACY WITH AN INSURABLE INTEREST

By 1930, FDR was at a crossroads. He was back on the path he felt had always been destined for him. He was governor of New York, but his heart was in Warm Springs. He spent as much time there as possible. He wrestled with questions about what would happen to Warm Springs if he died before there was a cure. He needed the perfect solution, and it needed to have scale and impact to help his fellow polio sufferers.

And he found it—in life insurance.

FDR thought about life insurance a little differently than how it's usually used. Typically, in life insurance, there is the owner, the insured, and the beneficiary. Clearly, FDR was the insured. And Warm Springs would be the beneficiary. But as for the owner, it would be more complicated. An owner of an insurance policy needs to have an *insurable interest* in the life

---

471 (Pushing The Fight On Infantile Paralysis 1927).
472 Some of the biggest supporters were like Henry Pope, whose daughter had polio. Pope became a trustee of Warm Springs. He donated $20,000. (E. Roosevelt 1948) page 633.

of the insured—that is to say, an economic stake where if the person died, it would result in financial hardship for the beneficiary.

When O'Connor completed the insurance application on October 8, 1930, he noted that if FDR died, the foundation would be forced to discontinue its existence.[473] They hoped the argument would hold.

But another financial question remained: even if the charity had an insurable interest, it wasn't clear who would insure him.

FDR's sunny optimism often willed things into being. His story to all who would listen, including the press, was that not only did the insurance companies he applied to feel he was insurable, but that he had the body of a thirty-year-old.[474] (He was forty-eight at the time.)

Behind the scenes, though, that wasn't exactly the story.

O'Connor determined that the right amount of coverage was $500,000 (or $10 million in today's dollars). This would be sufficient in keeping Warm Springs in business as well as pursuing the cure. The amount of $50,000 was a demarcation number with the insurance companies, as they often gave greater scrutiny to such transactions.[475]

But insurance companies were wary of such risk. Rather, they preferred to spread the risk through reinsurance. As a result, Warm Springs didn't seek one insurance policy for $500,000. They sought ten policies at $50,000 each.

And thus launched a complex pursuit of insurance.

Warm Springs contacted Robert L. Jones, who was a general agent of life insurance, and tasked him with procuring the policies. Jones selected the companies they would apply to, including Equitable, John Hancock, and Travelers, among others. Applications were made and medicals taken.

The first question out of the gate related to Warm Springs's insurable interest. On October 6, 1930, the MP and supervisor of applications queried Jones a serious question: Would FDR still be active with Warm Springs now that he was governor?

It was a reasonable question, considering it was not the norm for someone to be in such a high political position while managing a large charity.

---

473   From Life Insurance Application, dated October 8, 1930.
474   (G. F. Roosevelt 1930) This was a fact mentioned numerous times by the Roosevelt team. In fact, they even had doctors state that FDR's condition was comparable to a man of thirty. However, it was false.
475   Ibid.

Jones didn't blink. He explained that, yes, there still was an insurable interest as Warm Springs held property holdings of $1 million that were all brought about by the work done by FDR. FDR would still remain active in the organization. He was the "guiding spirit."

With that, no further questions arose on insurable interests.

The other problem that Jones had was, despite FDR's assertations that he was healthy "except for the polio," that wasn't really the case. When the underwriters of the ten companies had gotten back the results of the medical application, it was immediately stamped "substandard risk." In underwriting, this is not a good foreboding. Substandard risk means that the potential insured is a higher risk to the insurance company due to preexisting health conditions, and so the likelihood of paying out the claim was higher.

Jones knew that there was still the chance an insurance company would issue the coverage. But premiums would be higher.

If FDR had been unknown, the companies would likely not have issued coverage. But FDR was the governor of New York. People already were talking about him running for president. Jones knew he had an argument to push on the insurance companies.

The problem was that no one wanted to go first. Jones sent telegrams to all the potential insurers: Were they willing to take a risk?

The insurers were nervous. No one wanted to take the risk, but they also didn't want to be the one insurer who didn't insure FDR. Mutual Benefit Life replied first. They sent a telegram to State Mutual stating they were going to decline FDR due to polio. This did not bode well.

But the battle wasn't done. On October 15, 1930, a Western Union telegram went from the medical director of Equitable Life to the State Mutual Life Assurance Company. The query was straightforward: Had they decided to take a risk on the Roosevelt application? State Mutual replied: yes, they were issuing a $50,000 policy.

The first domino had fallen in FDR's favor.

When Mutual Benefit got word, they changed their stance. They would issue FDR a $25,000 policy.

In the end, the list of coverage looked like this:

- National Life Insurance Company $50,000—Annual premium $2,178.00
- Equitable Life Assurance Society $60,000—Annual premium $3,235.80
- Mutual Life $50,000—Annual premium $2,323.00
- Penn Mutual $50,000—Annual premium $2,178.00
- Travelers Insurance Company $50,000—Annual premium $1,680.50
- Massachusetts Mutual Life Insurance Company $50,000—Annual premium $2,178
- Guardian Life Insurance Company $50,000—Annual premium $2,178.00
- Fidelity Mutual Life Insurance Company $50,000—Annual premium $2,194.50
- The Columbian National Life Insurance $50,000—Annual premium $1,831.50
- Canada Life $25,000—Annual premium $1,131.23
- New England Mutual Life Insurance Company $25,000—Annual premium $1,117.50
- Mutual Life Insurance Company $25,000—Annual premium $1,161.50
- State Mutual Life Insurance Company $25,000—Annual premium $1,089.00

In total, FDR went above the $500,000 he wanted. Warm Springs Foundation had insured him for $560,000. But they paid dearly. Annual premiums totaled $24,476.53—a significant amount for 1930.

Louie Howe couldn't resist the photo op. After all, his guy was healthy—so healthy he was insurable. It was the next step to the presidency. Howe quickly arranged it: Roosevelt surrounded by others being presented with the $500,000 of insurance by Keith Morgan. The paper captioned it, "Rumors that Franklin D Roosevelt of New York, was in precarious health were dispelled when the executive was given $500,000 worth of life insurance."[476] The photo went national.

---

476 (Roosevelt Insured for $500,000 1930).

All the Presidents' Money

For the average American, $500,000 was an unheard-of sum. Clearly, if the insurers were willing to risk it, then they could too.

When FDR passed away in April 1945, within twenty-four hours, all the claims were filed, and the full amount was paid out. In the end, it was likely not too big of a risk for the insurers. They had fifteen years of premiums paid in, or $376,000. It ended up being a good risk for the insurance company.[477] FDR may have achieved a similar goal if he had just kept the funds and invested them—but he wouldn't have gotten the political optics of being insurable.[478]

Warm Springs Foundation had enough funds to keep going.[479] As the foundation evolved, it turned its attention to not just treatment but also seeking a vaccine cure. But remember I said that Elvis got his polio vaccine due to FDR? How did FDR take the work he did at Warm Springs and turn it into a vaccine? For that, we shift back to the 1930s when the Depression had decimated the Warm Springs donor pool. O'Connor was watching the annual revenue drop precipitously until, in 1933, they were running out of options. But then O'Connor had an idea for FDR: What if instead of chasing after large donors, they did something different? What if they had many donors each donating a small amount? Would that help?

And thus launched the president's birthday balls starting in 1934. A campaign was launched asking every American to pitch in a dime for the president's birthday. The proceeds would be split between the Warm Springs Foundation and local foundations. And boy did that take off. Across the country, millions of dimes were sent to Washington, DC, in honor of FDR.

The success of this campaign was such that in late 1937, FDR announced that they were going to launch the National Foundation for Infantile Paralysis. The organization launched in January 1938. Singer Eddie

---

[477] Keep in mind the insurance companies do the math not just on the risk of insuring an individual but also investing the funds to be there for when the policy pays out.

[478] On July 30, 1945, there was a Special Meeting of the Executive Committee of the Board of Directors of Georgia Warm Springs Foundation. In the meeting minutes, it was noted that the "Foundation was the beneficiary under certain policies of insurance on the life of the late President and that the proceeds received from such policies amounted to $560,000.00, and the Chairman recommended that this sum be set up as a Reserve for future capital expenditures at the Foundation." (Meeting Minutes of Adjourned Special Meeting of the Executive Committee of the Board of Trustees of Georgia Warm Springs Foundation July 30, 1945).

[479] It is now the Roosevelt Warm Springs Institute for Rehabilitation and is operated by the State of Georgia.

FDR and Elvis Get the World All Shook Up

Cantor was enlisted to bring publicity to it. As he worked with FDR's team, he said, "We should just call it a March of Dimes." The dimes rolled in. They still supported the work at Warm Springs, but O'Connor used larger allocations of the donations to support scientists seeking a vaccine. And then in 1955, one was ready. Jonas Salk had cracked the code. A year later, in 1956, Elvis would get the vaccine, and the number of young people vaccinated would soar.

Subsequently, polio isn't the scourge today that it once was. We rarely hear of anyone getting it. And that takes us back to high-impact charity. For FDR, the impact was personal. But his intent shows one of the key examples of building metrics around charitable giving. He wanted scale to create real impact in the world, hence the need for a large annual insurance premium. It wasn't enough for him to find a cure for himself. He wanted a cure for other polio sufferers, then other Americans, and finally the world. Ultimately, over 2.5 billion children have been vaccinated against polio.

PART III

The Wealth Builders

Chapter Eight

LADY BIRD BUYS A RADIO STATION

If you ever asked me what is the best thing you could do financially, my answer would be quite succinct: get married and stay married.

It might seem like an odd answer, but the truth is being married gives you a greater chance of building wealth. Studies of wealth in America consistently find that married couples have more wealth than remarried couples, with $640,000 in assets versus $450,000 on average. And both married and remarried couples have more money than divorcées and never-married individuals who both only have, on average, $167,000 in assets.[480] Part of this is that married couples today are often doubly blessed with having two working spouses.

As someone who works with couples on their personal finances, I have found the strongest balance sheets are often when both spouses work together to effectively navigate their financial challenges. Personal finance isn't easy—nor is marriage. But when done right, it is a joint vision working together. And it can actually be a fun adventure as the relationship and net worth grow.

I am often surprised that when I am interviewed by prospective clients, I am never asked about how my husband and I manage our money. To me, it is an important question because it tells you a lot about how I will work with you.

In my marriage, I run the day-to-day aspects of our money. But my husband is an equal partner in decision-making on anything strategic in our financial life. We talk about money all the time in our house and are

---

480   (Wilcox 2021).

very clear with each other's hopes and goals. We enjoy the problem-solving we have to do to understand our money and make our finances stronger.

But my husband once pointed out to me something that I think about a lot. Given all our conversations, he's relieved he never has to worry about how I will handle our finances in the event he predeceases me. That's why whenever I work with a couple where one spouse says they aren't really interested in money, I make it clear: it is really important that they engage. Marital finances are a team sport.

Studies have consistently shown that money in general has a huge impact on the quality and satisfaction of a relationship. (The data is a bit more spotty when it comes to financial issues triggering divorce.) The more financial stresses, like debt, on a relationship, the more challenging things become. Further, if a money issue does not get resolved and is recurrent, it can undermine the marriage.

The goal of any married couple should be to focus on what academics call "financial harmony." Financial harmony is the ability of a couple to create a shared vision that allows for a unified purpose and direction in order to create intimacy. There will be some conflict at times but due to the connection to the bigger picture, these conflicts can be navigated to a successful resolution.[481]

Presidential marriages are often a source of fascination (and gossip). When you look at the relationships between the presidents and their First Ladies, they're fairly egalitarian. Often, there is a shared vision. They are connected to each other and help each other problem-solve.

In researching the presidents, I was often surprised to find that the best way to understand the presidents was through the First Ladies. It reminds me of that scene in the 1995 movie *The American President*, starring Michael Douglas and Annette Bening. After a couple of awkward first encounters dating each other, President Andrew Shepherd and his girlfriend have a frank discussion in his bedroom:

> President Andrew Shepherd: Do you know what your problem is?
>
> Sydney Ellen Wade: What's my problem?

---

481 (Garbinsky, et al. 2020) page 3.

Lady Bird Buys a Radio Station

President Andrew Shepherd: Sex and nervousness.

Sydney Ellen Wade: Sex and nervousness is my problem?

President Andrew Shepherd: Yes. Last night when we were looking at those place settings in the Dish Room, I realized those place settings were provided by the first ladies. And I'll bet none of those first ladies were nervous about having sex with their president husbands. And do you know why?

Sydney Ellen Wade: No, but I'm sure you'll explain it to me.

President Andrew Shepherd: I will. Because they weren't presidents when they first met them. That's not the case here.[482]

That's a pretty important point. When the First Ladies met their husbands, they were simply regular guys. After all, Harry Truman had to court Bess for nine long years before she finally agreed to marry him. Theodore Roosevelt's future wife, Edith, was his childhood next-door neighbor. And Grace Coolidge first glimpsed her future husband Calvin through a window where he was shaving in long underwear and a hat. It brings us to a unique phenomenon of a number of successful marriages and money: a significant number of presidents married up financially. Washington, Lincoln, Eisenhower, and Clinton are just a few that come to mind. They chose women who had means—whether their own or self-created—and rose up to meet them. And their wives—Martha, Mary, Mamie, and Hillary—all had faith that their spouses would find a way to manage. As a result, their marriages became more of an equal partnership financially.

Over the course of those marriages, their finances grew. Today, we're used to presidents leaving office to a life of great wealth. But that wasn't always the case.

Choosing which presidential marriage's finances to examine here was difficult. But when I examined the various marriages, I saw something

---

482 (Reiner 1995).

about certain aspects that we can emulate in order to create financial success. In some marriages, for example, a perfect dance where both partners play a part can create financial and marital harmony. In others, understanding that no matter how solid or long a marriage, we all come from different experiences, which makes communication key. And finally, certain financial behaviors are really a money disorder. It is necessary to have connection and trust with your partner so that these behaviors do not destabilize the relationship.

LBJ AND LADY BIRD FREQUENTLY DANCE A PAS DE DEUX

Seeing a couple that meshes well can be like watching a pair of ballroom dancers glide across the dance floor. It's smooth and elegant, with both partners working together to create an image of flow, dexterity, and style. You aren't really able to see where one partner stops and the other begins.

These are the best relationships when it comes to managing personal finances. Couples who make decisions together don't always agree, but you feel that when they're working through financial problems, they're truly partners. They stand out to me because these couples are rarer than you might think. They are a true example of financial harmony.

There is a couple that has worked with me for years. He's a former CEO, and she's a senior marketing executive who also has a chain of successful restaurants. They're smart and direct and know exactly what they want. They argue points and feel they're smarter when they do it their way. Working with them is not for the faint of heart. Their tenacity when they're tackling a financial issue together is impressive.

Recently, we worked through a transaction to buy a winery in Italy. From the outset, it seemed like a challenging idea. They wanted to hire someone to run the winery and operate a villa to use a few months a year. They hoped to reside at the villa a couple of months a year.

Don't worry, my first question to them was simple: "Wouldn't it be easier to just rent out the most expensive villa on a vineyard every year?" But alas, no—they wanted to take on this project together. The interesting thing about their negotiation to pursue this endeavor was how they worked together. They sat in every meeting, read every document, and negotiated every point together. They were aligned on a vision, and no one was going

Lady Bird Buys a Radio Station

to get in the middle of this partnership. It was an elegant dance of a married couple who were equal in every way.

A number of presidential couples could dance a financial pas de deux with style and flair like those two, but one couple did it so well, they fooled us all: Lyndon Baines and Claudia "Lady Bird" Johnson. LBJ spent the majority of his career in the mastery of power and persuasion. He was so good at it that Lady Bird seemed like the little housewife in the background. But she was a powerhouse in her own right, and their personal finances reflected that. In fact, Lady Bird was a bit of a badass. You wouldn't have thought that based on how she was portrayed in the media in the 1960s. She seemed so quiet and reserved. But you can't judge a book by its cover.

Lady Bird grew up differently from other young girls of the 1920s. Motherless by the time she was five, she had a steely yet calm demeanor. She needed that because her father had a strong personality. She once said, "My father was a very strong character, to put it mildly. He lived by his own rules."[483]

Business was something her father prided himself on and "all his life was concerned with a good investment and did manage to make many of them for most of his life."[484] Lady Bird had another influence, her namesake Uncle Claud. Uncle Claud wanted her to go to Harvard Business School and would sit with young Lady Bird and discuss opportunities she should consider in business and the stock market.[485] Not the norm in the 1920s.

These conversations with the men in her life made an impact on her; underneath her calm exterior, Lady Bird wanted to go to college, which wasn't a typical ambition during those times. But she wouldn't be deterred. She briefly attended a junior college and then matriculated at the University of Texas at Austin. During her time in Austin, she stood out even more from her college classmates. Lady Bird had been driving since she was thirteen years old, and she would navigate a big Buick around campus. She had an account at Neiman Marcus, and she also was clear on her ambition: she wanted to become a journalist, and she graduated cum laude in 1934 with a degree in journalism.

---

483   Lady Bird to Jan Jarboe Russell, "Lady Bird Johnson: The Early Years," https://www.pbs.org/ladybird/earlyyears/earlyyears_index.html.
484   Transcript Claudia "Lady Bird" Johnson Oral History Interview, August 12, 1977, by Michael Gillette, Internet Copy, LBJ Library, page 4.
485   Idem, page 29.

Earning a degree changed her; she felt university "certainly made me more assured, more aggressive in tackling the world and trying to find out just what my thing is, just what can I do."[486] Now she just had to figure out what it was she wanted to take on.

But life happened before she could embark on that career path. She met LBJ at the office of a mutual friend in Austin in September 1934. She later said, "I do believe before the day was over he did ask me to marry him and I thought he was just out of his mind. It was very—I'm a slow, considered sort generally, and certainly not given to quick conclusions or much rash behavior."[487]

LBJ was immediately smitten when he met Lady Bird. But he was acutely aware that she was a "rare bird" in many ways. She had grown up in a different financial situation than he had. He was anxious about how to financially provide for Lady Bird. Just a month after meeting, he wrote her,

"About the financial angle dear, I'm sure the salary will be some less than I'm making here but much more when the buying power is taken into consideration. It isn't enough for the two of us tho' and the salary following graduation won't be. It is bad to fall in love with a girl who has handsome comforts and advantages but it is worse than bad to attempt to make her happy with a nominal salary after marriage....No Honey, I haven't overestimated what my Bird should have."[488]

The Johnsons had financial compatibility in their skill sets. Right out of the gate, it allowed for a very balanced approach to their finances. And what is so important here is that before they married, LBJ and Lady Bird were having key conversations about money. It might sound obvious but even today in the 2020s, it has been found that only 51 percent of all couples talk money before the wedding.[489]

Marriage suited the personalities of Lady Bird and LBJ. LBJ was like the ambitious business-minded men she had grown up around. Lady Bird was adept as a political wife and discovered that LBJ was forward-thinking

---

486 (Claudia Johnson, Oral History Interview 1977) Interview III, page 39.
487 Ibid.
488 Letter Lyndon Johnson to Lady Bird Taylor, dated October 27, 1934, Lyndon and Lady Bird Johnson's Courtship Letters, Personal Papers of Lyndon and Lady Bird Johnson, LBJ Presidential Library, accessed July 27, 2023, https://www.discoverlbj.org/item/pp-ctjandlbj-letters-lbj-10-27-34.
489 (Bank 2019).

Lady Bird Buys a Radio Station

when it came to money. Reflecting back almost fifty years later, Lady Bird noted his openness. "He was very determined that I should learn all about his finances. In fact, he was an extremely open person, far more open than I was. He would say, 'We've got—' it seems like he made $267.00 a month. That does seem very small, doesn't it? I believe maybe he got a raise to $325.00."[490]

Together, they came up with a plan to bolster their finances: Every month they spent $18.50 on a $25 bond. The bonds paid a 5 percent return and acted as the ballast for their finances.[491] They were also a team when it came to the day-to-day blocking and tackling. Lady Bird handled the budgeting; she liked the ability to balance a checkbook. She was the more frugal of the two and took steps to keep their bank account in the black. In comparison, LBJ focused on strategy and the big picture, but was known at times to spend a little more than he should. Basically, they were really good dance partners.

The idea that both of them would be engaged with their finances was an interesting one in the 1930s—and probably made the Johnsons cutting edge for the time. When marriage and personal finance are studied, women's voices are seen as more equal when they can contribute income to the bottom line. This equality has been linked to women's greater participation in the labor market.[492]

But at the time, Lady Bird wasn't working. She helped in her husband's congressional office, but it didn't pay. Although she didn't earn a paycheck, she had an inheritance of $67,000 from her mother (paid in annual installments) and land in Alabama. Lady Bird herself didn't "remember ever worrying financially, really. I knew Daddy would come to my rescue if I needed him to, and also I very early got the feeling that somehow or another Lyndon would manage."[493]

---

490   (Claudia Johnson, Oral History Interview 1977) Interview V, page 22.
491   Ibid. It is interesting to note that LBJ and Lady Bird were very comfortable buying bonds. In a write up of their net worth in the 1970s, *Time* magazine noted that they had $400,000 of municipal bonds in their asset base—or about 3 percent of their total net worth (at the time) of $14 million.
492   (Pepin and Cohen March 2021).
493   (Claudia Johnson, Oral History Interview 1977) Interview V, pages 21–22.

Throughout her life, Lady Bird would mention how LBJ came from a more challenging financial background. But he wasn't intimidated by her money. In this respect, the Johnsons were ahead of their time. The Pew Research Center has shown that while marriage typically increases the economic status of the wife, there are more marriages in the 2020s where the wife is not only wealthier than the husband (whether through earning power or assets brought into the marriage) but is also greater educated.[494]

This unique characteristic is common today in many successful ultra-high–net-worth marriages. For over fifteen years, I've worked with a couple that met right out of college and married. They've raised three kids, and the husband has successfully climbed the career ladder to become CEO of a Fortune 500 company. When we started working together, they were worth less than $1 million (including their house). Today, they are ultra high net worth and have complex asset base where everyday decisions can be overwhelming. But they wouldn't have been successful without the wife's input.

She is the budgeter and approver in the marriage. She came into the marriage with an equal education and from a family with better finances. She might have decided to stop working a few years into the marriage to care for the children, but she never abdicated. She stayed an engaged participant. And because of her point of view, the couple have made charity a key component of their wealth philosophy. She once said in a meeting, "Our children will have enough; we must do more for others." That comment opened the door for millions to go to charities that support women struggling with domestic abuse and child trafficking. Similar to Lady Bird and LBJ, their marriage and their finances are a well-choreographed pas de deux.

Yet despite working well together, Lady Bird was aware that LBJ wanted real financial success. This was no secret—family, friends, and political supporters were well aware of his ambitions. Some of this came from deep-seated anxiety. LBJ had seen his father die penniless. He also saw numerous colleagues get voted out of Congress and have to take low-paying jobs. Like we saw with his predecessor Truman, LBJ was afraid of ending

---

494   (Pew Research Center 2010).

Lady Bird Buys a Radio Station

up broke.[495] Having an outside business could help build wealth—and alleviate his financial fears.

Eight years into their marriage, an interesting business opportunity came their way.[496] An Austin radio station had launched in 1939 but had struggled to take off for five years due to regulatory issues. Lady Bird herself noted, "It was part-time, low-capitalized, only nine employees, in debt to everybody in town, went off the air at sunset, had everything against it."[497]

Word got around that the little station was up for sale.[498] Lady Bird found it "was within our price range."[499] Lady Bird used $17,500 from her inheritance and bid on KTBC[500] dependent upon FCC approval. LBJ would not be an owner, and as a result, the Johnsons felt this mitigated any conflict of interest with LBJ's congressional role.[501] Johnson's political opponents later claimed that LBJ strong-armed the owners into letting them buy the station. Whether or not that was true, the station was, by all accounts, "run-down" and "terrible."[502] The equipment didn't work, and it was stretched financially.[503] And the fact that the station was on the air only until sunset meant it failed to reach a sizable demographic of listeners at a time when radio was the center of the entertainment universe.

In 1942, $17,500 was a lot of money, the equivalent of $300,000 in 2024 dollars. Furthermore, her purchase was a symbolic transfer, as Lady Bird noted that "what I inherited from my mother was in my daddy's hands

---

495   (Caro 1990) pages 80–82.
496   It should be noted that the Johnsons had wanted to buy a newspaper called the *Jefferson Jimplecute* but the negotiations didn't really go anywhere.
497   (Claudia Johnson, Oral History Interview 1977) Interview XVI, page 67.
498   It should be noted that many of the Johnsons' enemies and foes made much of this—implying that the Johnsons took advantage of LBJ's position. I am not going to opine on that—I am solely focusing on the personal finance aspect of it. The best description of this is Chapter 6 of Robert A. Caro's *Means of Ascent: The Years of Lyndon Johnson*.
499   Ibid.
500   Lady Bird says in her Oral History for the LBJ Library that it was $17,500, but she wasn't sure. In some places, it was quoted at a price as high as $41,000. Regardless, it was a large sum.
501   One of the controversies surrounding the radio station was that her application was approved in twenty-four days. The owners of the option to purchase had been waiting three years for approval.
502   Transcript Harfield Weedin Oral History Interview 1 by Michael Gillette, internet copy, LBJ Library, 2/24/1983.
503   Ibid.

and I wasn't in need of getting it. I was perfectly glad to leave it, but the time had come when we could make use of it."[504]

Now what Lady Bird was referencing was a very nuanced area of estate planning law. Most of the time, when a couple marries, their property and income become marital property. Thus, in the event of a divorce, this property would be part of the division of the assets. However, in the event one of the spouses inherits assets, those assets do not become marital property unless they are specifically merged. As a result, Lady Bird's inheritance was strictly hers, and LBJ had no ownership interest.

A SHARED VISION

Lady Bird and LBJ had decided early on that they had two goals with the radio station. First, they wanted to improve the quality of radio programming in Austin. In the letters going back and forth on a close to daily basis between the Johnsons in 1943, LBJ wrote that "we must be able to give the people better programs and programs of a nature that they will enjoy more than any other station. Generally speaking, I think we have already made arrangements for the news and music part. I think in order to meet the above goal this must be supplemented by a lot of variety and imagination."[505]

Second, they wanted the station to be profitable. LBJ was clear they didn't want to be like FDR's son Elliott who owned radio stations. Those stations were, in LBJ's words, "top heavy in expense."[506] Both Johnsons were on the same page when it came to keeping the business expenses down. LBJ defined the financial strategy in that "this total over-all expense per month should not be in excess of $2,500 or $2,750. It would be extremely difficult to keep it within this figure, but it does give you something to check on, look at, study and thoroughly analyse [sic]."

Lady Bird quickly responded with the work she was doing on her end. When she examined the books, however, she realized she was in a bind. In the sale, she had inherited some accounts receivable and a lot of ac-

---

504 Transcript Claudia "Lady Bird" Johnson Oral History Interview XVIII, by Michael Gillette, Internet Copy, LBJ Library, page 12. It should be noted that her inheritance was increased when her namesake, Uncle Claud, died the prior year.
505 Letter Lyndon B. Johnson to Claudia "Lady Bird" Johnson, dated April 1, 1943.
506 Ibid.

counts payable.[507] The station was running at a big loss. In fact, it was losing $1,000 a month (or almost $20,000 in 2024 dollars).[508] She needed to make a move—and fast. She brought in a key manager to help her run the station and update obsolete and outdated equipment.[509] She chased after her accounts receivable. She laid off employees she had inherited. As Lady Bird recalled in her later years, "There were years when I signed all the checks, and knew what big decisions needed to be made and had the opportunity to say something about them and sometimes did."[510]

A BIGGER OPPORTUNITY SET

It soon became clear to both of them that cutting expenses would merely keep the station afloat. They needed to actually grow the revenue. Together, LBJ and Lady Bird realized it needed to be a full-time station out of the gate. Given LBJ's experience with governmental agencies, in June 1943, Lady Bird applied for more wattage for twenty-four-hour programming and moved the station to a better building despite a hefty $4,450 bill to get it ready for the station.

Lady Bird's pregnancy in 1943 caused LBJ to engage deeper in the management of the radio station. One area he sought to grow revenue was in advertising. In order to do so, he took a calculated risk. Despite it being a small market, advertisers and listeners wanted national programs on the radio. Luckily for him, given his role in Congress, he was able to get a number of key meetings in New York City. He shared with Lady Bird that "tomorrow I hope to see [William] Paley of the Columbia Broadcasting Company and also the SeSac people. I will write you upon my return and tell you what happened."[511]

---

507 Transcript Claudia "Lady Bird" Johnson Oral History Interview XVIII, by Michael Gillette, internet copy, LBJ Library, page 12.
508 Transcript Harfield Weedin Oral History Interview 1 by Michael Gillette, internet copy, LBJ Library, 2/24/1983, page 26.
509 Ibid., page 16.
510 Transcript Claudia "Lady Bird" Johnson Oral History Interview XIX, by Michael Gillette, internet copy, LBJ Library, page 38.
511 Letter Lyndon B. Johnson to Claudia "Lady Bird" Johnson, dated April 1, 1943. SESAC was founded in 1930 and is the Society of European Stage Authors and Composers.

The mix of political charm and radio ownership got him what he wanted: a CBS affiliation. LBJ and Lady Bird would be able to bring key programs to the market, and advertisers started to pay a premium.

And what a premium they paid. In the first months Lady Bird owned the station, the ad revenue was approximately $3,000 a month. By 1945, it was over $15,300 a month. LBJ and Lady Bird had achieved what they had wanted: financial stability and success.

When LBJ became vice president, he and Lady Bird put the station and its assets into a blind trust. By that point, the Johnsons were no longer involved in the day-to-day running of the station. Yet interestingly enough, the importance of their business even resonated on the most difficult of days. In her diary entry on November 23, 1963, among the chaos of the JFK assassination, Lady Bird noted that the cabinet "came in with a list of things I must do immediately. Sell my house, possibly sell my business (KTBC)…just the simple things of going on living."[512]

By the mid-1960s, the net earnings exceeded $500,000 annually. This "seed money" would be used to accumulate other assets including land as well as investing in the markets. But interestingly, LBJ was extremely private about the radio station, with even historian Doris Kearns Goodwin noting that "he kept the doors to his financial history tightly closed, assuming even in his most unguarded moment, the posture of an Horatio Alger figure who rose from rags to riches by hard work, determination, pluck and luck."[513]

Almost thirty years after LBJ had passed, the Johnson family sold their remaining stake in the radio station for $105 million to an Indianapolis radio conglomerate.[514]

GEORGE AND MARTHA REALLY NEED TO TALK

One piece of presidential trivia that I have always found fascinating is that George Washington was an amazing dancer. His dance of choice? The minuet. And it is not an easy dance to do. It's a slow, stately ballroom dance

---

512 (C. L. Johnson n.d.) Diary entry, November 23, 1963.
513 (Kearns Goodwin 1991) pages 98–100.
514 (Hachitt 2003).

executed in triple time. But apparently, the father of this country could cut quite the rug on the dance floor.[515]

Back in Washington's time, how a couple danced together was more than just flirtation. It was also a subtle communication of social status and courtship.

While nuance in dancing creates a smoothness on the dance floor, straightforward communication between spouses is a very important thing in financial planning. I often find that spouses are about 90 percent aligned on their planning. They might agree they want to own a home, retire to a sunny state, or buy a new car. Those are the easy money communications between couples.

That remaining 10 percent can create some real challenges, and couples might disagree on that 10 percent for any number of reasons. The reason could be simple and straightforward in that one spouse prefers to invest more heavily in stocks while the other prefers real estate. However, I can tell you that the 10 percent differential usually goes deeper than that.

In any marital relationship, any interaction about money is a loaded question. Both spouses come from different homes where money was taught through words and actions. Money translates to emotion in a marriage. These emotions can range from controlling to deprived to overly generous. You name it, and money attaches to that emotion. Studies on money and marriage often focus on situations where money is not discussed between spouses. One of the most prevailing reasons for this is that the household is shouldering significant debt. That debt creates anxiety.

Anyone who has dealt with an anxiety-driven discussion with their spouse will know how fast the discussion can go downhill. To keep the relationship going, many people will opt to just avoid the topic and hope it fixes itself on its own. Unfortunately, that tactic generally leads to the opposite desired result. The money problem gets bigger, and the spouses avoid talking about it more.

Finally, in today's world, we also have to layer in the fact that many households are two-career homes. Women are making money that allows

---

515 For more insight into the dancing skills of our first president, check out Mount Vernon's take at https://www.mountvernon.org/george-washington/athleticism/on-the-dance-floor/. According to the Mount Vernon records, Washington was dancing well into his fifties and sixties.

for more equality and parity in the home. But in return, this can make men feel stifled in their role in the marriage.

Basically, what I'm saying is that money can be a big issue in any relationship. The best way to work through money issues is through communication and connection. And if you don't communicate well, it can cause a lot of frustration for your spouse.

Perhaps this is best illustrated in the marriage of George and Martha Washington. By all accounts, the marriage was a love match between the two. Martha was a young widow whose first husband was decades older than she, but his death left her a very wealthy woman. In fact, don't even think your school history lessons told you the truth of what she looked like.[516] She was stunning.

Washington was quite a striking man, especially by eighteenth-century standards. At six feet three inches, he towered above his shorter contemporaries and was a good-looking man whose exploits on the military field made him appear quite dashing. As you can imagine, they were drawn to each other at first glance. In today's parlance, Martha swiped right.

The Washingtons were quite successful in combining their lives—and fortunes—in marriage. George had done well in building his own finances, but by marrying Martha, he became one of the wealthiest men in the country. In a custom not often used today, he was responsible for her dower property. And as a result, he became the custodian for land and, tragically, slaves who were part of that dower property.

In twenty-first-century America, we don't have second spouses holding dower estates, but an aspect of Washington's situation is still relevant to how we operate today. In the event that someone dies without an estate plan—or intestate—the state will step in and award the surviving spouse a one-third interest. This is pretty much the law of the land across the United States. In Martha's case, her first husband didn't have an estate plan. She received one-third of the estate as a life interest, and the remaining two-thirds went to her minor children. However, until they reached the age of major-

---

516 In recent years, historians have started to reassess our vision of Martha. Rather than the little old lady in her later years, they have focused on the fact that Martha was a beautiful and smart woman who was very sought after. You can learn more at https://www.smithsonianmag.com/history/martha-washington-life-elusive-historians-180976983/.

ity, their portion of the estate had to be managed. Washington stepped in to help in this role when he married Martha.

The Washingtons grew their wealth over the decades they were married. They were a couple with great communication and had a strong connection. In fact, Martha even traveled with Washington and stayed with him and the army during the Revolutionary War.

While the Washingtons managed their marriage well, an incident at the end of their lives was a result of poor planning—very poor estate planning. After he left the presidency in March 1797, Washington assumed he would finally live the life he wanted with Martha at Mount Vernon. He had dreamed of this moment—of working on his lands and spending time with the woman he had been married to for forty-two years. But while he worked hard overseeing the properties, he had another focus in mind: how he wanted his estate to pass.

As 1799 began, Washington was in a happy place. His beloved granddaughter, Nelly Parke Custis, had recently married, and he had settled down into his new life. Sometime between mid-May and July 9, 1799, he drafted his will.[517]

Now, Washington had a lot of experience with estate planning. For over 130 years prior to his death, his ancestors had written wills, including his father and his elder brother. Washington knew that it was important to be clear and concise. He had also served as executor in others' wills and understood that administration could be challenging. Trust me—no one enjoys being an executor. It's a nightmare of a role that requires a lot of patience and organizational skills.

Washington's asset base was complex. Not only did he have Martha's dower property, but he owned land from Virginia to New York, as well as stocks and bonds, livestock, and the Mount Vernon estate. The total value at the time was roughly $780,000—or the equivalent of $20 million today.

Washington wrestled with how to dispose of the assets and like many today, he was plagued with competing interests in the event he predeceased Martha. How could he have the assets pass smoothly so he could protect his wife if he died first?

Washington was known for his prudence in thinking through a problem, and he felt time was on his side. In July 1797, he came up with the

---

517   (Prussing 1927) page 12.

solution to write not one but two wills. The two versions reflected the struggle he was feeling internally: whether to free his slaves at his death. He figured he would determine, as time passed, which version was a better fit.

Unfortunately for Washington, he had much less time than he imagined. Just five months later, Washington's personal secretary, Tobias Lear, noted that on Thursday, December 12, 1799, Washington rode out to his farm and that "rain, hail, snow falling alternately with a cold wind" had soaked Washington."[518] The next day, Washington awoke with a cold that worsened over the next forty-eight hours.

He was fluish and had a throat infection and, due to the ineptitude of contemporary doctors, became worse. It seems incomprehensible to us today, but he hovered near death due to a condition called quinsy,[519] where an abscess forms between the tonsils and the throat wall. It is survivable, if treated correctly. If not, the abscess worsens until pus is inhaled. This aspiration is life-threatening.

Since death wasn't uncommon in those days in those circumstances, Washington knew he had to address his estate plan immediately. As he lay sick in bed on Saturday, December 14, at about 4:30 p.m., Lear noted that Washington asked Martha to bring his two versions of the will to him. He reread both and made a fateful decision: with a flick of his hand, he threw one version into the fire. A short time later, he passed away.

As mentioned above, the issue that Washington struggled with in his estate plans was slavery. As disgusting as this sounds to modern ears, Washington had 317 slaves at Mount Vernon. Of this group, 123 slaves were his property and could be freed at his command. The remaining 194 slaves were technically Martha's dower slaves, part of her late husband's estate over which Washington had less control.

Given the love match and constant communication between Washington and Martha, you might think he would have discussed with her how he was thinking about the problem. I have sat in many estate planning meetings where the impact of a disposition is debated and thought through. I like to play out with both spouses exactly how the money will

---

518 (Death of Washington: Letters and Recollections of George Washington 1932) The description is that of Tobias Lear's from his diary on the last days of Washington.

519 "8 Facts About George Washington's Death," George Washington's Mount Vernon, https://www.mountvernon.org/george-washington/death/8-facts-about-george-washingtons-death/.

Lady Bird Buys a Radio Station

flow. Informed spouses can often keep each other from making poor decisions because they can call out potential issues. But Washington didn't do that. He didn't involve Martha at all in drafting the estate plan; he failed in his communication with her.

Once he passed away, she got a shocking surprise when his fifteen-page will was probated. In it appeared this key provision:

> Upon the decease (of) my wife, it is my Will & desire th⟨at⟩ all the Slaves which I hold in ⟨my⟩ *own right*, shall receive their free⟨dom⟩.[520]

Or to put it more succinctly: Washington stated that he wanted his slaves to be freed upon Martha's death.

At first glance, this phrasing doesn't seem so bad. It's along the lines of setting up a qualified terminable interest property trust (QTIP) in estate plans today that allows a surviving spouse access to assets. (We saw this earlier with Warren Harding's estate plan.) He didn't want to disrupt his wife's lifestyle just because he had passed. In fact, 170 years later, Eisenhower did something similar for his wife, Mamie. They had spent almost two decades building and residing at the Eisenhower farm in Gettysburg, Pennsylvania. In Ike's will, he stipulated that the farm would pass to the National Park Service but not until after Mamie's death. Mamie survived Ike for ten years before this disposition occurred.

By not discussing this with Martha and by not thinking about the repercussions, Washington put Martha in a precarious situation. If their slaves would be freed at Martha's death, what would prevent one of the slaves from murdering her to seek freedom for all of them? That's where communication comes in. If Washington had explained this to Martha,

---

[520] George Washington's Last Will and Testament, 9 July 1799, Founders Online, https://founders.archives.gov/documents/Washington/06-04-02-0404-0001. The full provision says, "Upon the decease of my wife, it is my Will & desire th⟨at⟩ all the Slaves which I hold in ⟨my⟩ *own right*, shall receive their free⟨dom To emancipate them during ⟨her⟩ life, would, tho' earnestly wish⟨ed by⟩ me, be attended with such insu⟨pera⟩ble difficulties on account of thei⟨r interm⟩ixture by Marriages with the ⟨dow⟩er Negroes, as to excite the most pa⟨in⟩ful sensations, if not disagreeabl⟨e c⟩onsequences from the latter, while ⟨both⟩ descriptions are in the occupancy ⟨of⟩ the same Proprietor; it not being ⟨in⟩ my power, under the tenure by which ⟨th⟩e Dower Negroes are held, to man⟨umi⟩t them."

she might have pointed out the unintended implications of his estate disposition.

Yet, Washington's error is not uncommon in the estate-planning world. In their book, *Preparing Heirs*, Roy Williams and Vic Preisser noted that in their research of wealthy families, 70 percent of all estate plans fail in transfers *within the family* with the main reason being issues around communication.[521] This is no surprise. While Washington and Martha were a love match, researchers find that "most couples chose not to talk about their finances as it closely relates to feelings, such as success, competence, safety and security."[522] Slavery was a highly fraught topic that was further complicated by the fact that many slaveowners believed they did care for their slaves and were acting in their best interests. It may have been a conversation that Washington was simply uncomfortable with or one that Martha was unwilling to have.[523]

Further researchers find that couples struggle to discuss finances as it can relate to childhood experiences. In Washington's case, as a child, Washington saw his mother suffer under his father's will. As his mother, Mary, was the second wife, upon his father Augustine's death, she lost access to most of the marital assets. They passed to Washington's brother. This would have made an imprint on young Washington. At the end of his life, those earlier emotional experiences may have been triggered. Rather than communicate with Martha his intent, he made the decision to use his estate plan to protect her from the struggles his mother had, inadvertently making her a potential target.

Now given Washington's revered position in society, his will was published, first in newspapers and eventually into a book. The press shared the more interesting parts of Washington's will. Newspapers in certain areas of the country and the world praised Washington on freeing his slaves and claimed that Martha had already done so.[524] It made the Washingtons out to be magnanimous and warm-hearted individuals.

---

521 (Williams and Preisser 2010) pages 2–3.
522 (Grobbelaar and Alsemgeest 2016) page 271.
523 Historians have made the case that Washington's will and its manumission of his slaves was a statement of his growing anti-slavery viewpoint.
524 (Bell's Weekly Messenger 1800).

Lady Bird Buys a Radio Station

But the truth was, Martha was terrified. Not only did she lose her beloved husband, but she knew her death would free her slaves. The publication of his will also meant the slaves knew the provisions.

Now, Washington had given Martha a life estate in his slaves and other assets. But at her death, once the slaves were freed, Washington's will intended for Mount Vernon and his papers to pass to his nephew Bushrod Washington.

Bushrod was a judge in Virginia. One day, following Washington's death, Bushrod gave notice to his peers that he had been called to Mount Vernon by Martha. The reason she called him was clear: there had been an attempt to set fire to Mount Vernon, and it was thought that the slaves had set it.

Bushrod, along with Chief Justice John Marshall, arrived at Mount Vernon. Given the urgency of the situation, Bushrod and Marshall advised Martha to take the following action: she should emancipate the slaves immediately to prevent anything worse from happening.[525]

As the year anniversary of Washington's death approached, Martha received a visitor from the capital. First Lady Abigail Adams had traveled thirty-six miles to come to see the grieving Martha. Adams herself was no fan of slavery.

Usually, the conversation of First Ladies is private. But front of mind was a document that Martha signed on December 15, 1800. The document was a deed of manumission that would free Washington's slaves on January 1, 1801.

Martha was anxious. She confided to Abigail that "with all her fortune finds it difficult to support her family, which consists of three Hundred souls."[526] But Martha also shared that "In the state in which they were left by the General, to be free at her death, she did not feel as tho her Life was safe in their Hands, many of whom would be told that it was [in] there interest to get rid of her."[527]

---

525 (Binney 1858) pages 25–26. This story is recounted by Horace Binney in his biography of Bushrod Washington. They were contemporaries and there is no reason to believe this to be untrue. The only issue is the time frame Binney proposes is that this occurred a few years after Washington died. However, Martha issued the deed of manumission just more than a year after his death.
526 Letter Abigail Adams to Mary Smith Cranch, dated December 21, 1800.
527 Ibid.

Ultimately, just a year after Washington died, Martha freed their slaves via a deed of manumission. The unintended consequences of the poor estate drafting were mitigated. And she herself died just a short while after Washington. An imperfect end to a wonderful love story.

THE DANGERS OF MONEY DISORDERS ON A MARRIAGE

When it comes to money, a marriage can have miscommunication at times (like the Washingtons), or they can have mismatched financial skills (like we saw previously with Reagan and Jane Wyman and budgeting). However, when working with these couples, you focus on trying to find common money beliefs (building a radio station together like the Johnsons) in order to work through these financial challenges.

But there are some financial behaviors that are classified as *money disorders*. A marriage can be undone when these behaviors undermine stability. Psychologists break money disorders into the following: compulsive buying, gambling, hoarding, financial enabling, financial denial, financial dependence, and enmeshment.[528] These mental health challenges are more common than you might think.

It is easier to see these disorders when working with a couple because the spouses often reflect what the other's behavior is causing. It is not uncommon to find that one spouse "acts out" more than the other spouse and is seen as the cause of the problems. Studies have found that negative financial behaviors ultimately have an impact on the satisfaction and stability of an intimate relationship.

But sometimes these behaviors are concealed. That's when we enter the world of financial infidelity. Financial infidelity is defined as "engaging in any financial behavior expected to be disapproved of by one's romantic partner and intentionally failing to disclose this behavior to them."[529] Concealment is a key aspect of this behavior. Examples include hiding purchases and debt or lying about income or expenses. The reasons behind financial infidelity can vary from the need for control in a relationship, financial disagreements between couples, differing financial values, and lack of trust.

---

528 (Taylor, Klontz and Lawson 2017) page 125.
529 (Garbinsky, et al. 2020) page 1.

Lady Bird Buys a Radio Station

In a 2023 survey, the National Endowment for Financial Education found that two in five Americans have committed a financial deception in a current or past relationship.[530] Researchers point out that while they are quite prevalent, they are hard to track because the behavior remains hidden and hard to observe. But they are often a key cause in divorce.

Abraham Lincoln might know a few things about money disorders. He became financially successful—at times due to his wife, Mary, and at times despite her. The Lincolns struggled throughout their marriage to be open and honest about money due to conflicting financial backgrounds and a plethora of challenging money disorders. The repercussion was that they often were dissatisfied with the relationship.

Lincoln was realistic about his financial origins. During the 1860 presidential election, Lincoln spoke to J. L. Scripps of the *Chicago Tribune* about his beginnings. William Henry Herndon recounted the exchange: "'Why, Scripps,' said he, 'it is a great piece of folly to attempt to make anything out of me or my early life. It can all be condensed into a single sentence, and that sentence you will find in Gray's Elegy,

> *"The short and simple annals of the poor."*
> That's my life, and that's all you or anyone else can make out of it.'"[531]

Lincoln didn't see his poverty as unique. Rather, it was just how things were. Yet, despite being poor and self-taught, Lincoln eventually made his way to Springfield, the capital of Illinois, on April 15, 1837.[532] Upon his arrival, his friend and confidante Joshua Speed described Lincoln leaving New Salem and heading to Springfield on a borrowed horse with "no earthly goods but a pair of saddle-bags."[533]

---

530 (National Endowment for Financial Education 2021).
531 (Herndon 1888) Story as recounted by Herndon from a letter John L. Scripps to William H. Herndon, dated June 24, 1865. No one can study Lincoln without giving great thanks to his former law partner, William H. Herndon. After Lincoln's death, Herndon collected contemporary recollections of Lincoln. The recollections that were sent to Herndon are available online at the Northern Illinois University Digital Library.
532 I always find it fascinating that Lincoln enters Springfield on April 15, 1837, and dies twenty-eight years later on the same day.
533 Letter from Joshua Speed to William H. Herndon, dated 1865.

All the Presidents' Money

Springfield was the social and political center of Illinois in the 1840s. Despite his impoverished background, Lincoln was on his way to success as an attorney as he was interesting, charming, and knew how to tell a story. He was welcomed into the social scene, learning firsthand about wealth and politics.

At six feet four inches, Lincoln stood head and shoulders above most people he met. As he made the social rounds, he met Mary Todd, a wealthy socialite from Lexington, Kentucky. She was living in Springfield with her sister and was taking part in the debutante season there. She was only five feet two inches, and this difference in height wasn't the only sharp contrast between the two. Well-educated and vivacious, Mary came from money and was accustomed to a certain lifestyle.

Yet, there was something that both Lincoln and Mary did have in common: challenging childhoods. While her family had means, Mary was one of sixteen children, often overlooked, and could only get attention from her father when she had a conflict with her stepmother.

For Lincoln, courting Mary gave him access to high society. Mary's sister, Elizabeth Edwards, was married to Ninian Edwards, the son of the Illinois governor. Her sister's home in Springfield was a large, luxurious two-story home on Quality Hill, nicknamed Aristocracy Hill. Guests were greeted in French. And their parties were ones not seen in the area at all with dancing, music, and violins.[534] It was the crème de la crème.

Lincoln had no real context for this highbrow world. Leonard Swett, a contemporary of Lincoln's in the early 1840s described him as poor and "his ideas of money were always far from lavish. I never knew him to refuse to spend for anything he needed. Yet he was always rigidly frugal and in no way indulged, in himself or others, idleness or wastefulness."[535]

Not surprisingly, Lincoln used humor to mitigate any discomfort he felt in Mary's world. He would often joke that God only needed one "d," while the Todds needed two.[536]

---

534 (Strozier 2016).
535 Letter Leonard Swett to William H. Herndon, dated January 15, 1866. Also discussed in (Burlingame, *An American Marriage: The Untold Story of Abraham Lincoln and Mary Todd* 2021) page 100.
536 (Strozier 2016) page 221.

Lady Bird Buys a Radio Station

Though Lincoln and Mary were from different backgrounds, both were clever and ambitious. They were drawn to each other. After a tumultuous courtship, they married, despite her family's misgivings about Lincoln's more uncouth beginnings.

From the get-go, the marriage seemed mismatched. But the real disconnect was when it came to money. Today when people marry, we tell them to have talks about values and life goals, including personal finance. Sharing common financial goals is a way to build connection and intimacy. Yet, this likely didn't occur in the Lincoln marriage. For all his skills as an amazing orator, contemporaries often noted that Lincoln often avoided direct discussions with his wife.

As newlyweds, Mary was surprised to learn how lean their finances were. She was used to living with her father's money and then in her sister and brother-in-law's wealthy household. Lincoln was doing moderately well as an attorney with an income of $1,500—enough to afford a good lifestyle in Springfield.[537] But what Mary didn't realize was that Lincoln's expenses exceeded his income. He was still paying down debts from earlier failed business ventures and supporting his parents. At the end of each month, they were often in the red. Whether he disclosed this to her prior to their wedding isn't clear.

In order to keep costs down, the newlyweds rented a room. Lincoln wrote to Speed, "We are not keeping house, but boarding at the Globe Tavern…[o]ur room…and boarding only costs us four dollars a week."[538]

While Lincoln was often away working, Mary was alone, pregnant, and confined to the limited quarters they had at the Globe. Prior to her marriage, Mary had been waited on by servants (in fact, her family owned slaves), received guests in drawing rooms, and was the belle at parties. She had never known the level of financial straits they were in. The financial stress was traumatic for her. When their first son, Robert, was born, another boarder recalled that "Mrs. Lincoln had no nurse for herself or the baby. Whether this was due to poverty…I do not know."[539]

---

537 (Pratt 1943) page 85. Pratt indicates that from 1840 to 1850, Lincoln was earning $1,500 to $2,000 annually.
538 (Pratt 1943) page 83.
539 (Pratt 1943) Sophie Bledsoe who lived at the Globe Tavern recalled being a six-year-old who cared for the infant due to Mary being unable to at times.

All the Presidents' Money

The Lincolns struggled to financially make it work. But the financial challenges, along with Lincoln's constant life on the road in the legal circuit, undermined the marriage. Finally, a savior appeared. Mary's father came to town to meet her new husband and child, and bestowed a myriad of gifts: twenty-five dollars in gold coins, eighty acres of land in Illinois worth $1,200, and even an annual annuity of $1,100.[540] Further, he gave Lincoln a legal case that resulted in a nice settlement for the Lincolns.[541]

Lincoln saw no issue in accepting his father-in-law's generosity to a point. Lincoln prized his sense of integrity, which would cause tension with Mary. She noted once that "he is too honest to make a penny outside of his salary."[542] But their financial challenges had made an imprint upon Mary. She struggled more with acute stress and emotional dysregulation. With an absent husband, she started to display odd behavior related to money.

Within their new home, Mary scrimped on household expenses. Yet, she hoarded excess funds to pay for luxurious items. At one point a stunning bolt of silk was available. Rather than buying just enough for herself, she bought the entire bolt—she didn't want anyone else to have it. Spending became a way to self-soothe.

At first, this behavior was easy to hide as Lincoln was often traveling the legal circuit and rarely home. But as time went on, it got harder to hide. When Lincoln would return home, he made the rounds around town to pay open invoices and was chagrined by her acquisition of luxurious goods. Unfortunately for Mary, while her husband cared for her, he did not know how to help her. Rather, he avoided the issue and simply paid whatever bills he received.

Now, on first glance it would be easy to write off Mary's spending as simply someone who lacks financial discipline. I am sure Lincoln probably thought this at times. But spending can be a symptom of a whole host of mental health issues, ranging from obsessive-compulsive disorder to bipolar disorder to general anxiety. Or if the spending is hidden, it might mean a lack of trust. Today, the priority would be to involve a mental health profes-

---

540 (Pratt 1943) page 67.
541 (Baker, Mary Todd Lincoln: Managing Home, Husband, and Children 1990).
542 (Keckley 1868) page 129.

sional who can help them. For a spouse, it would mean working with their partner on agreeing to a set spending pattern and having regular check-ins.

But for the Lincolns, these things did not happen. Rather, as time went on, they were further pulled apart due to grief from the loss of their son Eddie in 1850. They entered a pattern very early on that defined them for years: Mary acted in an over-the-top manner (or what historians often label "histrionics"), often creating a lot of drama while Lincoln withdrew from her emotionally. His withdrawal would cause her to create more and more chaos.

THE CHALLENGES CONTINUE IN WASHINGTON

Becoming the president and moving to Washington, DC, only amplified the situation for the Lincolns. Two months after Lincoln's 1861 inauguration, Mary made the first of many trips to New York City to enjoy shopping on the Ladies' Mile, an area of the city filled with department stores. A. T. Stewart was a particular favorite. Newspapers became accustomed to reporting her spending sprees. One article by the *New York Herald* noted that Mary was seen "from the early hours…until late in the evening…ransack[ing] the treasures of the Broadway dry good stores."[543] Her purchases were often for clothing but what was shocking was the quantity and quality of the items she acquired. She had chinchilla coats and shawls in different fabrics that cost between $50 to $2,000.[544] Stories of three hundred pairs of gloves being ordered made the rounds. Not only was her spending getting out of control, but she was also keeping the level of debt a secret.

Lincoln struggled with his wife's spending yet was conscious that they were living a very anxious life with a war going on. Then the worst happened: their eleven-year-old son Willie died of typhoid fever. Grief compounded an already delicate financial situation.

Three weeks after Willie's death, Elisha Whittlesey, the comptroller of the Treasury, received a letter from the president. It read:

---

543 (Fleischner 2003) This section relies heavily on Fleischner's commentary on page 272.
544 (Fleischner 2003) page 272.

All the Presidents' Money

Private   Executive Mansion
Washington, March 11, 1862

Hon. Elisha Whittlesey

My dear Sir:

Once or twice since I have been in this House, accounts have been presented at your Bureau, which were incorrect. I shall be personally and greatly obliged to you if you will carefully scan any account which comes from here; and if in any there shall appear the least semblance wrong, make it known to me directly.

Yours very truly,

A. Lincoln

Like all presidents, the Lincolns were responsible for financing the entertainment and food in the White House. It was surprising that he would get involved in an accounting error while a war was going on. But Mary's financial behaviors were starting to have an impact on the White House. Relations with her husband's private secretaries John Hay and John Nicolay had deteriorated so much that they called her "Hellcat" behind her back.[545] Lincoln may have felt that this might be the perfect time to get this confusion cleared up from the White House dinner thrown in honor of Prince Napoleon on August 3, 1861.

The story was one that was typical of Mary and her financial management. She put together a White House dinner that included all the touches—food, wine, and flowers. She herself was dressed to the nines. But when it was time to pay the bill for the party, Mary balked.

White House entertainment expenses were long thought to be the responsibility of the president, but Mary boldly presented a $900 invoice for

---

545   Letter John Hay to John Nicolay, dated April 4, 1862.

the dinner to Caleb Smith, the secretary of the interior. This was a dilemma for Smith. When he spoke to William Seward, the secretary of state, he learned that Seward had thrown the same exact dinner the night after the one at the White House—same chef, same food, same everything. But Seward's bill was only $300. Smith was furious. He denied the payment of the dinner bill. But Mary wasn't to be daunted. Rather, because the White House gardens were using manure coming from her horses, she wrote up a bill for the manure totaling $300 and sent it to Smith. Smith fumed, but he knew it wouldn't serve the president well if this became a scandal. He paid the manure invoice and put the issue to rest.

Nine hundred dollars might not seem like much, but it has the same purchasing power as $30,000 today.

Lincoln realized that he had to make sure this never happened again, hence the letter requesting the invoices be sent to him. He didn't want Mary to be padding her pockets in order to shop.

FINANCIAL INFIDELITY REARS ITS UGLY HEAD

As the Lincoln presidency continued, financial infidelity began to enter the relationship. Mary's dressmaker, Elizabeth Keckley, recalled that Mary opened up about her financial issues in 1864. She explained to Keckley that she had "contracted large debts, of which [Lincoln] knows nothing, and which he will be unable to pay if he is defeated."[546]

Mary went on to explain the intensity of the debt. "I owe altogether about twenty-seven thousand dollars; the principal portion at Stewart's, in New York." (This would be the equivalent of $525,000 in 2024 dollars.)

Mary believed Lincoln was unaware of her behavior. She shared with Keckley that "if he knew that his wife were involved to the extent that she is, the knowledge would drive him mad....He does not know a thing about any debt...If he is reelected, I can keep him in ignorance of my affairs; but if he is defeated, then the bills will be sent in and he will know all."[547]

While Mary committed her own form of financial infidelity, Lincoln wasn't a completely innocent party, either. Lincoln focused on aggressively saving while in the White House. When they left Springfield, they had

---

546 (Keckley 1868) page 129.
547 (Keckley 1868) page 130.

just over $9,000 in interest bearing notes, a little cash, and a home worth $5,000.[548] His presidential salary of $25,000 moved him into a different bracket. Upon his arrival in Washington, DC, he opened a bank account at Riggs & Co. and deposited his monthly paycheck. As the excess balance grew, he bought Treasurys with yields ranging from 5 percent to 7.3 percent, often with the interest paid in gold.[549]

By April 1865, his net worth had risen over four years from $15,000 to $85,000.[550] Yet, he was selective about what he shared with Mary and didn't always give her the full financial picture.

The Lincolns never got to resolve their financial infidelities and problems. However, Lincoln may have been trying to.

On the day he died, he spent time with Mary. With the war ending, he was turning toward the future. In one of their final conversations, he tried to address her overspending by doing something I see spouses do all the time: he understated their financial situation in an attempt to potentially rein in her spending. He said:

"We have laid by some money, and during this term we will try and save up more, but shall not have enough to support us. We will go back to Illinois, and I will open a law-office at Springfield or Chicago, and practice law, and at least do enough to help give us a livelihood."[551]

Ultimately, the Lincolns were an example of how money disorders can undermine the connection in a marriage. It isn't clear if he could have stabilized her spending or been more transparent with her if he had lived. More than likely, the Lincolns would have carried on in the same manner and never been able to have the connection they both wanted.

One final postscript in the messy finances of the Lincolns: Lincoln died intestate. The estate took two and a half years to be probated. It was split in three equal shares of $36,765.60 each ($770,000 in 2024 dollars) between Mary and their two surviving sons, Robert and Thomas ("Tad").[552]

---

548 (Pratt 1943) page ix.
549 (Pratt) pages 182–185.
550 (Pratt 1943) page 125.
551 (Pratt 1943) page 125.
552 (Pratt 1943) pages 139–140. It should be noted that the executor, Justice David Davis, found the Lincoln financial affairs in good condition. When Mary died in 1882, she was a bit more prepared than Lincoln as she had executed a will.

A MODEL MARRIAGE

As I said earlier, the best way to grow wealth is to get married and stay married. Yet, it is often said that in most marriages, the arguments are around two things: sex and money. While financial planning cannot help with the first, it can with the second. Because being a true financial partner allows for better financial decision-making.

Chapter Nine

MEET GEORGE WASHINGTON—THE ULTIMATE AMERICAN HUSTLER
(OR GRIT)

George Washington, Woodrow Wilson, and Herbert Hoover: three men, three different time periods in America. All three were smart and ambitious. None of them were born into wealth. All three would go on to be president. Yet, as they all embarked on their early careers, only two would develop unbelievable wealth. Was it nurture or nature? Or was it grit?

Angela Duckworth's 2016 book, *Grit*, defines it as the "perseverance and passion for long-term goals" and states that it involves "working strenuously towards challenges, maintaining effort and interest over years despite failure, adversity, and plateaus in progress."[553] Stamina is a key component here, and that comes down to the old adage that advises focusing on the marathon, rather than the sprint. Grit is a key component of financial success. It's not the only one, but in the right environment where there is opportunity, grit can be the differentiator in building wealth.

Using grit to manage financial behavior has been found to have an impact on net worth, lowering debt and lessening financial distress: the greater the grit, the greater the shaping of wealth. And certain personality traits, like grit, are often developed in childhood. Researchers at Washington University in St. Louis decided to see if gritty savers are "better savers by virtue of their wealth or due to diligent choices that benefit their long-

---
553 Duckworth, 2007 study, pages 1087–1088.

term economic health."[554] What they found is that "gritty individuals save more due to a different propensity to make certain financial choices that build wealth."[555] These individuals can tap into their determination and focus on the long-term goals. As a result, this intensity causes "gritty people [to] have positive long-term financial outcomes not only because of greater career attainment, but also because of better financial behaviors—even under duress."[556]

The basic skills of strong finance—budgeting, connecting with your future self—are the tools that allow grit to prosper with finance: from growing your asset base to paying down debt. And even when financial behaviors cause a negative situation, grit can allow an individual to regroup and pivot. Failure is also a key component of developing grit. Without failure, we don't have that moment of self-reflection to figure out what went wrong.

THE GRITTIER THE BETTER

A lot of presidents had great financial grit, but George Washington was the master of financial grit. Long before he became president, Washington was a first-class hustler. He was incredibly passionate about succeeding and building wealth. And he was wired to persevere so that he could rise in economic status. The hurdles in front of him were substantial, yet he was able to overcome them. He was very focused on becoming financially successful.

To understand why Washington was such a hustler, it might come down to a book he borrowed when he was thirteen from his neighbor William Fairfax. Borrowing a book from your neighbor seems like an odd indicator of grit, but it wasn't just any book—it was the 1679 tome called *The Compleat Surveyor* by William Leybourn. At the time Washington borrowed it, he was at a crossroads in his life after the death of his father, Augustine.[557] For Washington and his mother, it was a devastating blow to their security. It wasn't that Washington's father died penniless—quite the contrary. But

---

554 (Jason Jabbari 2021) page 6.
555 Ibid.
556 (Jason Jabbari 2021) page 18.
557 (Knollenberg 1964) page 4. There is very little in this historical record on Washington's relationship with his father. Washington only mentions his father three times in over twenty thousand pieces of personal correspondence.

Meet George Washington–The Ultimate American Hustler

his father already had an heir in George's older half-brother Laurence. In the social-economic status of the eighteenth century, it wasn't a great place to be. To be fair, he was starting out better than many, but Washington was going to have to hustle or be resigned to struggle.

Washington's mother is often maligned by historians. She's seen as a burden and unlikable. Her relationship with her famous son is often described as strained.[558] And there is truth to that. At times, Mary could complain and nag him. She would guilt him into paying her expenses later in life. But like most women, she understood the need to create security, and over the course of her life had to weather financial ups and downs. To understand where Washington's grit came from, we need to explore Mary's story.

Mary was the daughter of an elderly planter and likely an indentured servant. She lost her father when she was three years old and her mother at the age of twelve.[559] Given the precariousness of her situation, Mary was placed in a guardianship under a man named George Eskridge. When Mary turned twenty-two, Eskridge introduced her to Augustine Washington, a recent widower. Mary was considered a highly valued bride due to the fact that her dowry was significant, with at least one thousand acres of property and three slave boys.[560] Mary and Augustine married soon thereafter and would have six children, including her eldest, George, who was born in 1732.

Mary was dependent upon her husband, and she understood that at his death, his sons from his first marriage, Laurence and Augustine Jr., would inherit the majority of Augustine's assets and that she would live at Laurence's whim. But her survival instinct was strong. And she wasn't afraid to speak up in a time when a woman's input wasn't appreciated. Mary was, in many ways, a great teacher of grit.

When Augustine died in 1743, Mary's financial stability became precarious. Like a lot of gentlemen of his time, Augustine's asset base was land

---

558 "Mary Ball Washington," George Washington's Mount Vernon, https://www.mountvernon.org/library/digitalhistory/digital-encyclopedia/article/mary-ball-washington/.
559 (Saxton 2019).
560 Ibid. As a result of her parents' deaths, Mary had inherited two parcels of land, a good horse and saddle, and three slave boys.

rich with little liquidity.[561] His estate consisted of over ten thousand acres of land and forty-nine slaves.[562] As expected, he left the majority of his assets, including Mount Vernon, to twenty-five-year-old Laurence.

As his second wife, Mary had inherited a life estate on Ferry Farm and some land. But this inheritance was really for her first-born son, George, to be given to him at age twenty-one. If Mary were to remarry, she would have to guarantee that her children would still receive their inheritance from Augustine. Washington himself didn't fare so well in the estate plan. He got some plots of land in Fredericksburg, but his father didn't stipulate that George's education should be paid for, and for the rest of his life, Washington regretted that he didn't have a chance to go to college.

WASHINGTON FINDS HIS PASSION

With college out of the question, Washington focused on learning through books. He learned math and geometry and even trigonometry. But at some point, in 1745, Washington approached his neighbor Fairfax and asked if he could borrow a book on surveying. Growing up in Virginia made it clear that the way to money and power was in land, so George studied the rules of surveying. In the pages of the borrowed book, Washington wrote out complex math equations.[563] He studied the rules of surveying land. He was focused, and learning about land was slowly becoming a passion.

Despite their father's estate plan and a fourteen-year age gap, Washington and Laurence were close. Laurence was incredibly well-connected and had an interest in helping his little brother navigate potential career options. Among his many contacts, Laurence was close to a group of planters—Robert Jackson, Nathaniel Chapman, Daniel McCarty, James Thompson, and Anthony Strother—who were also his father's executors. This group of older men saw potential in young Washington. They also wanted to help protect Laurence's interests. As a result, they came up with a pretty interesting idea on how to help young Washington proceed in life. Rather than a formal education, they felt he needed an adventure to give

---

561 (Neill, Washington and Orme 1892) page 269.
562 (Ellis 2004) page 8.
563 "Original Washington Book Returns to His Mount Vernon Estate," George Washington's Mount Vernon, https://www.mountvernon.org/about/news/article/original-washington-book-returns-to-his-mount-vernon-estate/.

him life experience. Laurence proposed Washington join the Royal Navy as a midshipman. It would pay twenty-three shillings a month, which is approximately $283 in today's money.[564] Washington was excited by this idea. He knew that the military would be a way for him to make his way in the world.

Despite Washington's eagerness, as he was only fourteen, his mother needed to be consulted. At first, Mary agreed with the group that it was a path Washington should consider. But then she started wavering, eventually opposing the idea.[565] An exchange of letters between the group made it clear that Mary was being "difficult."

On September 18, 1746, Robert Jackson wrote Laurence, "I am afraid Mrs. Washington will not keep up to her first resolution. She seems to intimate a dislike of George's going to sea, and says several persons have told her it is a bad scheme."[566]

While Laurence and his friends were frustrated, Mary had a reason to be wary. It was fairly common for a third of the midshipmen on a boat to not survive due to disease. Plus, her brother Joseph Ball had chimed in support of her position. He also gave her an interesting piece of financial advice, given Washington's eagerness and ambition. He wrote her in a letter: "He must not be too hasty to be rich, but go on gently, and with patience, and things will naturally go."[567]

How Washington took the news, we don't know. He was probably pretty disappointed and not thrilled with his mother. But part of Washington's ability to persevere and be scrappy reflected another key component of grit—the power of the pivot. While joining the navy would have given him income, when those plans did not materialize, he moved onto the next opportunity.

A UNIQUE OPPORTUNITY

Learning the art of surveying is not easy. It requires technical knowledge as well as experience in the field. After almost three years of studying, Wash-

---

564 Eric W. Nye, "Pounds Sterling to Dollars: Historical Conversion of Currency," accessed Thursday, March 14, 2024, https://www.uwyo.edu/numimage/currency.htm.
565 (Knollenberg 1964) page 4.
566 Neill, page 271.
567 Ibid., page 272. Also discussed (Knollenberg 1964) page 7.

ington received an invitation from William Fairfax—his neighbor who had lent him the book.

William Fairfax was no ordinary neighbor. He was a wealthy and well-connected man who owned significant land holdings throughout Virginia—more than five million acres (as in Fairfax, Virginia, is named for his family). He was also Laurence's father-in-law. Fairfax had taken on the role of a surrogate father to Washington, and Washington welcomed the arrangement.

One day in 1748, when Washington was sixteen, Fairfax invited him to join a proper survey trip. Fairfax had considerable lands he wanted his son George Fairfax to survey. Washington jumped at the opportunity to join. The group, which also included James Genn, the county surveyor of Prince William County, rode to the western part of Virginia to survey Fairfax's land in the Shenandoah Valley. The team was very experienced in surveying. Washington observed and learned as the fairly large team laid out lots in the land tract.

An eager student due to his enjoyment of both math and the wilderness, Washington discovered on the trip that work as a surveyor appealed to him. It was also earning him money. He noted in his journals, "A doubloon is my constant gain every day that the weather will permit my going out; sometimes six pistoles."[568] In colonial America, a doubloon was a Spanish gold coin, worth roughly eight dollars at the time.[569] Pistoles were worth half a doubloon.

Basically, Washington was thrilled to be making, as we say, some "coin."[570] He found it motivating. The trip reinforced something in Washington about continuing to persevere. He realized the potential opportunities that being a surveyor held. And it was a position that did not have a barrier to entry for him.

Over the next three years, Washington would work surveying the Fairfax holdings all around the Shenandoah Valley and Northern Neck. He

---

568   Ibid., page 272.
569   "Doubloon," Encyclopedia.com, May 23, 2018, https://www.encyclopedia.com/history/united-states-and-canada/us-history/doubloon#:~:text=DOUBLOON%20was%20a%20Spanish%20gold,%247.84%20from%201786%20to%201848.
570   Washington might have been onto something. In 2014, the first gold doubloon struck in the United States by his neighbor in 1787, sold for over $5 million. https://www.dailymail.co.uk/news/article-2535881/Gold-doubloon-worth-16-two-centuries-ago-expected-fetch-5-MILLION-auction.html.

Meet George Washington–The Ultimate American Hustler

conducted over 190 surveys in the area. And with the money he earned, he bought his first piece of land: a 552-acre plot on Bullskin Creek in the lower Shenandoah Valley.[571]

WASHINGTON'S PASSION BECOMES A CAREER PATH

He quickly embarked on steps to become a surveyor by obtaining his surveying license from the College of William and Mary, which was authorized to issue such licenses.

But Washington wasn't just any guy getting a surveying license. He had his well-connected brother as well as an advocate in his neighbor Fairfax. And his connections paid off. At age nineteen, he was rewarded with an appointment as the official surveyor of Culpeper County.[572] This was no side job. It was a formal appointment with the Crown, and Washington took an oath to His Majesty's government. He was the youngest person ever appointed. The position was lucrative with a salary of £100 annually. This might not sound like a lot but when converted to the present day, it was £22,744.[573]

Washington worked very hard at surveying, and it became his passion. He enjoyed the process and accuracy needed. Washington also enjoyed learning more about land. He was able to parlay his one surveyor role into another that also paid £100 a year. And as his skills grew, he realized he was quite the saver. Washington tracked meticulously every penny he generated. And for good reason—he knew having land would help him grow his wealth and establish his place in society. By the time he was twenty-one, he owned over 2,300 acres in Virginia.

And then something happened that Washington couldn't have expected. In 1752, his brother Laurence died of tuberculosis. One unique provision in their father's estate was that should Laurence "dye without heir of his body Lawfully begotten," Washington would inherit Mount Vernon at age twenty-one. As his brother didn't have any heirs, Washington came into possession of the 2,500-acre estate.

---

571 (Knollenberg 1964) page 9.
572 There is some dispute about the age George was when he took this role.
573 "£100 in 1750 is worth £27,786.99 today," Official Data Foundation, https://www.in2013dollars.com/uk/inflation/1750?amount=100.

All the Presidents' Money

As a successful surveyor and landowner, Washington could have just stopped pushing, but he didn't—this is where he excelled. And he had never given up on his earlier goal of serving in the military, so he used the connections he had cultivated to secure an appointment as a major and was given a dress rank with another income of £150 annually. He would soon be going off on expeditions to negotiate with the French and then running for the House of Burgesses. Each success was built off the one before it. And in soldiering, when he was successful, he was able to add land grants in Ohio to his growing net worth.

As Washington kept climbing, his biggest leap was still to come—but not to commander of the Revolutionary forces or president. Rather, his marriage would propel him to the biggest financial success.

As for the book that started his journey, despite his relationship with Fairfax, he never returned it. It remained in his library for fifty-four years.

What was key for Washington early on in propelling him toward success was that he could not afford to fail. He had no safety net, and that precariousness helped build up his tenacity and drive—or grit—to succeed. And there are few success stories as inspiring as Washington's—from self-educated surveyor, to general commanding the Continental Army, to the nation's first president. And his financial success is equally impressive.

For anyone who has seen the musical *Hamilton*, Washington is back to the stoic character we know him as. But there is a reason Washington picks Alexander Hamilton. He sees his earlier self in Hamilton looking for "his shot." It's implicit bias at work. We find it easier to hire people who we feel inherently comfortable with and who remind us of ourselves. He understands that Hamilton has not just the smarts—but also the grit to succeed. And like Laurence and Fairfax who helped him, it's not lost on Washington that Hamilton being his aide-de-camp will help give entry into a hard-to-access world.

There is something about Washington's story that is a lot like a quote from actor Will Smith, who said:

> "The only thing that I see that is distinctly different about me is I'm not afraid to die on a treadmill. I will not be out-worked, period. You might have more talent than me, you might be smarter than me, you

Meet George Washington–The Ultimate American Hustler

might be sexier than me, you might be all of those things—you got it on me in nine categories. But if we get on the treadmill together, there's two things: you're getting off first, or I'm going to die. It's really that simple, right?"[574]

I have to tell you, if it was young George Washington up against Will Smith on that treadmill, I'd pick Washington to outlast him.

Oh, and when Washington died, his estate was valued at $780,000 in 1799 dollars. If we convert that value for today, it's closer to $400 million.

PASSION + PERSEVERANCE = QUITTING?

Washington makes grit look easy. I mean, c'mon, is it really that simple as getting a book on surveying and then wealth is yours for the taking? We all know that is as true as the story of Washington cutting down the cherry tree and not telling a lie.

Building wealth is hard as it comes from a series of choices that you have to hope pan out, along with having passion and perseverance. These stories always sound much better in retrospect. Fourteen years after leaving office, Bill Clinton himself noted that "I think I had the lowest net worth of any American president in the 20th century when I took office."[575] For years after graduating from Yale Law School, Clinton made sacrifices financially in order to move ahead politically. But his real wealth building grit occurred post-presidency. With a path paved by Jerry Ford, Clinton took it to the next level. The times had evolved since Ford, and Clinton was an international figure. When the *Washington Post* looked into Clinton's post-presidential activity, they found that almost half of Clinton's speaking engagements from 2001 through 2013 were overseas. His total payments for his speeches in that time frame: $104.9 million.[576]

But do you blame him? He had an opportunity set and he went after it. (And if he hadn't embraced this gritty side of wealth building, the pundits would probably give him a hard time for not maximizing his wealth.)

---

574 Will Smith in an interview with Tavis Smiley on June 17, 2011. The clip can be seen at this link: https://www.youtube.com/watch?v=doqS35FfcUE.
575 (W. J. Clinton 2014).
576 (Rucker, Hamburger and Becker 2014).

Clinton might have made a lot of money, but he physically pushed himself to get there.

When it comes to wealth building, is there a point at which you are best served by quitting? That may sound counterintuitive, but in recent years, with the greater focus on personal well-being, quitting is seen as empowerment. In the post-pandemic workplace, the rise of quiet quitting (or not putting in full effort) occurred nationally as workers rethought their roles in the workplace. But really quitting might be a chance to rework grit to a financial endgame that an individual finds more worthy.

WOODROW WILSON IS HEADED TO ATLANTA

If you had to pick a president who had financial grit, Woodrow Wilson might be a pretty good bet. Incredibly smart and ambitious, he always seemed like a man with an eye on the prize. In recent years, Wilson's reputation has been taking a beating for a variety of reasons. But what's shocking when looking at Wilson's personal finances is that despite being a driven person, he really didn't have the drive to build wealth. He was financially *grit-less*.

Born right before the Civil War in Virginia, Wilson came from a long family line of ministers, including his father, Joseph Ruggles Wilson. His intelligence and drive got him into Princeton University, followed by the University of Virginia Law School. Unfortunately for Wilson, he struggled with his health, ultimately finishing his law degree from his parents' home. By 1881, he was ready to embark on a legal career. After such a pedigree in his educational life, it would only seem logical that he would be poised for a successful and lucrative career with the drive to build great wealth, and it would be easy to assume that the pursuit of riches was included in that drive.

Wilson was incredibly close to his parents—and to his father, in particular. As he began to make his plans on where to start his career, he turned to his father for guidance, and between the two of them it was decided that Atlanta offered the best prospects. In the early 1880s, Atlanta was an interesting place in terms of a growth economy. It was the beginning of a boom time. Henry W. Grady, editor of the *Atlanta Constitution*, would later in 1886 make a famous speech to the New England Society in New York City, grandly naming it the "New South." No longer was it a city based on an agricultural economy. The Civil War was over, and the city had been rebuilt. Atlanta was the future.

At the time Wilson was considering making the move to Atlanta, the population was roughly thirty-seven thousand inhabitants. And the population was growing exponentially.[577] The idea of setting up a law firm in such a fertile market appealed to Wilson. And of course, it wasn't lost on him that Atlanta was the capital of Georgia, in the event his interest turned to politics. Wilson was always fascinated by the political arena.

Wilson was clear on the opportunity set ahead of him, writing a friend, "*After innumerable hesitations as to a place of settlement, I have at length fixed upon Atlanta, Georgia*. It more than any other Southern city offers all the advantages of business and enterprise."[578]

Wilson was confident that he was making the right choice as to where to establish himself as an attorney. But first he needed to figure out how to practice law and make a living in Atlanta. And thus, he launched one of the most challenging years of his financial life.

AN OPPORTUNITY FULL OF POTENTIAL

Now, Atlanta was booming, and so was the practice of law. At the time of Wilson's arrival, Atlanta already boasted 143 attorneys in practice, not an unreasonable number, considering all the changes occurring. But that should not have been a deterrent to success. After all, with persistence and talent, there should be more than enough legal work—especially for one as talented as Wilson.[579]

Yet, even out of the gate, Wilson was torn about practicing law. He wasn't sure it was the right path. He felt it might conflict with who he really wanted to be. His decisions began to reflect that uncertainty.

Instead of joining an established firm where he would receive mentoring and guidance, he opted to open his own practice with a fellow University of Virginia Law School grad named Edward Renick. They arranged to

---

577 In fact by 1890, the population had grown to sixty-seven thousand.
578 Letter Woodrow Wilson to Charles Talcott, dated September 22, 1881. Emphasis in original.
579 This assertion that there were too many lawyers for Wilson to succeed was debunked once the *Papers of Woodrow Wilson* was released.

share an office that cost nine dollars a month, and the firm of Renick and Wilson was born. However, Wilson very quickly came to the realization that he didn't like being a lawyer. Part of the problem was that he seemed to lack drive. Wilson and Renick were not a good combination, as they liked to read poetry together rather than practice law. And Wilson's father continued to give him a fifty-dollar allowance.

His father tried to convince him to give it more time, telling him in a letter, "It is a source of anxiety to me—your law distaste—an anxiety somewhat relieved however by the candor of which you acknowledge that state of your feelings…*All* beginnings are hard, whatever the occupation chosen—but surely a fair beginning must be made before the real character of the thing begun can be determined."[580] However, young Woodrow had already found a new outlet for his intellectual energies: writing political articles. Throughout 1882, he consistently wrote to friends with publishing connections while plodding along as a law partner.

The firm made a little money and wasn't a complete bust.[581] But Wilson felt the work was beneath him, grousing in a letter to a friend that "I am still following the young lawyer's occupation of *waiting*. One or two minute fees I earned—nothing more—though I have had business enough of a certain kind, the collection—or the efforts to collect numberless desperate claims."[582]

And there it is, in a nutshell, the growing frustration that Wilson felt. It was very common then that younger lawyers spent most of their time chasing down debt. Whether it was a settlement or even just getting paid by a client, this work filled his hours. Yet, rather than seeing this as a stepping stone or paying his dues, Wilson became resentful. This type of work and vocation was beneath him. Rather than see it as a transitory stage of his career, he put up his nose at the idea of a legal practice.

He mused that "the practice of law, when conducted for the purposes of gain, is antagonistic to the best interests of intellectual life…The philo-

---

580 Letter Joseph Ruggles Wilson to Woodrow Wilson, dated August 20, 1882. Emphasis in original letter.
581 (W. Wilson 1966).
582 Letter Woodrow Wilson to Robert Bridges, dated January 4, 1883. Emphasis in original.

Meet George Washington–The Ultimate American Hustler

sophical *study* of law—which must be a pleasure to any thoughtful man—is a very different matter from its scheming and haggling practice."[583]

Wilson's father tried to give him some perspective as to what was becoming his son's fixed mindset on the practice of law. "Immediate or even speedy success was not expected, at the outset, but *totus in illo* was and without the this-or-nothing motto, success if hardly possible and contentment altogether out of the question."[584]

QUITTING AS A SOLUTION

Finally, Wilson had had enough, and he quit the practice. But while he was ill-suited for lawyering, he was a perfect fit for another career path: academia. He decided to become a professor and applied to and was accepted into the doctorate program at Johns Hopkins.

Given his upbringing, Wilson's attitude was understandable. He grew up in a ministry, and in that environment, financial grit was not valued. Rather, he was taught to prioritize engagement in the greater world for personal and professional fulfillment. Money was a way to be comfortable, but not the goal. As a result, Wilson lacked the mindset and drive to create wealth.

And that doesn't make him unique. Although part of the American mindset is the idea that one should do better than the generation before them, not everyone is driven to be wealthy. In an oft-cited study from 2010, Americans don't see much of an increase in happiness once they make more than $75,000 a year (that would be $105,000 in 2023 dollars). But that just measures happiness. Recent surveys have found that to be comfortable financially, the number is much higher—$233,000 in income. And to feel financial freedom? $483,000.[585]

George Washington had to build tenacity and grit due to his position in life. But when Washington married Martha, he became guardian of her son, Jacky. Washington decided he would provide Jacky with all the opportunities he had not been given, including a top-tier education. But without

---

583 Letter Woodrow Wilson to Richard Heath Dabney, dated May 11, 1883.
584 Letter Joseph Ruggles Wilson to Woodrow Wilson, dated February 18, 1883. *Totus in illo* means, "To this I am wholly committed."
585 (Foster 2023).

hurdles and being backed by Washington and his wealth, Jacky squandered these opportunities.

Similarly, Wilson was backstopped by his family as he searched for the right path forward, living off his father's allowance. I tell my clients that when considering how best to instill strong financial skills in their children, they should always keep in mind the fine line between being supportive and being an enabler. Time and time again, I see wealthy families help set up their kids—first in college and then afterward as they are starting out. A good percentage of my clients' kids turn out fine, but some—even decades after their college graduation—are still getting an "allowance" from Mom and Dad and still haven't fully launched.

WILSON REMAINS THE SAME WHEN IT COMES TO MONEY

The real reason Wilson lacked the grit to build wealth was that he felt it was an unattractive characteristic. In fact, Wilson himself noted, "I can never be happy unless I am enabled to lead an intellectual life. The chief end of man is certainly to make money, and money cannot be made except by the most vulgar methods. The studious man is pronounced unpractical and is suspected as a visionary."

Wilson realized that being a professor was the "only feasible place for me, the only place that would afford leisure for reading and for original work, the only strictly literary berth with an income attached."[586] A few years after leaving Atlanta, Wilson was making $1,500 a year as an associate professor at Bryn Mawr College. It wasn't much, but it was enough for him because it made his dream job possible.

While he found the pursuit of money beneath him, here's a fascinating footnote about Wilson's financial story. And Wilson's academic career was nothing short of stunning, ultimately becoming president of Princeton University. One of the key components of that role: raising funds for the school. Wilson traveled around the country, exhorting alumni groups to open their wallets and support their alma mater. When it came to raising money for academia, Wilson not only did not act with disgust about money, but he actually embraced fundraising, becoming quite good at it.

---

586 (Berg 2013) page 92.

Meet George Washington–The Ultimate American Hustler

But he really didn't gain real financial stability until the presidency when he took Taft's advice in saving his presidential paycheck.

After his wife, Ellen, died in 1914 while he was president, Wilson married wealthy socialite Edith Bolling Galt within the following year. At that point, any money worries he might have had disappeared.

Remember, as I've said, a lot of presidents marry up.

When Wilson died in 1924, just three years after his presidential term ended, his net worth was not significant. He consistently ranks as one of our poorest presidents, along with Calvin Coolidge, Chester Arthur, and James Garfield. But given Wilson's views on wealth building, he would probably consider that a compliment.

HERBERT HOOVER SITS ON A GOLD MINE—LITERALLY!

My favorite story of grit is Herbert Hoover's. Hoover was unbelievable at managing money well. But given his background (as we saw earlier) as an orphan, he took grit and perseverance to a new level.

Hoover had a determination that couldn't be beat. Many of the presidents from Reagan to Ford loved Horatio Alger tales, but how Hoover made his wealth even tops those stories.

Hoover reminds me of a client of mine who grew up with very little money in Detroit, Michigan. His first job out of college was one that doesn't even exist today. In the 1960s, it was a novelty to have a television set in your hospital room and one that was expensive. As a result, hospitals required patients to pay for it. My client's job was to go from hospital room to hospital room in the 1960s and sell tokens to patients that would pay for the TV in their room. By the time he retired fifty years later, he had been the head of sales for an alcohol company with a personal net worth of $70 million. Learning the basics of selling in a hospital environment must have been difficult, but that experience helped him to master sales and, maybe more importantly to a salesperson, learn human nature as well. If he didn't have grit, he might not have lasted in that first job, which surely served him well in every job he held after. Hoover's story of grit is similar in that he was willing to stick it out in unfavorable conditions to get him where he wanted to be.

All the Presidents' Money

This part of Hoover's story begins when he's down to his last forty dollars and frustrated. A recent graduate of Stanford University with a degree in geology, he was horrified to find out that there were no jobs to be had at engineering firms. None of the bespoke firms that lined the streets of San Francisco or New York were hiring. The US economy was in a recession. The Panic of 1893 had been tough across the country. Industrial production was down 15.3 percent. Unemployment hovered between 17 percent and 19 percent.[587] Hoover himself noted years later that "I had lived all my life in hard times. But I had never heard of depressions."[588]

Hoover's college friends simply decided to wait it out. But he didn't have that luxury. As an orphan, he had always budgeted intensely to make ends meet. But now he was at the end of the money his parents had left to him and his siblings.

Never one to wallow, Hoover looked at the opportunity set around him and made a decision. He caught a train to the gold-mining districts of Nevada City and Grass Valley and looked for a job in a mine. He didn't care what he did; it just needed to pay. Hoover was able to get a job pushing a car in the lower levels of the Reward mine. It was a ten-hour shift and paid two dollars a day.[589] It was the lowest job on the totem pole. As he wrote to a friend, "I think it's invaluable to keep moving. I never stop anyway."[590]

Every day, he went down deep into the mine alongside the other workers. They were both fascinated yet worried by him. In his memoirs, Hoover recalled that the mine managers were skeptical of "them college educated fellers."[591] Here was a college grad, and yet he was as dirty and dusty as the rest of them. But for Hoover, it was eye-opening. His Stanford studies were theoretical versus the real experience of being deep in a mine. He was watching and observing. His hard work started to pay off, and he began to win the trust of the miners around him. In exchange, they taught him mining tips, which later became very useful to him.

Ultimately, the Depression hit the mining area as well, and Hoover was laid off. But he had saved one hundred dollars—and had a new skill set.

---

587 (Jalil 2015) page 323.
588 (Hoover 1951) page 24.
589 Ibid., page 25.
590 Letter Herbert Hoover to Nell May Hill, dated September 7, 1895.
591 (Hoover 1951) page 25.

Meet George Washington–The Ultimate American Hustler

HOOVER DEVELOPS HIS SKILL AND EFFORT

This story might seem like a blip in Hoover's life. But the truth is, it is probably (alongside his budgeting skills) the key to how he grew great wealth. He certainly valued his Stanford degree, but, as we've seen, Hoover was aware he needed something more to get ahead and wasn't averse to working hard to get it. He also understood that the "on-the-ground" education would be instrumental in getting him where he wanted to be later in his career.

I see a lot of parallels between Hoover and Washington. Hoover went into the mines to enhance his geology degree; Washington went on survey trips with Fairfax to enhance what he has learned in books. Their grit is enhanced by their ability to connect to their future self (remember that was one of the things that Thomas Jefferson was incapable of). Their sacrifice today would benefit them tomorrow.

In sharp contrast, Wilson couldn't see that sacrificing himself a bit to collect debts and build a law firm would give him the benefits of what he wanted tomorrow. And unlike Hoover and Washington, he had a backstop in the money his family provided him. There is nothing wrong with that approach, but his lack of grit in this circumstance limited his lifelong-earning capacity. It's no mistake that when we look at presidents like Clinton or Obama, they are similar to Wilson in not wanting to take the path of making money first (Obama hated practicing big law), but they were lucky to live in a time when their respective spouses could earn a living and enable them to chase their dreams.

At this point in Hoover's life, he didn't have a lot of money at all. In fact, he was basically broke. But he had a degree in geology from Stanford, and he had experience from working deep in a mine. So, what happened next? Let's take a look at the gritty moves that Hoover made.

GRITTY MOVE #1

Hoover was a standout geology student at Stanford. As a result, one of Hoover's Stanford professors introduced him to Louis Janin, a mining engineer on the Pacific coast who owned a firm. Hoover was hopeful he would hire him. Janin took young Hoover out for lunch (a lunch that Hoover noted cost more than he had in cash). Janin explained the workings of his firm but also told Hoover that unfortunately they weren't hiring any young analysts and that he didn't know any mines that were hiring.

However, there was a menial job open in the firm as a copyist, and Hoover jumped at it. Janin was surprised by the young man's eagerness for the position but hired him anyway.

Hoover enthusiastically embraced the copyist job, and a few months later, Janin approached him. There was an extensive engineering job in Colorado in need of an assistant. The pay was $150 a month plus expenses. To give context, the average American annual salary was $665.[592] Hoover was on his way.

He worked hard and jumped at opportunity after opportunity. In each new role, Hoover improved his skills. He worked harder than everyone else. In the company, his reputation grew along with his salary. And then Janin was asked by the prestigious British firm Bewick, Moreing and Company for help in finding an American engineer to run a mine in Australia. Janin didn't want to lose Hoover, but it was a huge opportunity that paid $600 a month. However, the home office wanted an experienced man who had to be at least thirty-five years of age. Hoover was twenty-two.

Bewick Moreing wanted the man for the job to stop by in London on their way to Australia. So, Hoover grew a mustache and went to London, listing himself on the White Star ocean liner *Britannic* "H. C. Hoover, Age 36, Mining Engineer."[593]

And Bewick Moreing seemed to buy it.[594]

GRITTY MOVE #2

From London, Hoover headed to Australia. Bewick had recently acquired mines in Western Australia. They wanted an American because American mining engineering was light-years ahead of Britain and Australia. Upon arrival, Hoover was transported back in time to 1849 and the California gold rush. Today, we romanticize that period of American history, but the

---

592 *Prices and Wages by Decade: 1890-1899*, University of Missouri, https://libraryguides.missouri.edu/pricesandwages/1890-1899#occupation.
593 (Burner 1979) page 26.
594 Hoover had to keep his charade up for the time he was in London, even while spending a weekend at Charles Algernon Moreing's country estate.

Meet George Washington–The Ultimate American Hustler

truth is that it was not a pleasant time. And Hoover found similar conditions. Dusty and dirty, everything was ripe for the picking in Coolgardie and Kalgoorlie, two towns in Australia that are still known for the gold industry today. Hoover wasn't wearing rose-colored glasses as he surveyed the site filled with tents and shanties. His letters to his family were filled with descriptions of the rustic and primitive nature of the area. He summed it up in one letter when he said, "It is a terrible place."[595]

Hoover often had to take Afghan camels to visit mining sites (later he would use a bike). Typhoid was a constant threat. Desert winds, along with high temperatures, made it barely livable. But he was also aware of the leg up he was getting on wealth building, being in such a rough environment. He joked to his cousin that "anybody who envies me my salary can just take my next trip with me, and he will then be contented to be a bank clerk at $3 a week the rest of his life, just to live in the United States."[596]

Hoover earned a reputation as the best mining engineer in the colony. He also developed a management style as he found the books poorly run and excess spending was bleeding the company dry. He immediately embarked—to all the Australians' horror—on a cost-cutting spree.

On the financial front, he was making more money than he ever thought he would. But Hoover the Quaker also knew he needed to see his wealth building as a community endeavor. The Quaker SPICES were at the core of his financial values.

Prior to leaving the United States, he worked it out with his friend Lester Hinsdale (yes, the same one from Stanford!) to manage his assets. First, he granted Hinsdale power of attorney to act on his behalf. Second, Hoover instructed Bewick Moreing to deposit £50 to £100 monthly in the Anglo California Bank in San Francisco.[597] In turn, Hinsdale disbursed the money to the Hoover family members who needed it.[598]

Hoover also made it clear to Hinsdale that any of the Stanford friends who needed help could also access the money. But Hoover insisted that

---

595 Letter Herbert Hoover to Burt Barker, dated October 25, 1897.
596 Letter Herbert Hoover to Harriette Miles, dated August 5, 1897.
597 The Hoover Library was gracious in sharing this file filled with letters detailing the money being sent back, along with every bank receipt for the deposits made in the US.
598 Hoover also expresses frustration in his letters home on how expensive it can be in Australia due to the need to join certain social clubs.

Hinsdale needed to be a "sphinx about matters of mine."[599] Hoover had no problem supporting people, but he wanted no acknowledgment.

Besides his family support, Hoover's finances were more sophisticated than ever. He continued to rely on the budgeting skills that had served him so well since childhood. He was investing in stocks and even owned a New England Mutual Life Insurance policy to protect his siblings in case he passed away unexpectedly. His childhood values allowed him to provide for others in good ways.

GRITTY MOVE #3

Hoover had been traveling around Western Australia to all the Bewick Moreing mines in an exercise to make the mines more efficient. He visited a small mine called Sons of Gwalia that was owned by some Welshmen. His geologist's eye caught something: the terrain looked like other geologic sites where gold had been found.[600] Rumors abounded that the mine could be valuable, but no one had been able to really show that.

Hoover's curiosity and ambition were raised. He knew he had a secret weapon in reviewing the mine: due to his experience, he was considered an expert "inspecting engineer."[601] Relying on his skills from Stanford and experiences in the mines in Sierra Nevada, Coolgardie, and Kalgoorlie, he went to work. But before he did, he cabled the company that they should seek an option on the mine.[602] By the time his twenty-four-page report for the home office was done, he was convinced that the Sons of Gwalia was a potentially rich gold mine, and that Bewick Moreing needed to move quickly to secure it. He proposed that they "purchase of a two-thirds interest for $250,000 and a provision for $250,000 working capital."[603] He also suggested that if the mine was acquired, Bewick Moreing should put it under his sole management.

---

599 Letter Herbert Hoover to Lester Hinsdale, dated April 14, 1897.
600 Hoover traveled a large portion of Australia on an Afghan camel. He found this mode of transportation so outdated that he pushed (and succeeded) in bringing the use of motor cars to the mining industry in 1903.
601 (Nash, *The Life of Herbert Hoover: The Engineer 1874 - 1914* 1983) page 67.
602 (Coughlin 2000).
603 Ibid., page 33.

Meet George Washington–The Ultimate American Hustler

Bold move—and it paid off. When Bewick Moreing cabled him back, they noted, "You will have entire management."[604]

In purchasing the mine, Bewick decided to appoint Hoover as manager for $15,000 a year plus expenses (the equivalent of a $500,000 salary in 2024 dollars).[605] He would also get a small share of the profit and be made a junior partner.[606]

GRITTY MOVE #4

Hoover inadvertently found fame along with the mine. In order for Bewick Moreing to finance the mine, they needed to be capitalized. As a result, they had an initial public offering on the London exchange for three hundred thousand one-pound sterling shares in January 1898. As part of the prospectus, Bewick Moreing circulated Hoover's report.

On the first day of trading, the shares doubled in value. And Hoover became a name known in London.

Hoover immediately went to work cutting production costs to maximize profits. Some of the changes he implemented to create efficiency only would have come from someone who had learned inside knowledge from working in a mine, such as having shift changes occur below ground. When he was done, in many ways, he had evolved mining into more of a modern-day business.

All the success brought more focus on Hoover. He started to believe his hype.

At one point, he vented in a letter to his brother that he was going to quit Bewick Moreing. The compensation wasn't enough. He wrote:

"I engineered the whole Sons of Gwalia deal out of which Moreing made $2,000,000 and never gave me a bean nor a share damn him. I'll fix his little game. It just happens that his business can't run without me and I will force him to make me managing director of Australia or tell him to the devil."[607]

---

604 Bewick, Moreing & Co. cable to Herbert Hoover, dated November 27, 1897.
605 Letter Herbert Hoover to Theodore Hoover, dated "late" April 1898.
606 (Hough 1977) page 69.
607 Letter Herbert Hoover to Theodore Hoover, dated 1898.

Over the next few months, he negotiated to be the head of the Sons of Gwalia mine. Finally, they gave in. Hoover noted to his brother, "I am entering into agreement to stay here 3 years an expect to leave with $150,000 or not a bean."[608] Along with the salary, they gave him a small percentage interest in the mine. Hoover's estimates of $150,000 would be the same as $5.6 million today. Not bad for a twenty-four-year-old orphan.

Hoover hit this one so far out of the park that Bewick moved him to China shortly thereafter to manage mines. The move allowed Bewick to promote Hoover into the partnership.[609] Over fifty years later, Hoover himself noted that the Sons of Gwalia mine had made $55 million in gold and $10 million in dividends. It finally closed in 1963 and by the end had been one of the most successful mines in Australian history.[610]

The income streams that he got from all of the mines that he helped develop allowed him to become one of our wealthiest presidents of all time.

CONSISTENT THEMES

To be clear—having grit alone doesn't create great wealth. Opportunity must be present. These three stories are ones of extremes. Yet each of them—Washington, Wilson, and Hoover—had opportunity. How they managed their passion and perseverance (or lack of) helped drive whether they had financial success. Wilson's story is one that is more common than we think. We often get in the way of our own financial success. If he had stuck out a law career in Atlanta, he might have found financial wealth. A lot of opportunities came his way that he simply lacked the passion to persevere on. And in his case, he was okay with not creating great wealth. He was looking to find satisfaction differently.

One consistent theme between Washington and Hoover is that they were both willing to work to find one way into the system to build wealth. They didn't care about discomfort. They didn't care about working hard. Instead, they had focus and perseverance.

---

608 Letter Herbert Hoover to Theodore Hoover, dated "late" April 1898.
609 Letter Herbert Hoover to Theodore Hoover, dated November 2, 1898.
610 (Hough 1977).

Chapter Ten

ULYSSES S. GRANT AND THE NEVER-ENDING GET-RICH SCHEMES
(OR LUCK)

Whenever I meet with a new client for the first time, I get to learn their story: education, career choices, and so on. Inevitably, there is a moment when the word "luck" comes out of their mouth. It could be the luck of meeting the right people at the right time. Or being at a company that took off and was a gamechanger. But I'm always amazed at how many of my wealthy clients note that luck played a part. (And usually the wealthier they are, the more they bring it up.)

Luck is studied by academics all the time. Researchers who study luck have identified two factors that determine how lucky a person will be: where you were born and what income bracket you were born into.[611]

When you take the first parameter, it is easy to see that our presidents were all lucky to be born in a country that, over the last 250 years, has offered a greater opportunity set than other countries. America is a country where a poor person can become rich.

Take Abraham Lincoln. The luck of being born in the United States is never more apparent than a short journey that started in New Salem, Illinois, where Lincoln lived for six years until 1837. His existence in New Salem was tough; he lived in a log cabin and struggled to survive as a storekeeper. Yet, seven years after leaving New Salem and moving just twenty-

---
611 (Frank 2016).

one miles away to Springfield, he was living in an upper-class home. Granted, he had help from his father-in-law in buying it, but you have to admit, luck may have played a hand.

But what about the second part, with the focus on income bracket? It's the answer to this question where certain presidents may have a little more luck than others: being a Trump, Kennedy, Bush, or Roosevelt, all from wealthy families—versus a Fillmore, Lincoln, or Van Buren, all born into poor circumstances. And when you have someone like Lincoln who was able to rise financially from starting at such a low-income situation, we find the story even luckier.

But what exactly is luck? Luck is defined as the "success or failure apparently brought by chance rather than through one's own actions."[612] Thus, randomness is often seen as the heart of luck. The *New York Times* economics writer and professor Robert H. Frank shared a great example of this in his book *Success and Luck: Good Fortune and the Myth of Meritocracy*. He told a story of randomness when it came to ice hockey. One unique fact about hockey is that 40 percent of all premier players in the world are born in January, February, or March. Yet, only 10 percent of premier players are born in the last three months of the year. Why is that? It relates to the cutoff date for participation in youth hockey leagues, which meant they were often older, bigger, and stronger. Just that little element of randomness changed the trajectory those players were on. It's an element of randomness that can impact your luck.[613]

But most of the time, luck with money isn't random. We have to add in the power of human influence. That opens up a whole other Pandora's box on the subject because that's where the presidents are interesting. They were born here, but they had to navigate various, often nuanced, situations to get lucky (or unlucky). These situations required skill, preparation, and even consistency.

SKILL VERSUS LUCK

Skill is an element that can really impact one's money and luck. In his studies on luck and success, Robert Frank found that people tended to

---

612 As defined by the Oxford Dictionary.
613 (Frank 2016) page 38. This story and others are recounted in his chapter on randomness.

Ulysses S. Grant and the Never-Ending Get-Rich Schemes

underestimate good fortune's role in success and were too quick to say bad luck was why they failed.[614] This is most common in investing.

I have a client I'll call Mr. Smooth (that's how he's known on X, formerly Twitter). Mr. Smooth is a venture capitalist and an incredibly successful one. He made early investments in companies that have gone on to be successful IPOs. He would tell you he's been incredibly lucky at investing in early-stage companies that have been able to grow. In fact, he's so modest, he would prefer that it be seen as luck.

But is it really luck? What he does requires a lot of skill. We know that because, if we delve into his experience, we see a mix of skills and personality traits that have helped him make strong investing decisions. He has studied businesses and knows the market and its cycles. In investing, his favorite line is that he's all about founders. That is a simple way of saying he's good at judging people and their skill sets. I can tell you in working with him that Mr. Smooth is also good at remaining emotionally objective. He doesn't make decisions based on fear, greed, and other such emotions that can lead to poor decision-making. He's consistent. That consistency creates luck.

Attributing Mr. Smooth's sound investment decisions to luck is simplifying a skill set that he has taken years to build. Luck is an easier way to explain it. But he's right—it's the skills and being lucky due to his consistency that allows him to be successful.

On the subjects of skills and luck, one of the best presidents to consider is Ulysses S. Grant.

Grant often becomes a favorite of anyone who studies him. He helped bring the country back together again during and after the bloody and brutal Civil War. He was so popular that when he died, his funeral, held in New York on August 8, 1885, had the largest attendance in the United States at that point: 1.5 million people. He was truly loved. As Lincoln once said, "I can't spare this man—he fights."[615]

He's a noble character with tremendous grit. After the first bloody day at Shiloh when the Union Army teetered precariously on defeat, William Tecumseh Sherman, who commanded a division at Shiloh, recalled coming

---

614 (Frank 2016) page 72.
615 This was recounted after the war by Pennsylvania politician Alexander McClure as a comment Lincoln made when Grant was criticized by others.

upon Grant under a tree in a downpour. Grant's collar was pulled up, and all Sherman could see was the light from Grant's cigar. Like many in the Union Army, Sherman felt defeated. He looked at Grant and said, "Well, Grant, we've had the devil's own day, haven't we?" Grant simply replied, "Yes. Lick them tomorrow though."[616]

Isn't that an awesome response? It tells you a lot about Grant. And lick them they did as the Union won the Battle of Shiloh.

Grant is often portrayed as being unlucky with money. He was at times a complete and utter financial disaster. Was he unlucky? I'm not so sure. I actually would argue that he had luck, but some of his personal character traits caused him to squander it.

Grant is an example where skill (or lack thereof) can have an impact on luck. And that's the quirky thing about luck—it is just one of several factors that cause financial success. You still need the basic building blocks of personal finance that we've previously discussed. Luck alone isn't enough.

THE AMERICAN WEST: A GREAT OPPORTUNITY SET

Historians often point to Grant's time in the West during the 1850s as the beginning of his bad financial luck. After the end of the Mexican War, Grant was in his late twenties and recently married. He bounced about in the army until he was eventually stationed first in California and then in Oregon. It was a challenging assignment for him. First, getting to the West Coast was not easy. On his journey, the military group he was with experienced illness and death. Second, his wife, Julia, was unable to join him due to pregnancy.

Upon arriving on the West Coast, Grant got his first look at an amazing opportunity set. California had only become a state in 1849. The discovery of gold in the foothills of the Sierra Nevada created an economic boom. The United States would be a very different country today without the gold rush. In many ways, Grant's arrival in 1852 was similar to Mark Zuckerberg's arrival in Palo Alto in 2004. It was fertile ground for anyone with an entrepreneurial mindset and the right business plan.

---

616 (Grant Had No Thought of Retreat 1894).

Ulysses S. Grant and the Never-Ending Get-Rich Schemes

Grant had an interesting skill set for this type of environment. In his time in Zachary Taylor's army, Grant had served as quartermaster.[617] This meant that he was in charge of procuring and distributing supplies to the army, as well as managing the barracks and the supply stores. It was a big job (and one that would help him manage the Union troops in the Civil War). But it gave him a skill set that most didn't have since he knew how to move items over long distances.[618]

Grant understood the opportunity set in front of him. He wrote Julia upon his arrival in August 1852, "I have seen enough of California to know that it is a different country from any thing that a person in the states could imagine in their wildes[t] dreams. There is no reason why an active energeti[c] person should not make a fortune ev[e]ry year. For my part I feel that I could quit the Army to-day and in one year go home with enough to make us comfortable, on Gravois, all our life. Of course I do not contemplate doing any thing of the sort, because what I have is a certainty, and what I might expect to do, might prove a dream."[619]

Grant was open to opportunity. He was open to leaving the army. Like others around him, he wanted to get rich—and the quicker the better, because then he could go home to Julia and his family.

GRANT EMBARKS ON A BUSINESS VENTURE

In the move west, Grant was aware of Elijah Camp, a civilian with experience in setting up army stores, who was also traveling with the army. Grant and Camp had gotten to know each other when Grant was stationed in Sackets Harbor, New York.[620] Grant casually noted in a letter to Julia that

---

617   Zachary Taylor had a huge influence on Grant. I love the fact that Grant got his love of unfancy uniforms from Old Hickory.
618   You might think I'm stretching here, but as Grant made his way west, so did Levi Strauss just a few months later in 1853. Strauss, a German-Jewish immigrant, had been tasked with bringing his family's dry good business to San Francisco after working in it in New York. It might seem like a no-brainer that Strauss would be successful, yet there were already 117 dry goods stores in San Francisco when he got there. So how did he succeed? Like Grant, he had a mastery of being able to get goods to San Francisco when a lot of his other competitors couldn't (in fact, most stores struggled getting any inventory at all). He worked with his brothers in New York to create a viable supply chain of goods across the country.
619   Letter U.S. Grant to Julia Dent Grant, dated August 20, 1852.
620   (Neal 2015).

All the Presidents' Money

Camp was likely going to be a sutler at the new fort. A unique army term, *sutler* referred to a civilian who was authorized to operate a store near a military camp, post, or fort. Typically, a sutler had to get a license from a military commander to set up shop. Being a sutler could be incredibly lucrative as these stores might be the only one for miles and thus would have a monopoly. But it was also hard work in terms of trying to procure goods from a distance.

By October 1852, Grant was stationed at Fort Vancouver in Oregon. He was living in the "Quartermaster's Ranch" at the fort with two other officers. The home was the nicest on the base and as a result was the social hub for the army.[621] Grant himself was "very much pleased with Vancouver."[622]

What happened next was that he started to go forward with his investments, or as Grant called them in the contemporary parlance, "a speculation."[623] He loaned Elijah Camp $1,500 as a seed investment in Camp's sutler store. He explained to Julia that the $1,500 investment with Camp "enabled him to buy, on credit, the house and a few goods where he keeps the store."[624] Grant believed that once the store was set up, he and Camp would split the profits. And in 1852, $1,500 wasn't a small amount of money. It's more along the lines of $60,000 today.

Grant saw it as a partnership with Camp, but Camp's behavior as the "partnership" progressed made it seem like less of a partnership and more of a simple loan. And there was no documentation for the business. If Grant had been my client, I would have told him to document it. Even when there are warm relationships, this continues to be important because money changes people's behavior. Even when my clients make loans to other family members, we have them document it. That way intentions and expectations are clearly set.

Pretty soon after the sutler's store opened, Camp approached Grant and offered to pay back the $1,500. Grant accepted the offer, although it was a deal he quickly regretted as Camp's sutler store started to boom. Camp wasn't just selling to the troops but to their families who had migrat-

---

621 *Fort Vancouver* (Washington, DC: Division of Publications, National Park Service, 1981), 120.
622 Letter U.S. Grant to Julia Dent Grant, dated October 7, 1852.
623 Grant consistently refers to all the business endeavors he makes as a "speculation" in his letters to Julia.
624 Letter U.S. Grant to Julia Dent Grant, dated October 7, 1852.

Ulysses S. Grant and the Never-Ending Get-Rich Schemes

ed west and the community around Fort Vancouver. The store was selling varied goods such as spices, coffee, clothing, and medicines.[625]

Grant lamented to Julia, "I was very foolish for taking it because my share of the profits would not have been less than three thousand per year."[626] And no wonder, as Grant estimated the store was generating $1,000 a month.[627] Yet, despite the store's success, Camp didn't pay back Grant. It was a verbal agreement between the two men—something of a gentleman's agreement. And from Grant's standpoint, he didn't see the risk. But Grant had spent his whole career in the military. When one gives or receives an order, one follows it. But business is far more cutthroat. And over the next few months, Grant started to learn this.

By February, Grant was still confident he would be repaid. He noted to Julia, "Mr. Camp owes me $1500 00 on a note that I hold against him, but it is not due for some time yet. If he lives and continues as prosperous as at present I would not give sixpence to have it secured."[628]

At some point, Camp paid Grant $700. But just six weeks after Grant wrote those words to Julia, Camp's store, which sold gunpowder, was destroyed in a massive explosion, and Camp took off without paying Grant the remaining amount he owed him.

Grant tried to reconcile this with his wife's queries on the investment. "You ask about Mr. Camp. Poor fellow he could not stand prosperity. He was making over $1000 00 per month and it put him beside himself. From being generous he grew parsimonious and finally so close that apparently he could not bear to let money go to keep up with stock of goods. He quit and went home with about $8000 00 deceiving me as to the money he had and owing me about $800 00. I am going to make out his account and send it to Chas. Ford for collection."[629]

But Grant added a cryptic coda in his letter to Julia. "I will some day tell you all the particulars of this transaction. I do not like to put it upon paper."[630]

---

625 (Neal 2015).
626 Letter U.S. Grant to Julia Dent Grant, dated October 7, 1852.
627 Letter U.S. Grant to Julia Dent Grant, dated June 15, 1853.
628 Letter U.S. Grant to Julia Dent Grant, dated February 15, 1853.
629 Letter U.S. Grant to Julia Dent Grant, dated June 15, 1853.
630 Ibid.

BAD LUCK OR BAD BUSINESS?

Clearly Grant didn't document the transaction. He should have had a written loan agreement with Camp, and that's what I would have advised him to do. When he agreed to be paid back, he should have secured that note against the business, and I would have advised him of that, too. And now he didn't want to give the details to his wife in a letter, which begs the question: What were those details? The other question we need to consider is whether partnering with Camp was even legal given Grant's role in the military.

Clearly, Grant is a horrible businessman. He undoes any luck he might have had. And he was lucky: Lucky to be stationed out west. Lucky to be quartermaster with a unique skill set. Lucky to be living in the social center of Fort Vancouver. Lucky to partner with a sutler store. Lucky to have the money to invest.

On one hand, we could argue he's naïve about people and about money. Naivete can actually be a useful trait in the start-up world as it encourages curiosity and risk-taking. However, in the rough-and-tumble world of the 1850s West, it made you a sucker.

Grant should have negotiated a tougher deal with Camp. Who makes a loan and then doesn't get paid any interest on the risk? Who agrees to get paid back instead of participating in the profits? Who doesn't secure his loan and feels the man's word is enough? He is too loyal to maximize his luck in wealth building. He lacks the ability to read scoundrels. As one historian put it, "Grant was always a sucker for other people's financial schemes."[631] His willingness to trust people financially (and later politically) often blew up in his face. And this is even when the signs are pointed out to him.[632]

And this is not uncommon. As mentioned previously, according to Frank, people have a "tendency to underestimate good fortune's role in success, while being too quick to embrace bad luck as an explanation of failure."[633] Why? Frank explained that people want to "think of themselves

---

631 (Korda 2004) page 5. Korda recounts how easily persuaded Grant and Julia were to consider the Upper West Side of New York for the General Grant National Memorial.
632 To be fair to Grant, his loyalty is some people is well-served throughout his career.
633 (Frank 2016) page 72.

Ulysses S. Grant and the Never-Ending Get-Rich Schemes

as highly competent and attribute their failures to events beyond their control."[634]

I have clients like Grant. They are corporate executives who have built their careers out of loyalty. And it makes it harder to advocate for themselves when it comes to financial opportunity. As we discussed earlier with my client Mr. Smooth, being objective is important in assessing a situation clearly. I would have told him he needed someone—an advocate or attorney of some sort—to help him think through his speculations and help protect himself from the downside risk.

In the months after the Camp debacle, Grant had a series of "speculations" that failed—selling ice, developing farmland, investing in a social club in San Francisco—and all are not undone by bad luck but rather another intervening force. Those forces included his loyalty as well as mismanaging risk.

A few years later, Grant realized he was going to be in New York near where Camp was living. And Camp was living quite a nice life in Sackets Harbor. Grant wrote Camp a letter to tell him he was coming to visit and wanted to discuss the unpaid $800 loan.[635] Camp got the letter and skipped town to Lake Ontario on his yacht to avoid Grant. Grant spent the last of his money getting to New York and found Camp gone. Grant landed in New York without a penny, defeated.

Talk about being out of luck.

CAN YOU CREATE YOUR OWN LUCK?

You can have luck and squander the opportunities it provides if you don't have the right skills, but what about making your own luck? Perhaps the better way to consider this is that there is luck in spotting the right moment or opportunity that comes our way. We need to be receptive to this and be prepared for when this luck happens. Preparation comes in learning the right skills and acquiring the right knowledge.

And as the Mark Twain quote says, "Clothes make the man."[636] This has certainly been true in the cases of some of our presidents. When you

---

634 Ibid., page 73.
635 (Perret 1997).
636 Twain's full quote is actually: "Clothes make the man. Naked people have little or no influence on society."

All the Presidents' Money

delve into the personal histories of those presidents who started out poor, there is usually a moment when they realize they need to dress the part to attract the opportunities.

Dressing well helps improve the odds of success. It can make the wearer more focused, confident, and accepting of risk.[637] Presidential trivia is riddled with this. Chester Arthur was renowned for his stylish wardrobe, culminating in stories that he had over eighty pairs of pants hanging in his White House closet.[638] Calvin Coolidge's largest donor, Frank Stearns, owned a department store. While he felt that Coolidge reflected the same values as his store, Stearns also knew that to increase Coolidge's odds of success in politics, Coolidge had to dress a certain way.[639] Even today in looking at photos of the Coolidges, you can see the fine details on their clothes—courtesy of Stearns. Fancy clothes are not exactly what one would think of when knowing Coolidge was "thrifty."

And when you already have the odds in your favor, it is something you think less about. John F. Kennedy had the luck to be born to a wealthy Massachusetts family. He had no worries about money and to him, jewelry, clothing, cars, and homes were not something to be aspired to—they just were. He had connections and had no need to impress them.

And the same thing is true for his clothing. In his younger years, JFK's clothing seemed like that of "hand-me-down clothing"—almost what a regular boy his age would wear.[640] By all accounts, he was a slovenly dresser and according to the Kennedy maids—simply messy.[641] It wasn't until he met and married Jackie that things changed because she shaped his wardrobe.

---

637 (Silvia Bellezza 2014).
638 What's funny is how things change by different eras. President Obama wanted to focus on making as few trivial decisions as possible as president in order to focus on the big decisions that often land on a president's desk. As a result, he made sure his wardrobe was the same color suits, ties, and shirts.
639 (Shlaes 2013) pages 133–134. Also from my discussion with Amity Shlaes on June 30, 2023. She notes that in the old photos you can see the expensive trim and accessories that adorned Coolidge's clothing.
640 (Horton 1964).
641 (Dallek 2004) page 52. Dallek quotes the Kennedy maids' complaints about JFK, including "the wet towels in a heap on the floor, the tangle of ties in one corner, the bureau drawers turned over and emptied in the middle of the bed in a hurried search for some wanted item."

Ulysses S. Grant and the Never-Ending Get-Rich Schemes

JFK's secretary, Evelyn Lincoln, noted, "After their marriage his suits fit perfectly, were conservatively cut and perfectly pressed....From a fumbling person who couldn't tie his own tie, and it was always too long, to an immaculate dresser."[642] But did it help him create luck in his personal finances? No, because he was already lucky enough to be the son of a very wealthy man.[643] The next president on our list of lucky ones came from circumstances very different from JFK.

HOW DOES CLOTHING CREATE LUCK?

Out of all the presidents, the president who created the most luck in his financials from how he dressed was none other than Martin Van Buren. He was also the last president to be born whose native language was not English. (In Van Buren's case, it was Dutch.) And he's one of only two presidents who attained the presidency without military experience or college, the other being Grover Cleveland.[644]

Known during his political career as "The Little Magician," Van Buren magically transformed himself from a poor boy into a wealthy man. Van Buren's family might have been on the poorer end of society, but he was born in one of the wealthiest counties in the entire country. And Van Buren had no fear of hard work and learning. To get Van Buren's luck—and ultimate wealth progression—you have to understand the Hudson Valley at the time of the American Revolution.

Wealthy Dutch immigrants had been in the country since the 1600s (including ancestors of another presidential family, the Roosevelts). But one family in particular just owned the area—the Van Rensselaers. The Van Rensselaers dominated the Hudson Valley. In fact, they owned over 750,000 acres in Columbia, Albany, and Rensselaer counties.[645] When the Van Rensselaers came to the country, so did the Van Burens. But the Van Burens were no Van Rensselaers. And even though it was the New World, all the hierarchies from Holland still applied. Growing up, Van Buren knew that his family didn't have means, as they owned a tavern, and that his

---

642 (Perry 2004) pages 40–41.
643 (Jensen 1977) In 1977, the *New York Times* estimated the Kennedy fortune between $300 and $500 million.
644 (Widmer 2005) page 9.
645 (Widmer 2005) page 21.

father was "a bit careless about money."[646] Furthermore, as a contemporary noted, the Van Burens "were humble, plain, and not much troubled with book knowledge."[647]

Luck can feel ephemeral. When you grow up poor in such a wealthy area like Van Buren did, any chance to "get your shot" is a stroke of luck—and you wouldn't want to let that fleeting moment pass you by. As an innkeeper's son, Van Buren knew he had to take chances to get ahead. Although he always felt insecure because he didn't get the education that others had, he knew he was clever.

Working at his father's inn, he watched the rhythm of people to learn and understand human nature, which allowed him to develop extraordinary attention to detail. He also had a chance to look at the clientele of the tavern. Aaron Burr, Alexander Hamilton, and other prominent people passed through the inn. And Van Buren took notes of how they behaved and how they worked the room.

His chance came when he was fourteen years old. Francis Sylvester, a local successful attorney, frequented his father's inn and approached Van Buren to see if he wanted to clerk in his office. In the early 1800s, you could study law under another attorney and gain entry to the bar.[648] It was a chance to rise up.

As one commentator described him, Van Buren was "impecunious, poorly educated and unrefined" in one of the wealthiest counties in the entire country.[649] Like Charlie Bucket opening up the Golden Ticket to meet Willy Wonka, Van Buren leapt at the opportunity. He knew at first the job would be "office janitor and errand boy," but that the role would also allow him to potentially learn the law.[650] Van Buren was ready for the arduous work where he would spend his days copying wills, indentures, deeds, and other law forms.[651] He was hell-bent on not being his father.

In fact, he really didn't like his father. In his sixties, Van Buren described his father as "an unassuming amiable man utterly devoid of the

---

646 (Widmer 2005) page 23.
647 (Crockett 1835) page 26.
648 It is incredibly interesting that more than 60 percent of American presidents are attorneys.
649 (Huston 2004) page 95.
650 (Shepard 1888) pages 36–37.
651 (Mushkat and Rayback 1997) page 17.

Ulysses S. Grant and the Never-Ending Get-Rich Schemes

spirit of accumulation."[652] What really made him burn was that his father had lost the money he had inherited from Van Buren's grandfather. His father's recklessness caused "his original property [that] was moderate [to be] gradually reduced until he could but ill afford to bestow upon his children the necessary for an education."[653]

One day in 1796, Van Buren set off on his first day of work as a clerk. As later described in a campaign bio, he was dressed in "coarse linen and rough woolens his mother had spun and woven."[654] Yet, by the end of the day, the homespun cloth had attracted dust and dirt to such an extent that Van Buren looked messy and disheveled. At one point, Sylvester told the young Van Buren that if one wanted to be a successful clerk, one must dress the part.

Van Buren got the message. He left the office and disappeared for two full days. When he reappeared, Sylvester was shocked to see his young clerk dressed in the same expensive suit his boss had two days prior. How he got it, history hasn't recorded. The likely answer is that he probably borrowed the money to have such a suit made. Van Buren understood that he had to invest in himself to help make his career, a notion many of us in our early careers also understand—and sacrificed so we'd have money to acquire the right wardrobe to get in the game.

He spent the next six years working for Sylvester building a reputation for hard work and smarts. And he looked the part. But what does that have to do with luck?

What if Sylvester had not given him the feedback but instead just fired Van Buren? He might have gotten another chance, but he may not have. In fact, he was pretty darn lucky to have a boss to give him that advice. We don't live in a day and age where that type of feedback is acceptable anymore. Van Buren was lucky Sylvester had that conversation with him. But Van Buren was also prepared for when this luck came. He had watched the politicians in his father's tavern. He had been honing his skills. And he listened to Sylvester. In his book *Chase, Chance, and Creativity: The Lucky Art of Novelty*, neurologist and Zen Buddhist Dr. James Austin described this luck as "favor[ing] those who have a sufficient background of sound

---

652   (Wildman 1925) page 177, quoting Van Buren's memoirs.
653   Ibid. Brackets added.
654   (Widmer 2005) page 27.

knowledge plus special abilities in observing, remembering, recalling, and quickly forming significant new associations."[655]

It's also a lesson about attracting opportunities—and, in turn, luck. It's a cliché, but you have to dress the part. Unlike Grant who squandered his luck, Van Buren showed us something different about luck. You can be incredibly smart and hardworking but oftentimes it is still the randomness of luck that propels you.

Just twelve years later, in 1808, Van Buren was earning $10,000 a year in salary (or over $200,000 in today's dollars) and was one of the most successful attorneys in the Hudson Valley.

During his presidency in the late 1830s, his love of the finer things in life led to constant criticism. But by that point, being a gentleman with refined taste had brought him so much luck, Van Buren remained true to who he had become.

CONSISTENCY + SKILL = LUCK

We have talked about the fact that all the presidents are lucky. Some are luckier than others. When reflecting on his life, Gerald Ford would say, "So I had a lot of lucky breaks I never planned on." Yet he would rationalize how that luck occurred. "But I would add this as a PS, and this is the point really. I said often, and I say today, 'The harder you work, the luckier you are.'"[656]

Now, Ford didn't do too bad financially. And since Ford, if I was to ask you about our contemporary presidents and if you thought they were wealthy, you would laugh and say, "Of course." Just look at Clinton or W or Obama with their book deals. Or Bush 41 from family money. And of course we have Trump. After all, Trump got hit with huge bond requirements by the state of New York only to have Truth Social go public on the same day.

But what about Jimmy Carter? Is he wealthy?

And I bet you would likely say, "Probably? Maybe? I don't know, but he's always building those houses for Habitat for Humanity?"

---

655 (Austen 2003) page 63.
656 (P. G. Ford, Ford-Cannon Interview for Ford Presidential Library 1990).

Ulysses S. Grant and the Never-Ending Get-Rich Schemes

Jimmy Carter is pretty stealth with his wealth. I mean, in the 2020s he and late wife Rosalynn were still using the furniture he built in the 1950s in their home. But the truth is, Carter is one lucky guy.

If you asked me who are the handful of presidents you should aspire to be like financially, I would have Carter near the top of that list. And the reason is that he's consistent. The truth is, when it comes to money, consistency is a big deal. Because if you are consistent, you have a good chance of also being consistently lucky.

One of the reasons Warren Buffet appeals to so many investors is that his advice is easy to understand. He has a good take on consistency. "Successful investing takes time, discipline and patience. No matter how great the talent or effort, some things take time; You can't produce a baby in one month by getting nine women pregnant."[657]

JIMMY CARTER AND HIS TWO OPPORTUNITY SETS

Carter grew up on a farm, but his family was pretty successful financially. He learned early on about how to make money and save. He also went to college and the Naval Academy. This wasn't a surprise to his family, as his mother, Lillian, noted years later that "he always wanted to go into the Navy."[658]

He was on the way up. In 1952, after six years in the navy, he had gotten access to a dream opportunity. He had been handpicked by Admiral Hyman Rickover to be an engineer on the nuclear submarine program in Schenectady, New York. It was cutting edge and only a few would actually be qualified for the work.

Rosalynn loved living in Schenectady. Their three sons were happy and healthy. They had everything they could want. Carter could even work regular hours in this new job and be home for the family. The Carters often told each other that this new job was "the best and most promising job in the Navy."[659] And Carter excelled. At one point Rickover noted in a pro-

---
657 (Buffett 1985).
658 (L. Carter 1978) pages 33–34.
659 (R. Carter 1984) page 35.

motion that "his leadership of the men assigned and his cooperation have been outstanding."[660]

Carter was making $300 a month. They managed their budget such that they were able to save seventy-five dollars every month.[661] Pretty soon, they hoped they would be able to buy a house. As part of the post–World War II generation, their opportunity set seemed better than anything they would have in Plains, Georgia, where they both had grown up.

A FORK IN THE ROAD

But their idyllic life was shattered in the early summer of 1953. Carter's father was diagnosed with pancreatic cancer. Carter rushed back to Plains to spend time with his father. Just a few weeks later, on July 22, 1953, Earl Carter passed away.

Carter reacted differently than most. He was devastated by his father's death at age fifty-nine. But rather than going down to help the family and then return to his normal life, he made a bold decision: he would give up his naval career and head home to run the farm.

In the post–World War II economy, this seems like madness. Carter would have been on his way to growing his wealth by simply continuing on the engineering career path. Serving as an officer on a nuclear submarine could open many doors.

And Rosalynn was livid. She had no interest in taking a step backward and returning to Plains. She had seen how hard it could be to eke out a living. Her father had died when she was a teenager, and she had seen her mother struggle to keep the family afloat.[662] Years later, Rosalynn would recount how hard she fought him about returning to Plains. She screamed and pleaded with him. She saw it as a dead end. And for her, the role of women on a farm was unappealing as it was back-breaking work.

---

660 (Rickover n.d.).
661 (R. Carter 1984) page 39. To give context, the median salary in the United States in 1952 was $3,900. Approximately 20 million American families made between $2,000 and $5,000 annually. This was the beginning of the middle class in the post-war world. See US Census Current Population Report: Consumer Income, dated April 27, 1954. Available at https://www2.census.gov/prod2/popscan/p60-015.pdf.
662 (R. Carter 1984) page 18. Rosalynn's mother was an only child. When she lost her husband, her parents pitched in to help but her mother (Rosalynn's grandmother) died soon thereafter, creating more financial issues.

Ulysses S. Grant and the Never-Ending Get-Rich Schemes

But there was a reason Carter wanted to go back. While he wanted to help his mother and brother Billy manage the farm, it was deeper than that. When Carter was home for the funeral, people kept coming up to him and telling him about the impact his father had on their lives. Carter learned things that he didn't know about the man his father was.

Rosalynn wrote in her memoirs about the situation. "Mr. Earl had quietly bought graduation clothes for children who couldn't afford new outfits; he had loaned money to farmers who bought his seed and fertilizer; he had helped support a widow in town for years after her husband died so she could make ends meet.…With Mr. Earl on his deathbed, many of his neighbors came to tell Jimmy about how much his father's life had meant to them."[663]

Even in his last moments, Carter's mother, Lillian, described how Earl "made Jimmy bring the books up. And I can't remember whether it was sixteen or eighteen…he cancelled notes for people he knew would be struggling hard."[664]

Carter himself came to a life-changing conclusion. He wanted a life that created significance for others. Furthermore, he felt he could still build that wealth that he and Rosalynn desired—but through the family farm. That wasn't going to happen being an engineer on a nuclear submarine. He would never progress to admiral. He needed to go home.

WHY BEING GRATEFUL CREATES LUCK

A lot about luck is how we react to the situations put in front of us. And what we are going to see is that Carter's reactions were anchored in being consistent—regardless of what he was dealing with. Carter also layered his consistency with intellectual curiosity. Dr. James Austin noted that luck "favors those who have a persistent curiosity about many things coupled with an energetic willingness to experiment and explore."

Earl had left the family "in good shape."[665] Carter had moved away from Plains more than eleven years prior. But his father, Earl, had kept growing the family's assets. As his wife, Lillian, noted after Earl's death, "He always had everything worked out. He planned for the future every

---

663 (R. Carter 1984) page 35.
664 (L. Carter 1978) page 21.
665 (L. Carter 1978) page 21.

day of his life."[666] At the time of his passing, the family assets included five hundred acres of land in Webster and Sumter Counties, a "thriving seed and fertilizer warehouse," as well as a fire insurance agency.[667] Additionally, Earl made loans to farmers; he would extend credit at the beginning of the farming season that the farmers would pay back at harvest, all while taking part in the state legislature.

From Carter's perspective, moving back would allow him to manage and continue growing the family assets. It would help his mother and younger brother Billy financially as well as support the over two hundred people who worked on their farms. And in many ways, he would be claiming his legacy that his father had grown from practically nothing. He could run the farm, create greater wealth, and continue with the philanthropy his father had started. He could also be an explorer and find new frontiers for himself and his family.

Carter went to work as executor of his father's estate. He quickly consolidated the assets and bought out his two sisters. The new corporation would be Carter and Rosalynn, his mother Lillian, and his brother Billy.[668] But even this was challenging because Lillian disapproved of Rosalynn being an equal partner with Carter.

Then things really got challenging. The move back was not easy. In Schenectady, they were saving and moving toward being affluent. Upon their return to Plains, they couldn't even afford a house. In fact, they couldn't even find one to rent. Their only option was government housing at thirty dollars a month. Rosalynn was less than thrilled as she moved in with Carter and their three young sons. Neighbors and family found her "aloof" and withdrawn. Yet her mother-in-law had some sympathy for her. Lillian later shared that Rosalynn "was so happy being in that (Navy) social life. It was just terrible for a couple to have to give that up and come back, but it was the only thing. It was the only way to save our business."[669]

Then came more bad news.

Carter's return to the family farm was not universally embraced. Billy had expected to run the farm after their father's death. He was infuriated

---

666 (L. Carter 1978) page 17.
667 (E. S. Godbold 2010) page 70.
668 (E. S. Godbold 2010) page 81.
669 (Thomas B. Ross 1976).

Ulysses S. Grant and the Never-Ending Get-Rich Schemes

by his brother and sister-in-law's return. Billy saw that they were usurping the legacy that Earl had created for him to inherit, not Carter. Within a few months, Billy left Plains and the farming to Carter.

Then came the inflation. As the US recovered from the Korean War, post-war inflation seemed inevitable. By early 1953, the Federal Reserve was already taking steps to tighten monetary policy as a way of tempering the projected inflation. It had an impact on the basic running of the farm. The country fell into a recession. Things were tough all over Plains. Then a drought hit. Peanuts, corn, and cotton crops all failed. The farmers around them were struggling, unable to pay their bills. Carter had no choice but to extend credit. The Carters were land rich but cash poor. The illiquidity put a harder squeeze on them.

Then Carter became even more illiquid. The Citizens Bank of Americus refused him a $10,000 loan unless he could get a cosigner. He eventually had to borrow funds from the fertilizer company. They couldn't catch a break. By the time the 1953 season ended, the Carters had barely made $200.[670]

Every time Rosalynn started to complain, Carter would respond the same way: that she should accept the situation and not give into displeasure. But that sentence is a powerful one. Carter said it because he wanted her to focus on gratitude—to appreciate the positives of the situation. Those who study luck often find that gratitude and consistency create an environment that generates greater luck. Why? Because the focus on the greater situation causes the elimination of self-interest.

Carter was not immune to money worries. He later recalled that "I owed $12,000 and did not know how I was going to pay it. If I could not collect my bills that month, I could not pay for the fertilizer I had already sold. It was gnawing away at [my] guts no matter what other good things were going on."[671]

However, by focusing on the overall picture and being grateful for his opportunities, he was able to turn it around. After the 1953 harvest ended, Carter realized that to grow the farm, he needed to learn more. He read everything available on modern peanut farming.[672] He enrolled in exten-

---

670 The stated amount varies, but in the range of $197 to $254.
671 (Bourne 1997) page 84.
672 (Thomas B. Ross 1976).

sion courses in agriculture at the University of Georgia. He sought out help from older, more experienced farmers. And he brought Rosalynn into the day-to-day running of the farm.

Slowly and steadily, he kept at it. The 1954 harvest was only marginally better than 1953. And he persisted at farming. He did not want to fail. Finally, the rains returned. It was a prosperous season in 1955. The Carter farm had a great harvest. The farmers paid back their loans to Carter, and he was able to start expanding the farm. Carter then stumbled on an extraordinary piece of luck. Rosalynn was an excellent businesswoman. By bringing her in to run the financial part of the business, Carter had inadvertently discovered that his wife had the right skills and acumen to scale a business.[673]

Their run of bad luck turned into a run of good luck. Over the next ten years, Carter and Rosalynn grew the business into a multi-million-dollar operation. They bought more acreage and expanded their warehouses. They also built a processing plant to shell and dry peanuts. His financial resiliency, much like everything about him, is often overlooked and underestimated.

In an article in *The Atlantic*, former Carter speechwriter and a friend of over forty years, James Fallows, noted that "Jimmy Carter has always been the same person.... Whatever his role, whatever the outside assessment of him, whether luck was running with him or against, Carter was the same. He was self-controlled and disciplined.... He was enormously intelligent—and aware of it—politically crafty and deeply spiritual. And he was intelligent, crafty and spiritual enough to recognize the inevitable trade-offs between his ambitions and his ideals. People who knew him at one state of his life would recognize him at another. Jimmy Carter didn't change. Luck and circumstances did."[674]

CONSISTENCY AND PERSISTENCE

Over twenty years after taking over the farm, Carter started to move into the arena to run for president. He disclosed that the Carter family holdings now included the "3,100-acre Carter Farms Inc. and a family partnership

---

673 (E. S. Godbold n.d.) Godbold speaks of Rosalynn's business acumen being one of the big benefits Carter had in scaling the business.
674 (Fallows 2023).

that buys and sells peanuts, gins cotton and sells fertilizer and insecticides to farmers in the Plains area."[675] Annual sales were $2.5 million. Carter also noted his and Rosalynn's personal net worth to be $558,628 ($3.5 million in 2023). His total assets were $999,689 with the farm factored in.[676] The press jumped all over it.[677] It was even higher than what President Ford reported. Ultimately, Carter's financial success was a testament to being consistent and being grateful for the opportunity.

DON'T OVERLOOK YOUR IMPACT ON LUCK

Skill, preparation, and consistency are elements that can also enhance your chance of luck with money. Grant might have had better luck in his future years if he had learned financial transaction skills. He needed to be measured and objective. He needed to understand the risks and create a margin of safety. And he needed to know his weakness was in trusting the wrong people. I have worked with clients who understand their weaknesses and ask me to keep them in check.

And what is tragic about him is that these mistakes occur again and again for him financially. It is only when he is dying of cancer that he writes his memoirs, thus ensuring his family's financial stability.

Van Buren and Carter both influenced their outcomes. And that's the lesson to take here. It is possible to manifest luck in your personal finances. But it takes a lot of work. Every one of my clients who have had financial success will be very clear about that. Luck occurred, but they had to be present when it showed up.

I have a client I have worked with for almost twenty years. She was an assistant controller when I first met her. Over the years I have worked with her, she is always the first one in the office at 6 a.m. and the last to leave. That work ethic has given her the ability to climb the corporate ladder to now being CFO of a major corporation. I'm sure today people might ask where her work-life balance is, but what she and my clients would say is that if you want to grow and gain wealth, you need to work hard. Luck will then find you, but it plays the long game.

---

675 (Horrock 1976).
676 (Thomas B. Ross 1976).
677 (Horrock 1976).

All the Presidents' Money

I'll end this with a quick client story. My client owned a marina in the South. This thing was an amazing moneymaker. It threw off seven figures like it was minting money. But he came to me one day and said it was time to sell. I told him he was nuts. There was no way we could generate as much yield for him as this income stream. But he was adamant. It was time. A few months later, he called me a few days after the marina closed. "You are never going to guess what happened," he said. "Eight hours after the marina closed, a freak storm hit the area. Hundreds of thousands of dollars of damage."

I was stunned. What timing.

He laughed. "Better lucky than good."

Was it? Or was it the years of working hard and understanding the business that allowed him to behave consistently to bring that luck? Either way, it is much easier to say he's lucky.

Afterword

When people hear I am writing a book on the personal finances of the presidents, I am usually asked either one of two questions:

Who was the worst with money?

Who was the best with money?

These two questions give me a lot of insight into how money and the presidents are perceived. We want to know the juicier personal information about these people. As I said earlier, it humanizes them and can even make us feel better about ourselves.

Yet, I ultimately believe that the reason people want to know the answers to these questions is to see if they can emulate the good behaviors and avoid the bad.

Here's the thing that most presidents learn on their journey: wealth happens at the intersection of opportunity and discipline. The first hurdle is having opportunity. For all of our presidents, they were able to get the opportunity. However, in today's world, it is much harder for most Americans to even access the right opportunity set.

It's the discipline part that is the greater challenge.

In my professional opinion, the three presidents who were the worst with their money (from the ones discussed in this book) were Thomas Jefferson, James Monroe, and Joe Biden. It is easy to see why: they all struggled with the basics of finance. They were unable to budget well, they didn't connect with their future selves, and their decision-making was flawed. Their financial issues were due to their poor management.

All the Presidents' Money

Yet, I believe all three were (and are) teachable and could be helped. They all wanted (and want) to improve their financial skills. For all their successes, financial stability seemed elusive. All three of them have felt that horrible feeling when we fail financially: shame.

By obtaining professional help from experts, along with consistent meetings to discuss their finances, they could become more proficient in money. In many ways, it's akin to hiring a personal trainer to lose weight and shape up. You have to put in the hard work on a consistent basis. It's not always fun, but it can be fulfilling and meaningful when real results occur.

As for the best, there are five that I believe show the best traits of those who are successful with money. These are the five whose behaviors I would encourage you to emulate in your personal finances:

Eisenhower is the perfect example of controlling one's emotions when managing their finances. He's cool, calm, and collected, and that is why he can execute strategy at the highest levels. When you get stressed about money, breathe deeply and think of Ike.

Reagan always connected with Americans, and it's because he's anxious like the rest of us. He was a master of budgeting. It helped him control his anxiety. Budgeting is such a dirty word in personal finance, but it is a great anti-anxiety mechanism.

Ford is one of the most inspiring personal finance stories because he embraces fearlessness. He isn't afraid to take a different path and be bold. That's really important in personal finance. Sometimes your choices will not be agreed upon by all of your friends and family. But like Ford, don't be afraid to also master the pivot.

Now, I would love to say Washington is my favorite president with money. And he's so good at so many of the skills. But due to his being a slaveowner, we always need to put an asterisk next to his name, as some of his wealth was made off of the backs of others.

But that doesn't mean we don't want to use some of his story for our own finances. Washington's grit (along with his budgeting) is something we all need to keep in mind when working with our money. Managing our personal finances is hard work and is a long game. Washington kept his eye on the prize the whole time, working through each issue that came his way, as personal finance is a daily engagement.

Afterword

But when it comes to the president who was the best with money, for me, it could only be Herbert Hoover. Hoover's financial life story is that of the hero's journey. At the right moments in his childhood, he learns about the basic tenets of personal finance. He budgets, he has vision, he is a risk-taker, and he has grit. And he's incredibly lucky in the opportunity set he comes across over his life. Hoover not only creates great wealth through his skills, but he also helps feed the world.

***

From these stories, you can see that building wealth at different times over American history is a journey. In April 2017, I took a journey that started this book. I had the opportunity to visit the Lincoln Presidential Site in Springfield, Illinois. But before I got to Springfield, I stopped in New Salem.

Lincoln lived in New Salem from 1831 to 1837. It is a rustic pioneer town with log cabins and dirt roads. I drove east seventy-one miles to Springfield to a house on the corner of Eighth and Jackson. Lincoln and Mary had purchased the house in 1844, and the contrast couldn't have been greater.

It had been only seven years from his arrival to the acquisition of one of the nicest homes in town. Now when you dig into Lincoln's finances, you find out he had some help from Mary's family. But the socioeconomic leap was unbelievable.

In reconciling this, I came across a story regarding Ike. On a visit to his hometown of Abilene, Kansas, after World War II, Ike reflected, "I have found out in later years we were very poor, but the glory of America is that we didn't know it then. All we knew was that our parents could say to us that the opportunity was all about us. All we had to do is reach out and take it."[678]

I found this quote as I neared the writing of this book. While Eisenhower was reflecting on his childhood in the 1890s, the quote resonated with me a little differently. In reading through the financial lives of our presidents, what struck me time and again is that regardless of the time period, whether it was Washington growing up in the 1750s, Hoover in the

---

678   (Morin 1969) page 11.

1880s, or even Jerry Ford in the 1910s, they all had a common hope that tomorrow would be better for them than today. That hope allowed them to engage with their personal finances and develop over their lifetime the ability to create and grow wealth.

Today I am not so sure this is the case. Yes, the American dream is still there but it is so much harder to attain. The tools and skills that prior generations had to propel themselves are no longer available. Budgeting is a useful tool—but only if the numbers have a chance to actually be reconciled. Today with challenging wage growth and incredible inflation, for many Americans it just isn't possible.

There is a lot of work that needs to be done. We cannot count on politicians to put forth the tools to fix the issues in our system. Rather we need to make sure that financial literacy is made available to all Americans in order to give them the skills they need to not only survive but to thrive financially in the twenty-first century.

Bibliography

1932. *Death of Washington: Letters and Recollections of George Washington.*

1967. "Archive: January 17, 1967 Statement of Governor Ronald Reagan on Tuition." *Ronald Reagan Presidential Library and Museum.* January 17. https://www.reaganlibrary.gov/archives/speech/january-17-1967-statement-governor-ronald-reagan-tuition.

1995. *The American President.* Directed by Rob Reiner.

ABC News. 2012. "Obama: I Only Paid Off My Student Loans Eight Years Ago." ABC News, April 24.

Adams, John. 1966. *The earliest diary of John Adams: June 1753–April 1754, September 1758–January 1759.* Edited by Lyman Henry Butterfield. Cambridge, Massachusetts: Belknap Press of Harvard University Press.

Adams, Lucas. 2014. "An Illustrated Account of 'The Great Die-Up' of the 1880s." *Modern Farmer*, April 2.

Aitken, Jonathan. 1996. *Nixon, A Life.* Regnery Publishing.

Ambrose, Stephen E. 1973. *Ike: Abilene to Berlin: The Life of Dwight D. Eisenhower from His Childhood in Abilene, Kansas, Through His Command of the Allied Forces in Europe.* New York: Harper Collins.

American Psychological Association. 2015. *Stress In America: Paying with our Health.* American Psychological Association.

Anthony, Carl Sferrazza. 2023. *Camera Girl: The Coming of Age of Jackie Bouvier Kennedy.* New York City: Gallery Books.

Armistead Jr, George H. 1956. "The Void Provision of a President's Will." *Tennessee Historical Quarterly* 15 (2).

Asch, Andrew. 2022. "Bird Streets Home Once Owned by Ronald Reagan Fetches $70M." *The Real Deal Real Estate News*, September 13.

Associated Press. 1978. "Fords Plan New Home." *The Sacramento Bee*, March 9: 8.

—. 1965. "White House China Set Reported Lost In Harding's Poker Game." June 28.

Austen, Dr. James. 2003. *Chase, Chance, and Creativity: The Lucky Art of Novelty*. Boston: MIT Press.

Baker, Jean H. 1990. "Mary Todd Lincoln: Managing Home, Husband, and Children." *Journal of the Abraham Lincoln Association*, 1–12.

—. 1987. *Mary Todd Lincoln: A Biography*. New York: W.W. Norton & Company.

Bales, Susan Ford, interview by Richard Norton Smith. 2010. *Gerald R. Ford Oral History Project* (July 25).

Ball, Dean W. 2021. "Calvin's Stocks." *Coolidge Quarterly*, March: 11–12.

Bank of America. 2023. *The 2023 Bank of America Study of Philanthropy: Charitable Giving By Affluent Households*. New York: Bank of America.

Bank, SunTrust. 2019. *2019 SunTrust Bank Harris Survey on Marriage*. SunTrust Bank.

Barrish, Cris. 2023. "1787 letter from cash-poor George Washington hailed as 'great discovery.'" *WHYY PBS*, February 20.

Baruch, Bernard M. 1935. "The Real Calvin Coolidge: A First Hand Story of His Life Told By The People Who Knew Him Best." *Good Housekeeping Magazine*, May.

Bell's Weekly Messenger. 1800. March 23.

Berg, A. Scott. 2013. *Wilson*. New York City: G.P. Putnam's Sons.

Berko, Malcolm. 1989. "Harken Energy Has A Blue-Chip List of Shareholders, Including Bush." *Tallahassee Democrat*, April 5: 46.

Biden, Joseph. 2008. *Promises To Keep: On Life and Politics*. New York City: Random House.

Biden, Joseph R, Pete Stephanopoulos, Amy Klobuchar, Bernie Sanders, Tom Steyer, Elizabeth Warren, and Andrew Yang, interview by Linsey Davis, Monica Hernandez, David Muir, Adam Sexton and

Bibliography

George Stephanopoulos. 2020. *Democratic Candidates Debate in Manchester, New Hampshire* (February 7).

Billings, Kirk Lemoyne, interview by Walter D. Sohier. 1964. *John F. Kennedy Presidential Library Oral Histories* (June 24).

Binney, Horace. 1858. *Bushrod Washington*. Philadelphia: C. Sherman & Son.

Borchers, Callum. 2023. "It's Summer, and Nepo Babies Are Coming to the Office." *Wall Street Journal*, June 1.

Bourne, Peter G. 1997. *Jimmy Carter*. New York: Simon & Schuster Inc.

Bradlee, Benjamin C. 1975. *Conversations with Kennedy*. New York City: Norton.

Bragdon, Henry W. 1967. *Woodrow Wilson: The Academic Years*. Cambridge: Belknap Press of Harvard University Press.

Brownstein, Ronald. 1987. "The Selling of the Ex-President : Nixon and Carter Just Wrote Books. Ford Had a Better Idea." *Los Angeles Times*, February 15.

Buffett, Warren. 1985. "1985 Annual Letter to the Shareholders of Berkshire Hathaway Inc."

Bureau, Consumer Financial Protection. 2020. *Building Blocks To Help Youth Achieve Financial Capability: Measurement Guide*. Consumer Financial Protection Bureau.

Burlingame, Michael. 2009. *Abraham Lincoln: A Life, Volume II*. Johns Hopkins University Press.

—. 2021. *An American Marriage: The Untold Story of Abraham Lincoln and Mary Todd*. Berkeley: Pegasus Books.

Burner, David. 1979. *Herbert Hoover, A Public Life*. New York: Knopf.

Burroughs, Bryan. 2010. "What's Eating Steve Cohen." *Vanity Fair*, July.

Bush, George H. W. 2000. *All the best, George Bush: my life in letters and other writings*. New York: Touchstone.

Bykowicz, Julie. 2020. "In His Own Words, Joe Biden Was 'Seduced by Real Estate.'" *The Wall Street Journal*, February 28.

C. Yiwei Zhang, Abigail Sussman, Nathan Wang-Ly, Jennifer K. Lyu. 2022. "How Consumers Budget." *Journal of Economic Behavior and Organization*, December: 69–88.

Campos, Paul F. 2002. "The Truman Show: The Fraudulent Origins of the Former." *Michigan State Law Review*. https://scholar.law.colorado.edu/faculty-articles/1580.

Carnegie, Andrew. 1889. *The Gospel of Wealth*. New York City: Carnegie Corporation of New York.

Caro, Robert A. 1990. *Means of Ascent: The Years of Lyndon Johnson*. New York City: Alfred A. Knopf.

Carstensen, Eldon Bernstein and Fred. 1996. "Rising to the Occasion: Lender's Bagels and the Frozen Food Revolution, 1927-1985." *Business and Economic History* 25 (1): 165–175. www.jstor.org/stable/23703112.

Carter, Lillian, interview by David Alsobrook. 1978. *Jimmy Carter Presidential Library Oral History Interview with Lillian Carter* (September 26).

Carter, Rosalynn. 1984. *First Lady From Plains*. Boston: Houghton Mifflin.

Chen, James, 2024. "Investing Basics: Due Diligence." Investopedia, January 18. https://www.investopedia.com/terms/d/duediligence.asp.

Circle, Penny, interview by Richard Norton Smith. 2008. *Gerald R. Ford Oral History Project* (December 5).

Citrifrost Corporation. 1940. "Letter to the Board of Directors of Citrifrost Corporation." Reproduced by The Richard Nixon Presidential Library and Museum, December 6.

—. 1939/1940. "Letter to the Stockholders of the Citrifrost Corporation." Reproduced by The Richard Nixon Presidential Library and Museum.

Clark, Laura. 2015. "The 1887 Blizzard That Changed The American Frontier Forever." *Smithsonian Magazine*, January 9.

Cleburne, Gregory. 1924. "Franklin Roosevelt Will Swim To Health." *Atlanta Journal*, October 26.

Clinton, Hillary. 2003. *Living History*. New York City: Simon & Schuster.

Bibliography

Clinton, William Jefferson, interview by David Gregory. 2014. *Meet The Press* (June 29).

Collins, Herbert Ridgeway, and David B. Weaver. 1976. "Text of the Will of Millard Fillmore." *Wills of the U.S. Presidents*.

Consumer Financial Protection Bureau. 2015. *Financial Well-Being: The Goal of Financial Education*. Washington DC: CFPB.

Coolidge, Calvin. n.d. "Letter Calvin Coolidge to Charles Merrill Dated November 29, 1929." *Merrill-Magowan Family Papers, Amherst College Archives and Special Collections*.

—. 1929. *The Autobiography of Calvin Coolidge*. New York City: Cosmopolitan Book Corporation.

Coughlin, William. 2000. "Into the Outback." *Stanford Magazine*, March/April.

Cramer, Richard Ben. 1993. *What It Takes: The Way To The White House*. New York City: Vintage Publishing.

Crockett, David. 1835. *The Life of Martin Van Buren*. Philadelphia: R. Wright.

Cunningham, Noble E. 2003. *Jefferson and Monroe: Constant Friendship and Respect*. Chapel Hill: University of North Carolina Press.

Dallek, Robert. 2004. *An Unfinished Life: John F. Kennedy, 1917–1963*. New York: Back Bay Books.

Danes, Sharon. n.d.

Daniels, Josephus. 1932. "Franklin Roosevelt As I Knew Him." *Saturday Evening Post*, September 24: 26, 29, 78–80.

Davis, Patti. 1992. *The Way I See It: An Autobiography*. New York: G.P. Putnam's Sons.

Deaton, Daniel Kahneman and Angus. 2010. "High Income Improves Evaluation of Life But Not Emotional Well-Being." *Proceedings of the National Academy of Sciences* 5.

DeFrank, Thomas M. 2007. *Write It When I'm Gone—Remarkable Off-the-Record Conversations with Gerald R. Ford*. New York: Berkley Books.

Dekom, Otto. 1976. "At Franklin Mint, They're Blase About Bicen." *The Morning News of Wilmington Delaware*, March 14: 47.

Democrat and Chronicle. 1874. "Fillmore and His Times." March 10: 2.

DeWitt, Dave. 2010. *The Founding Foodies: American Meals That Wouldn't Exist Today If Not For Washington, Jefferson and Franklin*. New York City: Sourcebooks.

Dimitri, Carolyn, Anne Effland, and Neilson Conklin. June 2005. *The 20th Century Transformation of US Agriculture and Farm Policy*. United States Department of Agriculture.

DiSilvestro, Roger L. 2011. *Theodore Roosevelt in the Badlands: A Young Politician's Quest for Recovery in the American West*. New York City: Walker Books.

Dixon Evening Telegraph. 1941. "In Their Blue Heaven." September 12: 19.

Doenecke, Justus D. 1988. *The Presidencies of James A. Garfield & Chester A. Arthur*. Lawrence: Regents Press of Kansas.

Duckworth, Angela. 2016. *Grit: The Power of Passion and Perseverence*. New York: Scribner.

—. 2016. *PBS Newshour*. May 12. https://www.pbs.org/newshour/economy/column-grit-or-quit.

Duke, Annie. 2018. *Thinking in Bets: Making Smarter Decisions When You Don't Have All the Facts*. New York: Penguin Publishing Group.

Dunbar, John. 2002. "Harken's Ivy League Underwriter." Center for Public Integrity, October 17.

Dunrud, Sharon M. Danes PhD and Tammy. 2005. *Children and Money: Teaching Children Money Habits for Life*. University of Minnesota.

Dusinberre, William. 2003. *Slavemaster President*. New York City: Oxford University Press.

Eisenhower, Dwight D. 1967. *At Ease: Stories I Tell To Friends*. Garden City: Doubleday.

Eisenhower, Mamie Doud, interview by Dr. Maclyn Burg and Dr. John Wickman. 1972. *Interview with Mrs. Mamie Doud Eisenhower* (July 20).

Eisenhower, Susan. 1996. *Mrs. Ike*. New York City: Farrar Straus & Giroux.

Ellis, Joseph J. 2004. *His Excellency*. New York: Alfred A. Knopf.

Bibliography

Fallows, James. 2023. "An Unlucky President, And A Lucky Man." *The Atlantic*, February 23.

Farlin, John D. 2008. "Charles E. Merrill: The Father of Main Street Brokerage." *Journal of the North American Management Society Journal of the North American Management Society* 3 (1): 3–12. https://thekeep.eiu.edu/jnams/vol3/iss1/2.

Federal Reserve. May 2022. *Report on the Economic Well-Being of U.S. Households in 2021 (SHED)*. Washington, DC: Federal Reserve. https://www.federalreserve.gov/publications/2022-economic-well-being-of-us-households-in-2021-dealing-with-unexpected-expenses.htm.

Finkelman, Paul. 2011. *Millard Fillmore: The American Presidents Series: The 13th President, 1850–1853*. Times Books.

Fitzgerald, F. Scott. 2004. *The Great Gatsby*. New York City: Scribner.

Fleischner, Jennifer. 2003. *Mrs. Lincoln and Mrs. Keckley*. New York: Broadway Books.

Ford, Jerry. August 7, 1958. "Your Washington Review."

Ford, President Gerald R., interview by James Cannon. 1992. *Ford–Cannon Interview for Ford Presidential Library* (April 25).

Ford, President Gerald R., interview by James Cannon. 1990. *Ford–Cannon Interview for Ford Presidential Library* (November 30).

Ford, Steve, interview by Richard Norton Smith. 2011. *Gerald R. Ford Oral History Project* (March 7).

Fort Worth Star Telegram (Fort Worth Texas). 1927. "Paralysis Cure Offer Sought By Many." August 15: 13.

Fossett, Peter. 1898. *Recollections of Peter Fossett*. New York City: New York World.

Foster, Sarah. 2023. "Survey: The average American feels they'd need over $200K a year to be financially comfortable." *Bankrate*, July 6. https://www.bankrate.com/personal-finance/financial-freedom-survey/.

Frank, Robert H. 2016. *Success and Luck: Good Fortune and the Myth of Meritocracy*. Princeton: Princeton University Press.

Franklin Mint. 1976. "Advertisement." *Fort Worth Star-Telegram*. November 21.

Gailey, Alex. May 8, 2023. "More than half of Americans say money negatively impacts their mental health, up sharply from a year ago." Bankrate. https://www.bankrate.com/personal-finance/financial-wellness-survey/.

Gallagher, Hugh Gregory. 1999. *FDR's Splendid Deception: The Moving Story of Roosevelt's Massive Disability—And The Intense Efforts to Conceal It From The Public.*

Garbinsky, Emily N., Joe J. Gladstone, Hristina Nikolova, and Jenny G. Olson. 2020. "Love, Lies, and Money: Financial Infidelity in Romantic Relationships." *Journal of Consumer Research* 47(1): 1–24.

Garrow, David J. 2017. *Rising Star: The Making of Barack Obama.* New York City: William Morrow.

Gately, Dermot. 1986. "Lessons From the 1986 Oil Price Collapse." *Brookings Papers on Economic Activity*, June: 237–284.

Gawalt, Gerard W. 1993. "James Monroe, Presidential Planter." *The Virginia Magazine of History and Biography*, 251–272.

n.d. *George Washington's Mount Vernon.* https://www.mountvernon.org/george-washington/martha-washington/the-deaths-of-george-martha/.

Gilbert, Robert E. 2005. "Calvin Coolidge's Tragic Presidency: The Political Effects of Bereavement and Depression." *Journal of American Studies*, April: 87–109.

Gladwell, Malcolm. 2000. *The Tipping Point.* New York City: Little Brown and Company.

Godbold, E. Staly. 2010. *Jimmy and Rosalynn Carter: The Georgia Years, 1924–1974.* New York: Oxford University Press.

Godbold, E. Stanly. n.d. "Jimmy and Rosalynn Carter: The Georgia Years, 1924–1974." Georgia Center for the Book. C-SPAN. Decatur, Georgia.

Golman, R., Hagmann, D., & Loewenstein, G. 2017. "Information Avoidance." *Journal of Economic Literature*, March: 96–135.

Greenberger, Scott. 2017. *The Unexpected President: The Life and Times of Chester A. Arthur.* Cambridge: Da Capo Press.

Bibliography

Grey, Gene. 1978. "Some Loose Change For Jerry Ford." *Press and Sun Bulletin (Binghamton New York)*, March 5: 17C.

Grobbelaar, Chrizann, and Liezel Alsemgeest. 2016. "The Relationship between Spousal Communication and Financial Arguemts and Stress Between Young Married Couples." *Journal of Social Science* 271–281.

Hachitt, Ann. 2003. "LBJ Family Signing Off From Radio Business in $105m Deal." *Austin Business Journal*.

Hailman, John R. 2006. *Thomas Jefferson on Wine*. Jackson: University Press of Mississippi.

Hall, Sherry. 2014. *Warren G. Harding & the Marion Daily Star: How Newspapering Shaped a President*. History Press Library Editions.

Hanson, Melanie. 2022. "Average Cost of College By Year." EducationData.org. January 9. https://educationdata.org/average-cost-of-college-by-year.

Hartford Business Journal. 2011. "GE pays $15M tribute to Reagan." *Hartford Business Journal*, February 7.

Harvard University. 2023. *375 Years of Financial Aid*. https://financialaid.hcf.harvard.edu/lady-mowlson.

Hasler, Andrea, Annamaria Lusardi, and Noemi Oggero. 2017. *Financial Fragility in the US: Evidence and Implications*. Washington, DC: Global Financial Literacy Excellence Center.

Herndon, William H. 1888. *Abraham Lincoln: The True Story of a Great Life*. Chicago: Belford-Clarke Co.

Hershfeld, Hal E. 2011. "Future self-continuity: how conceptions of the future self transform intertemporal choice." *Ann N Y Acad Sci*. 30–43.

Hillinger, Charles. 1977. "Expectation High at Hawaiian School." *LA Times*, July 17: 2–3.

Holley, Sallie. 1899. *A Life For Liberty: Anti-Slavery And Other Letters Of Sallie Holley*. New York: G.P. Putnam's Sons.

Hoover to Nell May Hill dated November 7, 1894. n.d. "The Correspondence of Herbert Hoover." Courtesy of Herbert Hoover Presidential Library.

Hoover to Nell May Hill dated September 7, 1895. n.d. "The Correspondence of Herbert Hoover." Courtesy of The Hebert Hoover Presidential Library.

Hoover, Herbert. 1951. *The Memoirs of Herbert Hoover*. New York City: The MacMillan Company.

Horrock, Nicholas M. 1976. "Peanuts Prove Profitable as Carter Empire Grows." *New York Times*, May 26.

Horton, Ralph, interview by Joseph Dolan. 1964. *John F. Kennedy Oral History Collection* (June 1).

Hough, Art. 1977. "The Hoover Hunt Is A Tedious Job." *The Cedar Rapids Gazette*, November 13: 59.

House of Representatives. 1958. "Individual Voting Record of Gerald R. Ford." *Eighty-Fifth Congress: Second Session*. Washington, DC. 7–11.

Huston, Reeve. 2004. "The 'Little Magician' after the Show: Martin Van Buren, Country Gentleman and Progressive Farmer, 1841–1862." *New York History*, 85(2), 93–121. http://www.jstor.org/stable/23183293.

In The Matter of Trading in the Securities of Harken Energy HO-2518. 1991. (SEC Investigation, August 21).

Insley, Jill. 1999. "Shopping Til You Drop." *The Guardian*, August 7.

Internal Revenue Department. 1941. "Delinquency Notice Social Security Tax." Reproduced by The Richard Nixon Presidential Library and Museum, May 29.

Internal Revenue Service. 2023. Internal Revenue Service. September 23. https://www.irs.gov/credits-deductions-for-individuals.

Investopedia. 2023. *Series Funding: A, B, and C*. December 22. https://www.investopedia.com/articles/personal-finance/102015/series-b-c-funding-what-it-all-means-and-how-it-works.asp.

Jaffray, Elizabeth. 1926. *Secrets of the White House*. New York City: Cosmopolitan Book Corporation.

Jalil, Andrew J. 2015. "A New History of Banking Panics in the United States, 1825–1929: Construction and Implications." *American Economic Journal: Macroeconomics 7*, July: 295–330.

Bibliography

Jason Jabbari, Joshua Jackson, Stephen Roll, and Michal Grinstein-Weiss. 2021. "Pinching Pennies Or Money To Burn? The Role of Grit in Financial Behaviors." *Social Policy Institute Research 47* 1–28.

Jeffers, H.P. 2000. *An Honest President: The Life And Presidencies Of Grover Cleveland.* New York City: William Morrow.

Jenkinson, Clay. 2006. *Theodore Roosevelt in the Dakota Badlands: An Historical Guide.* Dickinson: Dickinson State University.

Jensen, Michael C. 1977. "Managing the Kennedy Millions." *New York Times*, June 12: 107.

John Ameriks, Andrew Caplin, John Leahy. 2003. "Wealth Accumulation and the Propensity to Plan." *Quarterly Journal of Economics*, 1007–1047.

Johnson, Claudia "Lady Bird," interview by Michael Gillette. 1980. *Lyndon Baines Johnson Library Oral History Collection XVI* (January/February 29, 30, & 31, 1, 2, & 3).

Johnson, Claudia "Lady Bird," interview by Michael Gillette. 1977. *Oral History Interview* (August 14).

Johnson, Claudia Lady Bird. n.d. "Audio Diary and Annotated Transcript of Lady Bird Johnson."

Johnson, Lyndon B. n.d. "Johnson to OJ Weber." *The Correspondence of Lyndon B. Johnson.* Courtesy The Lyndon B. Johnson Presidential Library.

Joint Commitee on Taxation Staff. 2019. *Background Regarding the Confidentiality and Disclosure of Federal Tax Returns.* House Committee on Ways and Means.

July 30, 1945. "Meeting Minutes of Adjourned Special Meeting of the Executive Committee of the Board of Trustees of Georgia Warm Springs Foundation." Georgia Warm Springs Foundation Records.

K. Hoyer, M. Zeelenberg, & S.M. Breugelmans. 2022. "Greed: What Is It Good For?" *Personality and Social Psychology Bulletin*, 1–16.

Kandimalla, Sriskandha. 2023. "Ronald Reagan's Legacy: The Rise of Student Loan Debt in America." *New University—The Newspaper of the University of California at Irvine*, February 13.

Kansas Newspapers In Education. 2017. Eisenhower Foundation. https://www.eisenhowerlibrary.gov/sites/default/files/file/Chapter%2015%20College.pdf.

Kearns Goodwin, Doris. 1991. *Lyndon Johnson and the American Dream*. New York City: St. Martin's Griffin.

Keavy, Hubbard. 1941. "Jane Wyman, Married To Actor, Says Pooling of Income Helps." *The Tampa Tribune (Associated Press)*, September 18: 14.

Keckley, Elizabeth. 1868. *Behind The Scenes, or, Thirty Years a Slave, and Four Years in the White House*. New York: G.W. Carleton & Co. Publishers.

Keller, Hadley. 2016. "Which Administration Had the Chicest White House China?" *Architectual Digest*, October 11.

Kerr, Alexandra. 2023. *Financial Independence, Retire Early (FIRE) Explained: How It Works*. March 27. https://www.investopedia.com/terms/f/financial-independence-retire-early-fire.asp.

Killewald, Alexandra. 2016. "Money, Work and Marital Stability: Assessing Change in the Gendered Determinants of Divorce." *American Sociological Review* 81(4): 696–719.

Klein, Jeff Z. 2016. "Heritage Moments: The Shunning of Millard Fillmore." WBFO NPR, July 5.

Knollenberg, Bernhard. 1964. *George Washington: The Virginia Period 1732–1775*. Durham: Duke University Press.

Korda, Michael. 2004. *Ulysses S. Grant*. New York: Harper Collins.

Langella, Frank. 2012. *Dropped Names*. New York City: Harper.

Langevoort, Donald, interview by Gwen Ifill. 2002. "President Bush's Old Business at Harken Energy Corporation." PBS NewsHour (July 11).

Lanman, Charles. 1859. *Dictionary of the United States Congress*. Philadelphia: J.B. Lippincott & Co.

Lawrence, David. 1949. "Today In Washington." *Portland Evening Express*, January 18: 12.

Lincoln, Abraham. 1894. *Complete Works of Abraham Lincoln, Volume Two*. Edited by John G Nicolay and John Hay. New York City: Francis D. Tandy Company.

Bibliography

Lippman Jr., Theo. 1978. "Birth of a Salesman." *The Baltimore Sun*, March 9: 15.

Lurtz, Meghaan. 2019. "Future Self-Continuity: How Envisioning the Future Is Important to Financial Planning." kitces.com. October 16. https://www.kitces.com/blog/future-self-continuity-behavior-finance-habits/.

Mallon, Thomas. 2017. "When A New York Baron Became President." *The New Yorker*, September 4.

Marsh, Richard Dean. 1977. "James K. Polk and Slavery."

Martin, Mary M. 2020. *Financial Stress and Your Health*. Laramie: University of Wyoming Financial Literacy.

McCullough, David G. 2001. *John Adams*. New York City: Simon & Schuster.

McDougal, Jim, and Curtis Wilkie. 1998. *Arkansas Mischief*. New York City: Henry Holt & Co.

McGrath, Tim. 2020. *James Monroe: A Life*. New York: Penguin Random House.

McNamara, Robert. 2020. *History of Newspapers In America*. February 24. https://www.thoughtco.com/history-of-newspapers-in-america-4097503#:~:text=In%20the%20late%201880s%2C%20the,would%20appeal%20to%20common%20people.

Meacham, Jon. 2015. *Destiny and Power: The American Odyssey of George Herbert Walker Bush*. New York: Random House.

Meeder, Jay. 1978. "Testing Ford's Mettle At The Franklin Mint." *The Miami Herald*, February 27: 2A.

Melamed, Samantha. 2011. "Leading The Charge." *South Jersey Magazine*, October.

Menke, John D. 2011. "The Origin and History of the ESOP and Its Future Role as a Business Succession Tool." *Menke*. May 12. https://www.menke.com/esop-archives/the-origin-and-history-of-the-esop-and-its-future-role-as-a-business-succession-tool/.

Merriam-Webster. 2023. *Merriam-Webster Dictionary*. October 15. https://www.merriam-webster.com/dictionary/greed.

Miller, William Lee. 2002. *Lincoln's Virtues*. New York: Alfred A. Knopf.

Morella, Joe, and Edward Z. Epstein. 1986. *Jane Wyman: A Biography*. London: Robert Hale Ltd.

Morgan Stanley. April 2, 2015. *Oil Price Plunge Is So 1986*. Morgan Stanley Research.

Morgan, H. Wayne. 1998. *William McKinley and His America: Second Edition*. Kent: The Kent State University Press.

Morin, Relman. 1969. *Dwight D. Eisenhower: A Gauge of Greatness*. New York City: Simon & Schuster.

Morris, Edmund. 1979. *The Rise of Theodore Roosevelt*. New York City: Coward, McCann & Geoghegan, Inc.

—. 1979, updated 2010. *The Rise of Theodore Roosevelt*. New York City: Coward, McCann & Geoghegan, Inc.

Moscowitz, Milton. 1978. "Franklin Mint Profits Decline." *Fort Worth Star-Telegram*, January 25: 40.

Mushkat, Jerome, and Joseph Rayback. 1997. *Martin Van Buren: Law, Politics, and the Shaping of Republican Ideology*. DeKalb: Northern Illinois University Press.

Nash, George H. 1988. *Herbert Hoover and Stanford University*. Stanford: Hoover Institution Press.

—. 1983. *The Life of Herbert Hoover: The Engineer 1874–1914*. New York: W.W. Norton & Company.

National Endowment for Financial Education. 2021. *Financial Infidelity Survey*. The Harris Poll.

National Park Service. 2021. "An Introduction to Ulysses S. Grant's Classmates in the West Point Class of 1843." National Park Service. July 29. https://www.nps.gov/articles/000/an-introduction-to-ulysses-s-grant-s-classmates-in-the-west-point-class-of-1843.htm#:~:text=Within%20the%20ranks%20of%20the,academic%20curriculum%20of%20the%20academy.

NCAA. 2020. *Estimated Probability of Competing In College Athletics*. NCAA.

Neal, Patrick. 2015. *Elisha Camp—Sutler at Fort Vancouver*. February 15. https://www.nps.gov/fova/learn/historyculture/elisha-camp-sutler-at-fort-vancouver.htm.

Bibliography

Neill, Edward D., John Washington, and Robert Orme. 1892. "The Ancestry and Earlier Life of George Washington." *The Pennsylvania Magazine of History and Biography* 16 (3).

New England Historical Society. 2022. *John Adams Gets Into Harvard, Barely.* https://newenglandhistoricalsociety.com/john-adams-gets-into-harvard-barely/.

New York Times. 1952. "Eisenhower Taxes On Memoirs Cited." *New York Times*, September 28.

—. 1978. "Ford Uses Link To White House In Sales Venture." *New York Times*, February 23: Section A, Page 13.

New York Times News Services. 1978. "Memoirs of Fords." *The Sacramento Bee*, March 9: 8.

New York Times. 1956. "Presley Receives A City Polio Shot." *New York Times*, October 29: 33.

Nilsson, Jeff. 2015. "The Debt and Death of Thomas Jefferson." *Saturday Evening Post*, July 2.

Nixon, Edward, interview by Timothy Naftali. 2007. *Oral Histories of the Richard M. Nixon Presidential Library* (January 9).

Nocera, Joseph. 1998. "Charles Merrill: The Main Street Broker." *Time Magazine*, December 7.

Noland, Mary Ellen, interview by James R. Fuchs. 1965. *Oral History Interview for Harry S. Truman Presidential Library* (September 16).

Obama, Barack. 1995. *Dreams from My Father: A Story of Race and Inheritance.* New York City: Crown.

Obama, Michelle. 2018. *Becoming.* New York City: Penguin Random House.

O'Brein, Patricia. 1977. "Fords Leave Office Dancing." *Knight News Wire*, January 20: 2.

O'Brien, Andrew. 2021. "Elvis Presley Aids Fight Against Polio By Getting Vaccinated At 'The Ed Sullivan Show' In 1956." *Live For Live Music*, February 2.

O'Neill PhD & CFP, Barbara. 2011. "Steps Toward Financial Resilience." *Rutgers University—New Jersey Agricultural Experiment Station*, August.

Osborn, G.C. 1958. "Woodrow Wilson as a Young Lawyer, 1882–1883." *The Georgia Historical Quarterly* 126–142.

Oshinsky, David. 2006. *Polio: An American Story.* Oxford University Press.

Osnos, Peter. 2006. "Barack Obama and the Book Business." The Century Foundation, October 30.

Owens, Valerie Biden. 2022. *Growing Up Biden.* New York City: Celadon Books.

Oxford Dictionary. 2023. "Optics."

Packard, A.T. 1884. "Bad Lands Cow Boy." *Money In Cattle*, February 14: 1.

Pallardy, Richard. 2020. "History of College Scholarships." Saving for College. February 6. https://www.savingforcollege.com/article/history-of-college-scholarships.

Parmet, Herbert S. 1983. *JFK: The Presidency of John F. Kennedy.* New York City: Dial Press.

Paulson, Michael. 2016. "For a Young Donald Trump, Broadway Held Sway." *The New York Times*, March 6: Section C, Page 1.

Paul Arnsberger, Melissa Ludlum, Margaret Riley and Mark Stanton. 2008. "A History of the Tax-Exempt Sector: An SOI Perspective." *Statistics of Income Bulletin*, Winter.

Pepin, Joanna R., and Philip N. Cohen. March 2021. "Nation-Level Gender Inequality and Couples' Income Arrangements." *Journal of Family and Economic Issues*, 13–28.

Perret, Geoffrey. 1997. *U.S. Grant: Soldier & President.* New York City: Random House.

Perry, Barbara A. 2004. *Jacqueline Kennedy.* Lawrence: University Press of Kansas.

Pew Research Center. 2010. *Women, Men and the New Economics of Marriage.* Washington, DC: Pew Research Center. https://www.pewresearch.org/social-trends/2010/01/19/women-men-and-the-new-economics-of-marriage/.

Philadelphia Daily News. 1978. "Would You Buy A Coin From This Man?" *Philadelphia Daily News*, February 25: 2.

Bibliography

Piff, Paul, Daniel M Stancato, Stephane Cote, and Dacher Keitner. 2012. "Higher Social Class Predicts Increased Unethical Behavior." *Proceedings of the National Academy of Sciences*.

Piles, Mary. 2022. "The Infamous Two-Dollar Bill." February 22. Accessed March 27, 2024. https://www.cnbstl.com/about-us/news/the-history-of-the-two-dollar-bill.

Plummer Jr., William, and A.P. Peabody. 1856. *Life of William Plummer*. Boston: Phillips, Sampson & Co.

Pooley, Eric, and S.C. Gwynne, 1999. "How George Got His Groove." *Time*, July 12.

Pratt, Harry E. 1943. *Personal Finances of Abraham Lincoln*. Chicago: Lakeside Press.

Press and Sun-Bulletin (Binghamton, NY). 1927. "Pushing The Fight On Infantile Paralysis." August 15: 6.

Price, Thomas. 2023. *Comfort in My Retirement: President James K. Polk's "Mount Vernon."* https://www.whitehousehistory.org/comfort-in-my-retirement.

Prussing, Eugene E. 1927. *The Estate of George Washington, Deceased*. Boston: Little, Brown and Company.

Rayback, Robert J. 2017. *Millard Fillmore: Biography of a President*. Independently published.

Reagan, Neil, interview by Stephen Stern. 1981. *UCLA Oral History Program* (June 25).

Reagan, Ronald. 1990. *An American Life*. New York: Simon & Schuster.

Reeves, Thomas C. 1972. "The Search for the Chester Alan Arthur Papers." *The Wisconsin Magazine of History*, 310–319.

Rickover, H.G. n.d. "Report on the Fitness of Officers dated April 24, 1953 Carter, J Navy Records."

Rodkin, Dennis. 2010. "Renters Snap Up Obama's Former Condo." *Chicago Magazine*, August 4.

Romano, George Lardner Jr. and Lois. 1999. "Bush Name Helps Fuel Oil Dealings." *The Washington Post*, July 30: A1.

Roosevelt, Eleanor. 1949. *This I Remember*. New York: Harper & Brothers.

Roosevelt, Elliott. 1948. *F.D.R. His Personal Letters 1905–1928*. New York: Duell, Sloan and Pearce.

Roosevelt, Governor Franklin D., interview by Dr. E. W. Beckwith. 1930. *Newspaper Interview on Governor Roosevelt Accepting Delivery of $500,000 Life Insurance Policy In favor of Georgia Warm Springs Foundation* (October 18).

Roosevelt, Theodore. n.d. "Personal diary of Theodore Roosevelt, 1884." *Theodore Roosevelt Papers*. Library of Congress Manuscript Division.

Ross III, D. Bruce, and Ed Coambs. 2018. "The Impact of Psychological Trauma on Finance: Narrative Financial Therapy Considerations in Exploring Complex Trauma and Impaired Financial Decision Making." *Journal of Financial Therapy* 9 (2): 37–53.

Roth, Leland M. 1991. "Getting the Houses to the People: Edward Bok, the Ladies' Home Journal, and the Ideal House." *Perspectives in Vernacular Architecture*, 187–196.

Rucker, Philip, Tom Hamburger, and Alexander Becker. 2014. "How the Clintons went from 'dead broke' to rich: Bill earned $104.9 million for speeches." *The Washington Post*, June 26.

Sagamore Hill National Historic Site. 2023. *Theodore Roosevelt's Libraries*. August 15. https://www.theodorerooseveltcenter.org/Learn-About-TR/TR-Encyclopedia/Reading%20and%20Writing/Roosevelt%20Libraries.

Salinger, Pierre E.G., interview by Theodore H. White. 1965. *Oral History John F. Kennedy Presidential Library* (July 19).

Saxton, Martha. 2019. *The Widow Washington: The Life of Mary Washington*. New York: Farrar, Straus and Giroux.

Schwartz, Sybil. 1978. "In Defense of Chester Arthur." *The Wilson Quarterly*, 180–184.

Scofield, Merry Ellen. 2022. "How to Party Like a President: The Dinners Behind the Dinner Records of Thomas Jefferson." *Commonplace Online: The Journal of Early American Life*, May.

Severance, Frank Hayward. 1899. *Old Trails on the Niagara Frontier*. Buffalo, NY: The Matthews-Northrup Co.

Shales, Amity. 2014. *Coolidge*. New York City: Harper Perennial.

Bibliography

Shelley Stewart III, Michael Chui, James Manyika, JP Julien, Dame Vivian Hunt, Bob Sternfels, Jonathan Woetzel, and Haiyang Zhang. 2021. *The economic state of Black America: What is and what could be*. McKinsey Global Institute.

Shepard, Edwin M. 1888. *Martin Van Buren*. Boston: Hougton Mifflin.

Shlaes, Amity. 2013. *Coolidge*. New York City: Harper.

Shoop, Duke. 1948. "Truman Pay Step." *The Kansas City Times*, December 22: 1.

Silvia Bellezza, Francesca Gino, Anat Keinan. 2014. "The Red Sneakers Effect: Inferring Status and Competence from Signals of Nonconformity." *Journal for Consumer Research*, 35–54.

Slaughter, Stephen S., interview by Niel M. Johnson. 1984. *Oral History Interview with Stephen S. Slaughter* (April 19).

Snyder, Charles M. 1975. *The Lady and The President: The Letters of Dorthea Dix and Millard Fillmore*. Lexington: University Press of Kentucky.

Sobota, Lenore. 2018. "Illinois Bicentennial: Reagan's 'quintessential' story began at Eureka College." *The Pantagraph*, July 9.

Staiger, Matthew. 2022. "The Intergenerational Transmission of Employers and the Earnings of Young Workers." *Opportunity Insights Harvard University*, December: 1–93.

Stello, Heidi, interview by Megan Gorman. 2023. *Univesity of Mary Washington: The Papers of James Monroe* (August 8).

Stephen P. Roll, Samuel H. Taylor, and Michal Grinstein-Weiss. 2016. "Financial Anxiety in Low- and Moderate-Income Households: Findings from the Household Financial Survey." *CSD Research Brief No. 16-42*. St. Louis, MO: Washington University, Center for Social Development. 1–5.

Stephens, Joe. 2008. "Obama Got Discount on Mortgage." *The Washington Post*, July 2.

Story, Ronald. 1975. "Harvard Students, the Boston Elite, and the New England Preparatory System, 1800-1876." *History of Education Quarterly*, 281–298.

Stratford, Michael. 2013. "Obamas' Own Student Debt Topped $40,000 Each." *Insider Higher Ed*, August 26.

Strozier, Charles B. 2016. "Your Friend Forever, A. Lincoln: The Enduring Friendship of Abraham Lincoln and Joshua Speed." *Affinity: THE FRIENDSHIP ISSUE*, 204–228.

Sweet, Lynn. 2014. "Obama's Own Student Loans: $42,753 for Harvard Law School." *Chicago Sun-Times*, June 10.

Swift, Will. 2014. *Pat and Dick: The Nixons, an Intimate Portrait of a Marriage*. New York City: Threshold Editions.

Taft to Woodrow Wilson, January 6, 1913. n.d. *William H. Taft Papers: Series 8: Letterbooks, 1872–1921; Presidential; Vol. 47, 1912 Dec. 18-1913 Jan. 30*. https://www.loc.gov/resource/mss42234.mss42234-516_0220_0747/?sp=439&st=image&r=0.116,0.624,0.769,0.318,0.

Taylor, Colby D., Bradley Klontz, and Derek Lawson. 2017. "Money Disorders and Locus of Control: Implications for Assessment and Treatment." *Journal of Financial Therapy* 8 (1). https://doi.org/10.4148/1944-9771.1121.

The Atlanta Constitution. 1930. "Roosevelt Insured for $500,000." October 25: 6.

The Buffalo Commercial. 1867. "Organization of the Society for The Prevention Of Cruelty to Animals." April 5: 3.

The Buffalo Commercial. 1865. "The Art Gallery Inauguration Last Evening." February 17: 3.

The Bureau of Engraving and Printing. n.d. *Circulating Currency $1 Note $2 Note*. Accessed March 27, 2024. https://www.bep.gov/currency/circulating-currency/1-note.

The Cincinnati Enquirer. 1984. "Local Firm Plans Merger With Bush Exploration Co." February 16: 44.

The College Board. 2022. *Trends In College Pricing And Student Aid 2022*. New York: The College Board.

The Corpus Christi Caller. 1978. "Ford Boots One." *The Corpus Christi Caller*, February 25.

The Daily Advertiser. 1923. "President Harding No Longer A Journalist." *The Daily Advertiser*, June 29: 3.

The Federal Reserve. 2015. *The Panic of 1907*. December 4. https://www.federalreservehistory.org/essays/panic-of-1907.

Bibliography

The Indiana Democrat (Indiana, Pennsylvania). 1894. "Grant Had No Thought of Retreat." July 12: 5.

The Menke Group. n.d. *The Origin and History of the ESOP and Its Future Role as a Business Succession Tool*. https://www.menke.com/esop-archives/the-origin-and-history-of-the-esop-and-its-future-role-as-a-business-succession-tool/.

The New York Times. 1930. "Coolidge Buys A $45,000 Estate." *New York Times*, April 2.

—. 1878. "Will of Theodore Roosevelt." *New York Times*, February 17.

The News Journal (Wilmington, Delaware). 1926. "New Corporations." June 30: 4.

The Washington Post. 1890. "He Sells Oak View." *The Washington Post*, February 28: 6.

Thomas B. Ross, Ellis Cose, William Hines, Morton Kondracke, Tom Littlewood, David Murray. 1976. "Shattered Hopes, New Endeavor." *St. Louis Post Dispatch*, May 26: 3H.

n.d. "Thomas Jefferson's Monticello." *Extract from Thomas Jefferson to Cornelia J. Randolph: "a dozen Canons of conduct in life."* https://tjrs.monticello.org/letter/216?_ga=2.230859743.1147420860.1708292914-1950607593.1708292914.

Thomas Jefferson's Monticello. n.d. *After Monticello*. https://www.monticello.org/slavery/paradox-of-liberty/after-monticello/.

Thomas Jr., Michael G. 2018. "Why Financial Empathy Matters!" *Association for Financial Counseling & Planning Education Newsletter*.

Thorndike, Joseph J. 2016. "JCT Investigation of Nixon's Tax Returns." *Tax Notes*, June 14.

—. 2023. "Tax History: Did the IRS Drop the Ball When Auditing Nixon's Tax Returns?" *Tax Notes*, May 29.

Tough, Paul. 2023. "Americans Are Losing Faith in the Value of College. Whose Fault Is That?" *New York Times Magazine*, September 5: 31–39.

Tumulty, Karen. 2021. *The Triumph of Nancy Reagan*. New York: Simon & Schuster.

U.S. Currency Education Program. n.d. *The History of U.S. Currency*. Accessed March 27, 2024. https://www.uscurrency.gov/history.

Union College. 2016. *President With 80 Pairs of Pants*. September 21. https://muse.union.edu/newsarchives/2006/09/21/president-with-80-pairs-of-pants/.

United Press International. 1962. "JFK Donates Full Salary to Charity." November 14.

n.d. United States Military Academy West Point. https://www.westpoint.edu/admissions/prospective-cadets/cadet-fitness-assessment.

UPI Archives. 1982. "Jane Wyman found ex-husband Reagan 'a bore.'" November 26.

UPI. 1972. "Biden's Wife, Child Killed in Car Crash." *New York Times*, December 19.

Vaughn, Stephen. 1994. *Ronald Reagan in Hollywood: Movies and Politics*. Cambridge: Cambridge University Press.

Waldo, Richard H. 1935. "The Real Calvin Coolidge: A First Hand Story of His Life Told By The People Who Knew Him Best." *Good Housekeeping Magazine*, June.

Warwick, Jack. 1938. *Growing Up With Warren Harding*.

Wasserman, Pam. 2013. "Life Span and Life Expectancy." *Social Studies and the Young Learner*.

Weill, Sandy, interview by Richaed Norton Smith. 2011. *Gerald R. Ford Oral History Project* (January 24).

West, J.B. 1973. *Upstairs at the White House: My Life with the First Ladies*. New York City: Open Road Media.

Whitbeck, Sterling. 2020 (reprinted), original 1921. "Calvin Coolidge, Bank President." *ABA Banking Journal*.

White, Jack. 1973. "Nixon's Income Tax Bill was $1,670 for Two Years." *The Providence Journal*, October 3.

Whitman, Alden. 1972. "Basil O'Connor, Polio Crusader, Dies." *New York Times*, March 10: 40.

Widmer, Ted. 2005. *Martin Van Buren*. New York: Times Books.

Bibliography

Wilcox, W. Bradford. 2021. *Two Is Wealthier Than One: Marital Status and Wealth Outcomes Among Preretirement Adults*. The Aspen Institute and The Federal Reserve Bank of St. Louis.

Wildman, Edwin. 1925. *The Builders of America; Lives of Great Americans from the Monroe Doctrine to the Civil War*. Boston: L.C. Page & Company.

William R. Emmons, Ana H. Kent, Lowell R. Ricketts. 2019. "Is College Still Worth It? The New Calculus of Falling Returns." *Federal Reserve Bank of St. Louis Review*, 297–329.

Williams, Gladstone. 1953. "The Forgotten Man—An ExPresident." *The Sacramento Bee*, January 8: 34.

Williams, Roy, and Vic Preisser. 2010. *Preparing Heirs: Five Steps to a Successful Transition of Family Wealth and Values*. Bandon: Robert Reed Pub.

Wilson, Douglas L. 1991. "What Jefferson and Lincoln Read." *The Atlantic Monthly*, January: 51–62.

Wilson, Woodrow. 1966. *The Papers of Woodrow Wilson Volume 2 1881–1885*. Princeton: Princeton University Press.

Wood, Virginia. 1941. "Yes! A Honeymoon Can Last In Hollywood If..." *Screenland*, November: 30, 79.

Xiao, Jing Jian, and Nilton Porto. 2019. "Present bias and financial behavior." *Financial Planning Review*.

Yale Alumni Magazine. 2015. "The Cost of Yale: A History." *Yale Alumni Magazine*, May/June.

Yale University. 2023. *Yale University Student Accounts*. September. https://student-accounts.yale.edu/tuition-and-fees.

Index

PRESIDENTS

George Washington, xiv, 28, 30, 63, 64–65, 66, 76, 91, 117, 147, 148, 151, 156, 158, 164, 187, 196–197, 198–204, 215–223, 227–228, 231, 236, 260, 261–262

John Adams, 25–26, 32, 39, 46–47, 49

Thomas Jefferson, xiv, xvii, 3–9, 12, 15, 16, 22, 28, 35, 62–63, 64–69, 113, 231, 259

James Madison, xiv, 63, 66, 67, 68, 69

James Monroe, 62–69, 259

Andrew Jackson, 28, 106

Martin Van Buren, 28, 238, 247–250, 257

James Polk, 146–152

Zachary Taylor, 28, 146, 157, 241

Milliard Fillmore, 28, 30, 155, 156–162, 238

Franklin Pierce, 30, 158

Abraham Lincoln, xiii, xiv, xv, 28–32, 36, 38, 49–50, 106, 157, 187, 205–212, 237–239, 261

Andrew Johnson, 28, 30

Ulysses S. Grant, 32, 58, 76, 239–245, 250, 257

James Garfield, 229

Chester Arthur, 164, 229, 246

Grover Cleveland, xviii, 20, 28, 159, 247

William McKinley, xv

Theodore Roosevelt, 28, 90–94, 96–97, 126, 171

William Howard Taft, 117, 125–126, 130

Woodrow Wilson, 125–126, 130, 215, 224–229, 231, 236

Warren G. Harding, 8–16, 22, 75–76, 91, 130

Calvin Coolidge, 106, 116, 117, 130–139, 145, 187, 229, 246

Herbert Hoover, xvii, 54–62, 64, 74, 117, 138, 215, 229–236, 261

Franklin D. Roosevelt, xi, xii, xii, xiv, 37, 42, 156, 164, 166, 170–181

Harry S. Truman, 28, 29, 82, 103–106, 116–126, 164, 187, 192

Dwight D. Eisenhower, xv, 32–36, 49, 77–82, 89–91, 97, 105–106, 117, 164, 187, 201, 260–261

John F. Kennedy, xiii, xiv, 50, 156, 238, 246–247

Lyndon B. Johnson, xv, 10, 50, 105, 164, 189–196

Richard Nixon, xix, 82–90, 97, 103, 105, 127, 155, 162–166
Gerald Ford, 103–116, 123, 126–127, 161, 163, 223, 229, 250, 257, 260, 262
James Carter, 32, 107, 111, 156, 250–257
Ronald Reagan, xvii, 38–42, 49, 70–74, 108, 138, 204, 229, 260
George H.W. Bush, 38, 42–46, 49, 238, 250
William J. Clinton, xvii, 38, 47, 139, 141–145, 187, 223–224, 231, 250
George W. Bush, 38, 139–140, 238, 250
Barack Obama, 38, 47–49, 76, 231, 246, 250
Donald J. Trump, 38, 139, 140–142, 145, 165, 238, 250
Joseph Biden, xviii, 16–22, 38, 134, 259

FIRST LADIES

Martha Washington, 187, 198–204, 227
Abigail Adams, 203
Sarah Childress Polk, 147, 151–152
Abigail Fillmore, 158–159
Mary Todd Lincoln, xiii, 187, 205–212
Alice Lee Roosevelt, 92–94, 96
Edith Carow Roosevelt, 93, 96, 187
Ellen Axson Wilson, 229
Edith Bolling Galt Wilson, 229
Florence Harding, 11, 13, 15
Grace Coolidge, 130, 132, 138, 187
Eleanor Roosevelt, 166, 168, 170, 172–174
Elizabeth "Bess" Truman, 120–121, 123–125, 187
Mary Geneva "Mamie" Eisenhower, 78–81, 187, 201
Jacqueline Bouvier Kennedy, 246
Claudia "Lady Bird" Johnson, 10, 189–196
Pat Nixon, 83, 89
Elizabeth "Betty" Ford, 105–106, 111, 113, 116, 169
Rosalynn Carter, 251–257
Jane Wyman (ex wife of Reagan), 70–73, 204
Nancy Reagan, 74
Barbara Pierce Bush, 43–44
Hillary Rodham Clinton, 141–143, 187
Michelle Obama, 47–48, 122–123
Neilia Biden (late wife of Joe Biden), 17
Jill Biden, 20–22

PRESIDENTIAL MOTHERS AND FATHERS

Sara Delano Roosevelt, 168, 172
Mary Washington, 202, 217–218
Joseph Ruggles Wilson, 224
Frank Nixon, 82–83
David and Ida Eisenhower, 33
Nelle and Jack Reagan, 39, 70

Acknowledgments

When I started writing this book four years ago, I had no idea of how hard it would be to actually write a book and how many people would need to help me do it—including the presidents themselves.

Lucky for me, researching this book was a fun historical scavenger hunt for letters, documents, and other artifacts belonging to the presidents. In this search, I cannot say enough about the Presidential Libraries run by the National Archives. Their archivists do an amazing job in curating these artifacts and are willing to go far to help get the right answer. In particular, thank you to Spencer Howard of the Herbert Hoover Presidential Library-Museum, Virginia Lewick and the Franklin Delano Roosevelt Library, Randy Sowell and the Harry S. Truman Library, Stacey Chandler and the John F. Kennedy Presidential Library, Carla Braswell of the Richard Nixon Library and Museum, Stacy Davis of The Gerald R. Ford Presidential Library, and Youlanda Logan and The Jimmy Carter Library and Museum.

Of course, the Presidential Libraries only cover from Herbert Hoover to the present day. I also have to thank the organizations that help manage the legacies of the presidents from Washington through Coolidge. The individuals at these organizations include Amity Shlaes of The Coolidge Presidential Foundation, Samantha Snyder of The George Washington Presidential Library at Mount Vernon, Sherry Hall of The Warren G. Harding Presidential Sites, Bill Parke, Historian of the Unitarian Universalist Church of Buffalo (Millard Fillmore), Ryan P. Semmes Ph.D. of The Ulysses S. Grant Presidential Library, Heidi Stello of The James Monroe Museum at The University of Mary Washington, and Peggy Dillard of The Woodrow Wilson Presidential Library.

All the Presidents' Money

I am extremely indebted to Amelia Forczak who coached me through how to best explain all the great stories of the presidents. From storyboards to outlining, I never would have gotten this book over the finish line without her help. I also want to thank Nicole Sholly who helped me on copy editing.

Thank you to Maria Rosati who didn't give up on my idea, and to Ellen Archer who encouraged me to think through how to sculpt the book. I am appreciative of all the work Beth Davey did in taking my proposal and connecting it with the perfect editor. And thank you to Bruce Littlefield who read an early version and pushed me to expand as well as naming the book.

You can never overestimate the power of a great editor. I don't know how I got so lucky to work with Gretchen Young. She took in a first-time author and helped shape the book in a way I know I couldn't have done without her.

Thank you to Anthony Ziccardi and his team at Post Hill for making this a reality. I also can't thank Charlie Fusco and her amazing team enough for all their brand building and support.

I also want to thank my work colleagues who put up with a lot while I brought this book to life: Edward Kearney, Nicole Tanenbaum, Josephine Winder, Reed McCue, Natalie Wang and the entire Chequers team.

Special thank you to Bruce Gorman Jr, Brett Gorman, Leslie Schiavo, Jenna Laski, Austin Montgomery, Mark Gonzales, Gary LeFebvre, Kristina Kelley, Kristen Koss, Diane Koss, Joe Smith, Dave McMorran, Jerry Kronemeyer, Pat Ruedin, and Mike Kletchko.

I have been very lucky that I have learned so much from all the clients I have worked with over the years. I appreciate all they have taught me.

A very special thank you to my parents. To my dad, Bruce M. Gorman, for teaching me to have passion for history. And to my mom, Grace Ann Donato Gorman, for always pushing me to shoot for the stars. I love you both.

Finally, a thank you for my husband Roger Nabedian. You have been very patient in living with me and the presidents for the past few years. But I couldn't have kept going without your support and belief in me. I love you.

About the Author

Megan Gorman is the founding partner of Chequers Financial Management, a San Francisco-based firm specializing in tax and financial planning for high-net-worth individuals. *USA TODAY* recognizes Chequers Financial Management as one of the top 500 Registered Investment Advisor Firms (RIAs) in the nation. This female-owned business serves a diverse client base including entrepreneurs, corporate executives, and families with inherited wealth. Trained as an attorney, Megan thrives on the challenges of navigating complex financial landscapes.

Megan holds a B.A. in History from Bryn Mawr College and a JD from Rutgers School of Law.

Her past career includes positions at Goldman Sachs and BNY Mellon Wealth Management as well as being recognized as one of America's Top Women Wealth Advisors.

Currently, she serves as a Board of Trustees member for the National Endowment for Financial Education (NEFE) and chair of the Investment Committee managing a $200 million endowment.

Megan lives in Newport Beach, California, with her husband Roger.